Special Education

●◆ A REFERENCE HANDBOOK

CONTEMPORARY EDUCATION ISSUES

Special Education

A REFERENCE HANDBOOK

Arlene Sacks

A B C ⬤ C L I O

Santa Barbara, California • Denver, Colorado • Oxford, England

Library of Congress Cataloging-in-Publication Data

Sacks, Arlene.
    Special education : a reference handbook / Arlene Sacks.
        p. cm. — (Contemporary education issues)
    Includes index.
        ISBN 1-57607-274-6
    1. Special education—United States—Handbooks, manuals, etc.
I. Title. II. Series
LC3981.S33 2001
371.9'0973—dc21
                                    2001002700

This book is also available on the World Wide Web as an e-book. Visit www.abc-clio.com for details.

06 05 04 03 02 01   10 9 8 7 6 5 4 3 2 1

ABC-CLIO, Inc.
130 Cremona Drive, P.O. Box 1911
Santa Barbara, California 93116-1911

This book is printed on acid-free paper ∞.
Manufactured in the United States of America

☙ Contents

Series Editor's Preface   ix
Preface   xi

Chapter One: Overview   1

**The Development of Regular Education
    in the United States**   1
The Development of Special Education   2
    Special Institutions and Schools   3
    Growing Awareness of Special Needs   5
Legal Implications and Funding   7
Assessment and Evaluation   8
    *Formal, Informal, Norm-Referenced, and
        Criterion-Referenced Assessment*   9
    Functional Behavioral Assessment   9
    Learning Potential Assessment   10
Referrals, Eligibility, and Placement   11
**Assessment Issues When Providing for Dual Exceptionalities
    for the Gifted**   13
Individualized Educational Plan and Assessment   13
Types of Assessments for Exceptional Education Students   14
    Individual Tests of Intellectual Functioning   15
    Tests of Academic Achievement   15
    Assessment of Social/Emotional Behavior   15
    Assessment of Adaptive Behavior   16
    Assessment of Psychological Processes   16
Full-Service Schools   16
Mainstreaming   18
Inclusion   19
    Technology's Role in Classroom Inclusion   22
    *Realities of Inclusion for Regular and Special Education
        Teachers*   24
    Teachers' Experiences with Inclusive Classrooms   24

Brain Research   25
   "At-Risk" Children   26
   Controversy over Critical Learning Periods   30
Early Childhood Special Education   31
Head Start   32
Why Special Education Teachers?   33
Parental Involvement and the Need for Parent Education   36
References   39

Chapter Two: Chronology   43

Chapter Three: Special Education Curriculum   59

Curriculum Development Involves a
   Multidisciplinary Team   60
Curriculum-Based Assessment and Evaluation
   Approach   63
Including the Affective Domain   65
Encouraging a More Peaceful Environment   66
Multiple Intelligence and Its Impact on the Curriculum   69
Curriculum for Both General Education and
   Special Education   72
Community-Based Instruction and Curriculum   74
Discipline as Part of the Curriculum   76
Early Childhood Special Education Curriculum   78
Curriculum Accommodates Dual Exceptionalities   81
Inclusion in the Curriculum   82
References   85

Chapter Four: Special Education Programs and the Law   87

Section 504 of the Vocational Rehabilitation Act
   and IDEA Compared   88
Funding and Opposition   90
Charter Schools and Children with Special Needs   91
Technology Programs Based on the Law   92
Programs for At-Risk Infants and Toddlers   93
Policy versus Program Implementation   94
Special Education as It Is Impacted by Goal 1 of
   Goals 2000   95
References   95

Chapter Five: Special Education and Advocacy 97

The School as Advocate 97
Development of Advocacy Groups 98
Parent Advocacy 99
Popular Culture and Advocacy 100
Advocacy and Politics 103
References 103

*Chapter Six: Politics and the Special Education
Challenge* 105

The Development of Teacher Unions and Their Impact
on Special Education 105
Early Influence of Politics on Special Education Programs
for Young Children 109
Political Changes Affecting the Education of
Disabled Children 110
References 112

*Chapter Seven: Organizations, Associations, and
Government Agencies* 113

National Contacts 113
Advocacy and Legal Assistance 133
Free Medical Services 138
Federal Assistance 140
Fraternal Organizations 140
Wish Organizations 141
Free Medical Air Transportation 142
Transportation for Cancer Patients and Organ Donors 143

Chapter Eight: Selected Print and Nonprint Resources 145

Books and CD-ROMs 145
Guides and Reference Materials 154
Journals and Magazines 156
Web Directories 161
*Starting Points for Advocacy of Special Education
and Children's Services* 165
On-line Legislative Resources 166

Sites for Community Outreach   *166*
Toys   *166*
Videos   *169*
Educational Software Vendors   *172*
Adaptive Device Vendors   *178*
Enabling Device Vendors   *180*
Selected Internet Resources for Assistive Technology   *181*

Glossary   *185*
Index   *215*
About the Author   *235*

◆◆ Series Editor's Preface

The Contemporary Education Issues series is dedicated to providing readers with an up-to-date exploration of the central issues in education today. Books in the series will examine such controversial topics as home schooling, charter schools, privatization of public schools, Native American education, African American education, literacy, curriculum development, and many others. The series is national in scope and is intended to encourage research by anyone interested in the field.

Because education is undergoing radical if not revolutionary change, the series is particularly concerned with how contemporary controversies in education affect both the organization of schools and the content and delivery of curriculum. Authors will endeavor to provide a balanced understanding of the issues and their effects on teachers, students, parents, administrators, and policymakers. The aim of the Contemporary Education Issues series is to publish excellent research on today's educational concerns by some of the finest scholar/practitioners in the field while pointing to new directions. The series promises to offer important analyses of some of the most controversial issues facing society today.

Danny Weil
Series Editor

◆ Preface

"Special education," frequently viewed solely as an outgrowth of regular education, actually developed from several disciplines. Historical accounts describe special education as a product of superstition, abandonment, and elimination of such persons identified as mentally or physically disabled, whereas religious influences, primarily Christianity, gave rise to a more humane treatment of the disabled. Philosophers presenting early views of the differences between nature and nurture offered alternative theories regarding potential growth of persons with disabilities. Physicians who initially advocated treatment continued to develop supportive theories, which grew to include brain research. Artists eventually began to present a more humane picture of children and adults with physical disabilities, frequently placing them in paintings with aristocrats in order to attain a new view of these individuals. Through a combination of these developments, society slowly became both aware of and sensitive to the needs of persons with disabilities.

Understanding how special education developed as an outgrowth of regular education is necessary if one is to realize the current challenges and controversies of special education. In addition, knowing the special education success stories of John Lennon, Winston Churchill, and others can provide readers with a useful reality base.

In the United States, the Fourteenth Amendment and the civil rights movement of the 1960s laid the groundwork for the many special education laws set in place by federal and state legislatures as well as for the court cases decided in its favor. Head Start, a federal program developed in the 1960s, outlined provisions for young handicapped children. Over time, the rights of special needs students slowly but surely have been secured. Testing and assessment became specifically designed to make referral and eligibility to special programs more scientifically appropriate and less subjective.

Each law described, each program developed, and funding for each special situation has almost always been achieved through an adversarial situation; often taking years or decades and ultimately being resolved in the political world. Senators, presidents, and teacher labor unions have come to understand that they need to actively participate in the challenges facing special education.

Popular culture in the form of television, movies, and theater has—possibly without realizing it—become a vehicle for advocacy. Actors such as Tom Cruise, Dustin Hoffman, Cher, Anne Bancroft, Patty Duke, William Hurt, and Marlee Matlin have brought attention to issues of special education whether through theatrical roles or personal advocacy.

Now, many special-needs children who used to be isolated are included in normal classrooms. This new position comes with challenges for professions in all related fields of education. Curricula are being rewritten, and inclusive situations are being provided. The ultimate outgrowth of this is the greater acceptance of all children.

My intent in this book is to present readers with all the information they need to obtain full understanding of how special education can serve as a model for all education.

Arlene Sacks

Chapter One

◆◆ Overview

In today's research, terms related to the field of special education are frequently used interchangeably. *Children with special needs, disabled,* and *exceptional* historically have been used throughout the literature. For purposes of this reference text, the terms are used synonymously because all indicate services and education for children that fall outside of the regular education classroom. To develop insight into the vital issues and challenges concerning special education in the United States, one needs first to understand *special education* as it relates to *regular education.*

THE DEVELOPMENT OF REGULAR EDUCATION IN THE UNITED STATES

The desire to educate young citizens equally in the interest of a developing society became a cornerstone philosophy of America's forefathers. Though the Tenth Amendment of the U.S. Constitution gave states jurisdiction over education matters, no state required school attendance until 1840, when Rhode Island passed a compulsory school attendance law. By the mid-1880s, public schools throughout the country had adapted an age–grade level system, categorizing students into grade levels according to chronological age. Differences between students placed in this system became very obvious; strong students graduated to the next grade level while poor students were retained in the same level, or "flunked." In the early 1900s the National Education Association, a national organization for teachers, endorsed the Stanford-Binet Intelligence Scale tests as being a useful predictor of school success or failure. The tests introduced the concept of intelligence quotient (IQ), which became a significant factor in student stability placement. Through the 1940s and 1950s educational concerns emphasized nutrition (subsidized school cafeteria facilities were enacted in 1946) and proficiency in math and science. Not until 1965, with the passage of the Elementary and Secondary Education Act, were any federal educational programs in place to address the needs of children from low socioeconomic backgrounds. The Head Start program was one result of this act; it was developed in the belief that early educational intervention would increase the likelihood of later school success.

THE DEVELOPMENT OF SPECIAL EDUCATION

For most of our nation's history, schools were allowed to exclude certain children, especially those with disabilities. How the process of exclusion developed and where it began is quite a narrative.

Prior to the 1800s, superstition drove the treatment of persons with obvious disabilities, such as the severely retarded, mentally ill, deaf, blind, and physically disabled. Many children with disabilities were abandoned and left to die. Witch hunts, burnings, and exorcisms also were common means to an end for such "problem" children. Advocates of humane treatment for the disabled were few and far between. They include a Spanish monk named Ponce de Leon, who during the sixteenth century successfully taught deaf students to communicate; Juan Pablo Bonet of Spain, who developed a method of finger spelling for the blind during the seventeenth century; and Jacob Rodriguez Pereire, who simplified sign language and invented an arithmetical machine to teach students how to calculate. The English philosopher John Locke distinguished between idiocy (mental retardation) and insanity (mental illness) in 1690 by advocating the idea that there is no basic human nature, that our minds at birth could be opened to all kinds of stimuli.

In 1799, Jean Marc Itard, a French physician and educator, expressed his belief that idiocy could be treated through educational intervention. He went so far as to begin describing the concept of individualized intervention, sensory stimulation, and systematic instruction. He did so by taking responsibility for Victor, a 12-year-old "wild" boy found in the woods by hunters near Aveyron, France. The boy had developed no language, exhibited uncontrollable behavior, and was described as savage or animal-like. Hoping to cure his condition, Itard put Victor through a program of sensory stimulation. After 5 years, Victor had developed some verbal language and had become reasonably socialized to his new environment. This demonstrated two things: (1) learning could take place, even for individuals determined by professionals to be hopeless; and (2) appropriate treatment could be continued and expanded on by others (Hardman, Drew, Egan and Wolf, 1990).

The Spanish artist Diego Velazquez in several of his most famous paintings exhibited another example of a more humane attitude toward the disabled. Dating from the 1630s through the 1650s are Velazquez's famous depictions of court dwarfs. Unlike court jester portraits of earlier artists, these dwarfs are treated with respect and sometimes appear in the same painting as the royal family. An example of this is Velazquez's masterpiece "Las Meninas," or "The Family of Philip IV," completed in about 1656. In this enigmatic painting of Spain's royal family appear the child Infanta Margarita, two maids of honor, the king and queen of Spain, and most important to this issue, two attendant dwarfs.

Velazquez created other paintings depicting these members of the court. "El Nono de Vallecas" (1636) shows a dwarf named Francisci Lezcano, with additional characteristics of the mentally handicapped, seated on an outcropping of rock; the painting of a jester entitled "Calabacillas" (mid-1640s) depicts a dull-faced, crossed-eyed subject without mocking or exaggeration; and "El Primo" (1644) shows a jester who was in charge of the king's royal stamp. These paintings demonstrated that the dwarf—a disabled person—was capable of maintaining an esteemed role in royal society. Another painting by Valezquez, "Sebastian de Morra" (1643/4), shows how "Despite being deformed and a dwarf, his face and his straightforward and penetrating gaze show no hint of mental weakness whatsoever, though they do express a rather melancholy, introspective air" (Seraller, 1999, pp. 55–57).

Velazquez's paintings demonstrate a specific effort on the part of the artist—as well as the Spanish court, since it approved the portraits—to give respect and dignity to individuals with special needs. This is both ironic for a society functioning on a class system and courageous for its time.

Special Institutions and Schools

From 1800 to 1900 the first institutions for persons with special needs were developed in both the United States and Europe. Two conflicting objectives prevailed: (1) to offer humane treatment; and (2) to remove these people from general society. In 1817 Thomas Hopkins Gallaudet, an American minister and educator, established the first American residential school for the deaf. In 1832 Samuel Gridley Howe, an American physician and educator of the blind and deaf, founded the Perkins Institute for the blind. Additionally, Howe advocated public financial support for education and treatment of exceptional populations. In 1834, Louis Braille, a French educator, developed a system of reading and writing for the blind that is still used today. In 1837, Eduoard Seguin, a

French physician and educator, developed the first school for the intellectually retarded in Paris using the sensory motor method of application. In 1854, Seguin helped establish the first residential facility for the retarded in the United States.

In the mid-1880s, Dorothea Dix, an American educator and social reformer, secured reforms for mental institutions. She helped the American public view those institutions as hospitals for the "sick" rather than as prisons for the criminally insane.

Toward the end of the 1880s, Maria Montessori, an Italian physician and educator, developed theory, curricula, and instruction for early childhood education of normal and exceptional populations. This developed out of her experiences with the mentally retarded and the poor.

Also at the century's end, Alfred Binet developed the Binet-Simon Intelligence Test, the first scale for measuring intelligence and for determining mental age. Lewis Terman revised the Binet-Simon Intelligence Test for use with English-speaking children, which became known as the Stanford-Binet Intelligence Scale. Terman also produced the first longitudinal study of gifted children.

As the twentieth century dawned, Alexander Graham Bell, while speaking to members of the National Education Association (NEA), suggested the establishment of public school annexes for the education of the deaf, blind, and mentally challenged. In 1902, Bell urged that public "special education" be provided for children with disabilities so they could remain in their homes and communities. Work with Helen Keller, her teacher Anne Sullivan, and Captain Keller, Helen Keller's father, influenced Bell's philosophy of education. He grew to oppose segregated schools for students with learning handicaps.

Nationwide compulsory school attendance in the early 1900s flooded schools with thousands of new students, and policymakers had to find ways to deal with children who did not fit the mold. Many stayed in school until they could legally withdraw. In an agrarian society, there were plenty of jobs for unskilled and uneducated workers, so the social or economic ramifications of dropping out of school were few. But as the world changed, so did the issue.

Gradually, more public schools promoted special classes for children with learning handicaps. With the increased use of intelligence tests, it became easier for educators to diagnose children with potential academic difficulties.

In the first half of the 1900s, Alfred Strauss described the learning-disabled child (identified by the term "Strauss Syndrome"), thereby marking the beginning of the field of learning-disabilities research. Slowly, more regular classrooms began to accept mildly handicapped students, and school achievement for the disabled proved greater; however, it wasn't until the 1960s that the federal government took major legislative action to support special students in the educational process.

Growing Awareness of Special Needs

Since the 1960s there has been an avalanche of development concerning special education in the United States. Numerous court decisions and legislative acts now protect those with disabilities and guarantee that children receive a free and appropriate publicly supported education.

It is important to remember that parents and families are the heroes in this effort. Politicians such as President John Kennedy publicly shared information about his mentally retarded sister with the country, as did Hubert Humphrey regarding his grandchild with Down's Syndrome. As a result of this sharing, individuals with handicaps have become part of our public awareness.

Buehler and Dugas (1979) in their *Directory of Learning Resources for Learning Disabilities* give examples of famous people with learning difficulties, including the following:

Hans Christian Andersen (1805–1875), author of children's books: Wild variations of spelling and word formation in the handwritten manuscripts of this young man have led clinicians to conclude that he had a language disability—a fact that one might logically suppose would bar him from a literary career. It did not.

Thomas Edison (1847–1931), inventor: As a boy Edison was unable to learn in the public schools of Port Huron, Michigan. His parents withdrew him from school, and his mother undertook the slow, painstaking job of teaching the "three Rs" and other basic curriculum at home.

Woodrow Wilson (1856–1924), twenty-eighth president of the United States: Wilson did not learn his letters until the age of eight or learn to read until he was eleven. Letters from relatives consoled the parents because they believed the boy was so "dull and backward." At school, he excelled only when the subject had to do with speech. But then, wrote a biographer, "it has been noted that dyslexics not infrequently become fluent speakers, perhaps, in part, as a compensation for poor facility in reading and writing."

Winston Churchill (1874–1965), prime minister of England: This Englishman had considerable learning difficulties as a child. Recently, a "dummy" application was sent to his old boarding school; it was a duplicate of the application his family had actually submitted many years before, with only the name and personal data disguised. The school rejected the application out of hand, saying that the boy clearly would be unable to meet the school's standards.

George S. Patton (1885–1945), general and commander of the U.S. Third Army, World War II: Severely learning disabled, Patton could neither read nor write at the age of twelve. He overcame his difficulties to a sufficient extent to win appointment to the U.S. Military Academy at West Point, but even there, he had to hire a "reader" to help him get through his studies.

F. Scott Fitzgerald (1896–1940), one of America's leading novelists: As a boy Fitzgerald exhibited dreaminess, poor concentration, and a seeming inability to learn anything that did not present immediate, vivid interest. These characteristics caused his parents to doubt his ability to progress in school or in the world.

Nelson A. Rockefeller (1908–1979), governor of the State of New York, vice president of the United States: After watching a program on learning disabled children, this public figure wrote the following in *TV Guide* magazine: "I was one of the 'puzzle children' myself—a dyslexic or 'reverse reader'—and I still have a hard time reading today. But after coping with this problem for more than 60 years, I have a message of encouragement for children with learning disabilities. . . . Don't accept anyone's verdict that you are lazy, stupid, or retarded. You may very well be smarter than most other children your age. You can learn to cope with your problem. . . . Face the challenge. . . . Never quit."

John Lennon (1940–1980), songwriter, The Beatles: This young man from an English industrial city had persistent difficulties in school. Lennon's autobiographical writing at times sounds like the product of the language problems that he actually experienced (although it is comically intentional): "I attended to varicous schools in Liddypol. And still didn't pass—much to my Aunties supplies."

Many other renowned individuals throughout history were born with disabilities that did not stop them from achieving great goals. To wit:

- Jane Addams, Nobel Prize winner, social worker—physically impaired
- Ludwig van Beethoven, composer—gifted/handicapped
- Alexander Graham Bell, inventor—hearing impaired
- Louis Braille, teacher, creator of Braille writing system—blind
- Ray Charles, singer—blind
- Leonardo da Vinci, artist, inventor—gifted/handicapped
- Sir Isaac Newton, scientist—speech and language impaired

•◆ Franklin D. Roosevelt, U.S. president—physically impaired

•◆ Stevie Wonder, singer, composer—blind

Additional attention was brought to those with special needs with the passing of the Fourteenth Amendment, which aimed at securing rights for all persons regardless of creed, color, or condition. Professional and parent organizations, listed in Chapters 5 and 7 of this text, advocated educational equality for all students. The concept of "learning disabilities" emerged as an explanation of school failure as opposed to mental retardation. As a result, "special education" became a subsystem of "regular education." As this concept and more sophisticated learning strategies developed, the controversy of leaving some "special education" students in the "regular education" classroom with some additional aid has developed.

LEGAL IMPLICATIONS AND FUNDING

As evidence of the strength of the recent laws and funding allocated to special needs children, over 4 million children and youth (infants and toddlers) now receive special education and related services. Understanding the language and intentions of the laws empowers families to advocate more effectively for their children and strengthens their ability to participate as partners in their children's educational teams. This knowledge also assists professionals in understanding the intent of service delivery system, ensures protection of civil rights, and improves collaboration with other agencies and families. Because federal laws are often changed or amended regularly, keeping up to date on them is in the best interest of both the families of children receiving special education and the professionals who provide services to them.

Whenever Congress passes an act, it is given a number such as P.L. 94-142. P.L. stands for Public Law. The first set of numbers means the session of Congress during which the law was passed. For example, the 94 means the 94th session of the U.S. Congress. The second set of numbers identifies what number the law was in the sequence of passage and enactment during that session. Thus, the 142 means that this was the 142nd law that Congress passed and the president signed during the 94th session of Congress.

Laws passed by Congress reflect a general policy. Once the law is passed Congress delegates to an administrative agency within the executive branch the task of developing detailed regulations to guide the law's implementation. Federal regulations are detailed in the Code of Federal Regulations (CFR), which is available in most public libraries.

The CFR interprets the law and discusses each point of it. States and state agencies must comply with federal laws and regulations. In many instances states may go beyond what is required in the regulations (the federal minimum standards) so long as they do not conflict with federal regulations; for example, they may include gifted children in their special education programming. However, special education has elaborate sets of regulations regarding programming and procedures that must be provided in order for states to receive federal funding.

It is important to remember that there is no constitutional provision requiring that the federal government provide education—under the Tenth Amendment, regulation of education is reserved to the states. However, states are required under the due process and equal protection clauses of the Fourteenth Amendment to provide education on an equal basis and to provide due process before denying equal educational programming. Most laws providing for public education are generally state and local laws rather than federal laws. Although some educational programs, notably Head Start, are highly regulated by the federal government, education is still predominantly a state function.

You can become familiar with state laws and regulations by writing to your state's Department of Education for a copy of its State Special Education Law, regulations, recent amendments, policy, or court decisions related to children and youth with disabilities. For example, in order to receive federal funds for special education and related services under the Individuals with Disabilities Education Act (IDEA), every three years a state must have approved state plans to show that it intends to provide a free, appropriate education for all children and youth with disabilities. These plans must be made available to the public for review and comment before they are adopted and sent to Washington, D.C. Dates for review must be announced far enough in advance for parents and other interested persons to appear at hearings and express their views. Each citizen has a right to see a copy of state and local plans for educating children and youth with disabilities. Chapter 2 lists the laws, court cases, and significant acts that apply to special education.

ASSESSMENT AND EVALUATION

Whether dealing with regular education students or special education students, assessment and evaluation generally focus on a student's: (1) ability to learn, (2) achievement, (3) specific learning problems, (4) giftedness, (5) creativity, and (6) socioemotional adjustment. Any individual assessment is part of the greater whole, the total picture. Testing is only a small part of any assessment process. Data is also collected through student observations and interviews.

In the normal process, a student is placed in the regular school classroom, where he or she is screened to determine appropriate placement or curriculum. If during the basic screening process something in the child's behavior (academic, physical, or social) seems unusual or problematic, an appropriate screening may be implemented to see if there may be cause for special planning and special placement.

Formal, Informal, Norm-Referenced, and Criterion-Referenced Assessment

To better understand how assessments are undertaken, one should understand the difference between *formal* and *informal* testing as well as *norm referenced* or *criterion referenced.* Formal assessment involves tests of intellectual ability (sometimes referred to as learning aptitude); achievement tests; measures of specific abilities such as motor and language skills, auditory discrimination, and adaptive behavior; and social adjustment. Informal assessment includes systematic observation, work sample analysis, task and error analysis, interviews, and questionnaires (Gearheart and Gearheart, 1990, p. 4).

Norm referencing and criterion referencing refer to categories of tests. Norm-referenced tests are standardized at the time they are developed; that is, they are given to a large number of students in order to provide an index of "average" performance. An individual's performance on a test is compared to that of a national or local sample of students of the same age or grade level. Students who earn significantly higher or lower scores than their age mates or grade mates are said to perform "abnormally," hence the term "norm referenced." Criterion-referenced tests provide a measure of the extent to which individuals or groups have mastered specific curriculum content. Such tests are developed "by specifying the objectives or criteria to be mastered, usually in basic skill areas like reading and math, then writing items to assess mastery of those objectives or criteria. The results indicate the degree to which the content or skill representing a particular instructional objective has been mastered; they are used to describe what each pupil has learned and needs to learn in a specific content area" (Ysseldyke and Algozzine, 1990).

Functional Behavioral Assessment

A different type of assessment known as functional behavioral assessment (FBA) was developed from the field of educational psychology. It is the process of determining the cause of behavior before developing an intervention. By basing intervention on a specific cause, the application of assessment becomes more functional. To assess the causes (function) of behavior before analyzing and interviewing an individual, one uses functional assessments such as interviews and observations; in order to implement a functional analysis one manipulates different environmental events in order to produce specific behavioral changes.

Observing a person in his or her natural environment and analyzing what preceded the behavior, as well as what consequences followed the behavior, is basic to FBA. Trained behavioral analysts can help a multidisciplinary team create appropriate interventions that meet the needs the child's inappropriate behavior is providing. When devising an intervention program, realistic goals for students and management are important. Setting interventions focusing on positive behavior in small increments is most desirable.

Learning Potential Assessment

The purpose of conventional intelligence tests is to provide a measure representing stable characteristics of the individual they may serve within reasonable limits, as a reliable predictor of future performance. Viola (1997) believes this to be of little value for any educational endeavor "where the prescription of intervention procedures is to modify instructional procedures to enhance learning" (p. 65). In contrast, he suggests the *learning potential assessment framework,* which examines the process of learning and employs strategies facilitating the acquisition of new information and skills. It provides a student's response to intervention by using a test-teach-test format. Both Lev Vygotsky and Reuven Fuerstein have developed learning potential assessment devices. Vygotsky believed social influences are crucial to the learning process and that learning occurs due to a transfer of responsibility based on an interpersonal relationship between instructor and student; therefore, learning and cognitive development are enhanced by cooperative and collaborative experiences. Fuerstein similarly emphasized the importance of the social role between teacher and student in the cognitive potential for learning. Fuerstein assessed human potential and remediated cognitive deficits of all stages and ages of children through adolescence (Lerner, 1993).

The significance of a trained special education teacher is essential in this type of assessment due to the fact that the teacher provides the learning experiences, selects specific concepts to be taught, and interrelates them into the pupil's learning experiences. This learning strategy, or learning potential assessment, is an important part of experiential and cognitive assessment in that it provides detailed description of the student's response to intervention. The focus is not assessment for identification of *who is eligible* for special education services but rather *who is in need, how to meet those needs, and if this can be done in the regular or special education classroom.*

REFERRALS, ELIGIBILITY, AND PLACEMENT

Decisions regarding referrals, eligibility, and placement are specified by each school district. Several factors should be considered when placing a student in a particular setting: (1) the benefits to the student of being placed in a least restrictive setting, (2) the ability of the student to function in the setting, and (3) the intensity of services needed by the particular student. As a student progresses in a setting, a change of placement may be important in order to maximize that child's potential. A change of placement may also be necessary should a child be unable to function in a less restrictive setting. In addition, if the parents disagree with the evaluation of their child and so bring the case to a mediator, a decision in favor of the parents may necessitate a change of placement.

The referral process leads to screening. Referrals for young children are very different from referrals for older children because young children are often not referred from specific situations with professionals observing their success or failures in an educational setting. Often a young child will be referred through a program called "Child Find," which disseminates information in the form of pamphlets, newspaper articles, and local presentations that promote screening procedures for all incoming students. The purpose of this early screening is to identify children with potential learning problems before they identify themselves. Screening involves various measures to help identify children who may be "at risk" for special education services. Such screenings have been effective in identifying children with developmental delays and speech and language disorders, and it is believed that early identification may actually decrease the amount of (or even eliminate) special education services needed for many students in the future. There is no labeling of a child at this early stage, and the children, usually referred by parents, pediatricians, and others interacting with the children frequently, generally have positive experiences in special education settings.

Most referrals of older children, already in educational settings, come from teachers recognizing some learning problems. Teachers can refer a child for evaluation without the need for parental consent, though parents must be notified that a referral has been made. The parents must then give consent before any individual assessment of that child can be administered. Although referral timelines are not consistent in all states, ninety days is usually given to complete an evaluation based on a formal referral. Referrals have been criticized as sometimes being biased or disproportionate from certain groups. For this reason, the knowledge base and educational experience of the referring teacher should be considered, and all avenues to keep the child in the educational mainstream should be attempted first. Once a child has been assessed, if placement in a special education environment is determined to be a more positive experience, a detailed, individualized educational plan is developed.

Very different assessment techniques are used for young children, elementary school children, and middle and secondary school children. Additionally, each area of academics has developed specific tests and techniques to evaluate appropriate placement once any sign of abnormal learning is discovered. Within each age category there are not only specific tests for specific disciplines but also observational charts and checklists to make the experience more subjective.

Along with age and stage differences are concerns of language and cultural diversity. As McAfee and Leong (1997) point out, "Fair, impartial, and objective classroom assessment of all children must take into account the diversity found in most schools and centers. Of particular concern in contemporary society are sociocultural differences and individual differences" (p. 219).

Appropriate assessment is essential to the development of schools and communities that regard language, culture, and ethnic diversity as an opportunity rather than a problem. Teachers must be sensitive to the ways children and families from different cultures and backgrounds respond to the assessment approaches used and make adjustments as necessary. The wide variety of classroom assessment methods and contexts now available makes this possible (McAfee and Leong, 1997).

Assessment techniques for very young children (ages 0–5) usually involve not only the child but the parent(s) and other family members and are often required for purposes of family intervention services. Formalized testing for remedial or therapeutic purposes, as is used with older children, is not applicable to this age group. This presents many challenges and requires excellent communications skills on the part of educators.

Assessment of elementary, middle, and secondary school-age children is a complicated task involving formalized tests; informal assessments; cognitive and adaptive behavior scales; appropriate reading, math, and language instruments; assessments of sensory, perceptual, and motor skills; career, vocational, and transition-related assessment; and gifted, talented, and creativity assessment. It is important to remember that all these assessments must take into consideration the laws and regulations that apply to placement and special services. Additionally, effective instruction, setting specific objectives, and managing and evaluating such instruction are all part of appropriate assessment.

As there is no nationwide special education classification system, it is possible to diagnose a child as disabled in one state and not in another. Often, placement based on assessment and evaluation needs to consider the number of deficits, severity of disability, and the complexity and intensity of intervention. Assessment may be the emphasis, but multiple factors are considered before placement.

ASSESSMENT ISSUES WHEN PROVIDING FOR DUAL EXCEPTIONALITIES FOR THE GIFTED

Gifted students with disabling conditions remain a major group of underserved and underestimated youth (Cline and Schwartz, 1999). Often times, greater consideration must be given to the disability than to the superior intellectual ability; in such cases, appropriate assessment is a particular challenge.

To begin with, assessment processes such as standardized tests and observational checklists, which are necessary for appropriate curriculum development, require major modification when applied to children with so-called dual exceptionalities. Two examples are the hearing-impaired gifted child who cannot respond to oral directions and may lack vocabulary that truly reflects his or her complex thought processes; and the speech- and language-impaired gifted child who cannot respond to tests requiring verbal responses. Other examples include visually impaired gifted children who are unable to respond to specific performance measures—although their vocabulary may be advanced, they may not understand the meaning of words they use (e.g., color words); and learning-disabled gifted children who may use high-level vocabulary but cannot express themselves in writing.

INDIVIDUALIZED EDUCATIONAL PLAN AND ASSESSMENT

The Individuals with Disabilities Education Act requires that each special education student receive a full individualized educational plan

(IEP). This plan is the key to planning services for all children and youth with disabilities. The IEP team documents which parts of the general curriculum are relevant to each special education student. With regard to state assessments, if the student's current curriculum and program address areas parallel to part of the assessment, then only that part should be maintained. If the curriculum goals are unique to that student and not evaluated in a general assessment, the student cannot be assessed by that portion, and a modified assessment plan can be developed. Examples of modifications include deleting certain test items or sections, or substituting items and/or assessment tasks. Alternate assessments designed to reflect the individual circumstances of the student are intended to level the playing field for students with disabilities. These accommodations are intended to provide access to tests, not to alter the essential elements of the test.

Specific areas to be included in the IEP are present levels of educational performance, noted by test scores; and measurable annual goals, including benchmark and short-term objectives specific to the disability. Included with the objectives are ways to measure the child's progress or lack of it in the special education program. Objective testing to indicate real progress is the way to be certain the IEP goals are being achieved. If a child is not making progress as outlined in the goals, the IEP needs to be revised.

Special education programs rely on assessment procedures developed from the laws concerning persons with disabilities. Section 504 of the Rehabilitation Act and the Americans with Disability Act of 1990 require entities receiving federal funds to make accommodations for the handicapped in order to protect the individual's rights for being discriminated upon on the basis of a disability. If students are excluded from assessments that lead to special programs, their opportunity for postsecondary education and employment ultimately will be limited, thereby resulting in a form of illegal discrimination. IEPs must therefore be very specific so that there is a clear link between what the student was taught and what the assessments measured (Shriner, 2000).

TYPES OF ASSESSMENTS FOR EXCEPTIONAL EDUCATION STUDENTS

The following section offers the reader myriad assessments to be used in order to better place or develop instructional strategies to be included in an appropriate curriculum for the special needs child.

Individual Tests of Intellectual Functioning

- Kaufman Assessment Battery for Children (K-ABC)
- Kaufman Infant and Preschool Scale
- McCarthy Scales of Children's Abilities
- Stanford-Binet Intelligence Scale–Fourth Edition
- Wechsler Adult Intelligence Scale–III (WAIS-R)
- Wechsler Intelligence Scale for Children–Revised (WISC-R)
- Wechsler Preschool and Primary Scale of Intelligence–Revised (WPPSI-R)

Tests of Academic Achievement

- Basic School Skills Inventory (diagnostic version)
- Brigance Diagnostic Inventory of Early Development
- Kaufman Test of Educational Achievement (K-TEA)
- Key Math
- Test of Early Mathematical Abilities (TEMA)–2
- Test of Early Reading Ability (TERA)–2
- Test of Early Written Language (TEWL)
- Test of Written Language 2 (TOWL-2)
- Test of Written Spelling (TWS)
- Woodcock-Johnson Psycho-Educational Battery–Revised (achievement)
- Woodcock Reading Mastery Test–Revised

Assessment of Social/Emotional Behavior

- Behavior Evaluation Scale
- Behavior Problem Checklist (Quay and Peterson)
- Burke's Behavior Rating Scale
- Child Behavior Checklist (Achenbach)
- Children's Personality Questionnaire (CPQ)
- Devereaux Adolescent Behavior Rating Scale
- Devereaux Child Behavior Rating Scale
- Devereaux Elementary School Behavior Rating Scale
- Goodenough-Haris Drawing Test
- High School Personality Questionnaire (HSPQ)
- Minnesota Multiphasic Personality Inventory (MMPI)
- Piers-Harris Children's Self-Concept Scale
- Thematic Apperception Test
- Walker Problem Behavior Identification Checklist

Assessment of Adaptive Behavior

- Comprehensive Test of Adaptive Behavior (CTAB)
- Scales of Independent Behavior (SIB)
- Vineland Adaptive Behavior Scales (VABS)

Assessment of Psychological Processes

- Bender Visual Motor Gestalt Test
- Detroit Tests of Learning Aptitude (DTLA-2 and DTLA-P)
- Developmental Test of Visual-Motor Integration–Revised
- Test of Adolescent Language (TOAL-2)
- Test of Language Development–2 (Primary or Intermediate)
- Woodcock-Johnson Psycho-Educational Battery–Revised (cognitive)
- Woodcock Language Proficiency Battery

FULL-SERVICE SCHOOLS

The *full-service school* is a term that was coined in 1991 when the Florida state legislature passed statute 402.3026. This legislation supports the establishment of partnerships between the State Board of Education and the Department of Health and Rehabilitative Services for the purpose of identifying and meeting the needs of at-risk students (Dryfoos, 1994).

Coordination is the foundation of the full-service concept; diverse agencies are required to work together to provide integrated education, health, and social services to eligible families. The full-service school is an umbrella term that encompasses a variety of models, including family resource centers, school-based health centers, and community or neighborhood schools. Regardless of the label, its mission is to eliminate barriers to student achievement through programs designed to involve children and parents on the school grounds. The full-service school seeks to create a "one-stop" shop that will meet the needs of the diverse population it serves, with an expanded curriculum appropriate to both regular- and special education children. Programs at full-service schools often include parent education, life skills, adult basic education, teen pregnancy groups, dropout prevention, and substance abuse programs (Burnett, 1994).

As every community has its own characteristics, there is as yet no district or state-mandated blueprint for building full-service schools. They are, rather, ongoing projects that evolve as the needs of the community change. The foundation of the design is poured when specific questions are answered:

- ➥ Who will be the stakeholders in the community's school?
- ➥ What are the unique needs of the community?
- ➥ What special services need to be provided to respond to those needs?
- ➥ Where will these services be housed?
- ➥ When will they be delivered?
- ➥ How can the program ensure that services are delivered in a cohesive and effective manner?

A full-service school should reflect the best practices in community partnerships. This community involvement offers specific benefits for children with special needs if health services, transition facilities, and social services are involved in the education plan. Where collaboration is real, you are likely to find principals who are willing to lead and take some risks. They understand that the school alone cannot do the job of helping all children succeed and that sharing this responsibility means forging partnerships built on reciprocity, in which the school exchanges information, services, support, and benefits with its families and communities (Davies, 1996).

Key to the success of these cooperative relationships is the establishment of common goals and desired outcomes. Special education children require specific outcomes, goals, and objectives that must be reviewed annually. Their needs can be met more easily in a school community union that closely monitors the extent and integrity of its collaborations so as to avoid fragmentation and duplication of services. Ongoing communication between community participants and defined interagency agreements can minimize barriers to an effective service delivery plan. Sharing a facility allows for more practical use of space and increases opportunities for sharing information among educators and with families.

By linking schools with support services, families begin to view their neighborhood school as a hub for "inclusion" rather than "exclusion." In far too many communities across the country there are few interactions between family and schools. A change in the education and social service paradigm calls for a "whole family" philosophy. The creation of a full-service school partnership program that collaborates with community agencies can contribute to the elimination of basic barriers to family empowerment. In this way, schools and communities can work together to mitigate environmental conditions that place our children at-risk of school failure.

MAINSTREAMING

Mainstreaming refers to placing special-needs children in the least restrictive educational environment, the regular classroom. It is not to be confused with *inclusion,* which will be discussed later in this chapter. The concept of mainstreaming developed after federal laws were passed requiring students to learn within the "least restrictive environment" (LRE). Prior to that, special education was considered a separate situation with separate classes and, sometimes, separate schools. Mainstreaming was typically done on a voluntary basis when special education teachers received permission from general education colleagues for their students to spend time in the others' classroom (Brantlinger, 1997).

Under the new laws, although students could be categorized with separate learning difficulties, they still needed to be integrated into as normal an educational placement as possible. Because various educators, judges, parents, and advocates interpreted the laws' intent differently, several interpretations of mainstreaming developed. According to the National Association of State Boards of Education (1992), "mainstreaming refers to assigning a student with disabilities to a general education classroom for part or all of the school day" (p. 187). This means that a child with learning challenges in reading, for example, could be put in a special class for reading, but for the rest of the school day, the least restrictive environment might be the regular classroom. Similarly, if a child had reading and math challenges, he or she could still be placed with regular-education children for physical education, art, music, social studies, and science.

A myriad of situations developed with the hope of mainstreaming the special education student into the "mainstream" of society. The reasons for this were socialization, peer interaction, and movement out of special education classes as soon as possible. To assume (1) that physically placing students in regular classrooms would increase social interaction between the two groups, (2) that mainstreaming would increase the social acceptance of exceptional students by nonhandicapped peers, and (3) that special education students would imitate appropriate behaviors of regular class peers was taking a concept and making it a process based on hope—and a misinterpretation of public laws regarding appropriate environments and placements. Additionally, those most responsible for the act of mainstreaming a special education student into the regular classroom—the teachers—were the least prepared for this challenge. Regular education teachers had little training in dealing with individual differences and specific instructional processes developed for special-needs students. Preparing instruction for groups is very different from preparing an individualized plan. The roles and responsibilities of regular education teachers were never clearly defined in this process. In most cases, regular education teachers and their regular education students were not prepared for the mainstreaming process.

In 1992 the National Association of State Boards of Education (NASBE) completed a study group on special education and found poor outcomes with regard to the unnecessary segregation and labeling of children for special services, and the "ineffective practice of mainstreaming, which has splintered the school life of many students—both academically and socially." The study identified a vast bureaucracy that has developed to educate students labeled as disabled. "This bureaucracy is characterized by separate and parallel policies for special education students and staff; separate funding mechanisms; separate administrative branches and divisions at the federal, state, intermediate, and local levels; a system of classification for labeling children that is considered by many to be demeaning and nonfunctional for instructional purposes; and a separate cadre of personnel, trained in separate pre-service programs, who serve only students with diagnosed disabilities" (National Association of State Boards of Education, 1992, p. 187).

Choate's 1993 research indicates that there are no definitive answers regarding the most appropriate placement options for students with disabilities, and decades of studies have failed to produce a specific alternative for the most appropriate placement; some studies suggest gains due to regular rather than special education placement, while others do not. Important in Choate's findings are simple explanations influencing mainstreaming, such as: Schools and school systems vary in their mainstreaming practices; there are very few uniform process guidelines for mainstreaming; no two schools use the same assessment placement decisions or options; and instruments used to measure the effects of effective placement vary. These findings affect how one views the success or failure of mainstreaming and how well it compares, theoretically and in practice, with inclusion.

INCLUSION

From these discussions on mainstreaming and guided by the concept of the least restrictive environment, the concept of inclusion was created. For example, placing children within the least restrictive environment was interpreted to mean that to the maximum extent appropriate, children with disabilities are to be educated with nondisabled children. Special classes, separate schools, and removing disabled children from the regular educational environment can occur only if the nature of the disability is such that a regular education class with the use of supplementary aids and services cannot be achieved satisfactorily. According to the concept of inclusion, special education students should attend their home school with their age and grade peers, all day, in the regular education classroom rather than being pulled out of regular classrooms to receive special services. This is in accordance with the regular education initiative (REI), a position held by some special educators that students with disabilities should be served exclusively in regular education classrooms and should not be "pulled out" to attend special classes.

The inclusion system posits that support services should be brought to the child and presumes that the child will benefit from being in that class. Full inclusion connotes full-day placement for all students, regardless of handicapping condition.

Because the IDEA never uses the term *inclusion,* there is debate surrounding what is legally enforceable by the courts. Recent legal action, cited in Chapter 2, such as *Greer vs. Rome City School District,* 11th Circuit Court, 1992; *Sacramento City Unified School District vs. Holland,* 9th Circuit Court, 1994; and *Oberti vs. Board of Education of the Borough of Clementon School District,* 3rd Circuit Court, 1993, indicate that an inclusive setting appears to be the interpretation of the original law.

The initial targeted special populations were for students who were in the range of mild disability and had some academic proficiency. No longer will they be in special sections of the school building in general education classrooms with in-classroom support. Learning is no longer viewed in terms of all students completing all tasks at the same time; rather, a more fluid classroom environment and a lessening of the role of the regular classroom teacher in directing and controlling all activity has made inclusion possible. If students are encouraged to gain a deeper understanding of material as opposed to memorizing facts, and if regular education teachers are encouraged to work in collaboration with special education teachers, support personnel such as occupational and instructional therapists, and parents, an inclusive classroom offers the opportunity for team success. According to Galis and Tanner (1995), "a more moderate view of inclusion is that placement committees should use inclusion as one delivery model for providing the least restrictive environment in continuance of service delivery models" (p. 2).

The effects of inclusion are being felt not only in elementary, middle, and secondary schools but also in early childhood settings. In Malmskog and McDonnell's 1999 article *Teacher-Mediated Facilitation of Engagement by Children with Developmental Delays in Inclusive Preschools,* the authors state, "With normalized peer interactions identified as an important goal of inclusion, significant levels of adult-child interaction patterns may have a negative effect on overall development and social relationships" (p. 213). Their study's teacher-mediated intervention procedures provide an appropriate balance by providing high levels of modeling in an inclusive setting.

In India the Union Ministry of Welfare began in the 1970s to recommend integrating special education children into the common schools once their communication and daily living skills were at a functional level. This focus from special education to integrated education has developed in the 1990s toward inclusion similar to that in the United States. Anupreza Chadha (1999) points out several obstacles she believes prevalent in India:

- Does the country have the resources for equipping teachers with specialized skills/competencies, or making curricula disability sensitive, or addressing prejudices of children?
- Even in highly educational socioeconomic schools, only partial integration has been achieved. Most disabled children are integrated only for social activities, not in academic areas.
- Disability is described as a problem, not a priority. Building access and accommodations for the handicapped are not prevalent.
- Not all regular education teachers have the attitude that they are responsible for all children assigned to them, regardless of the handicap. (pp. 32, 33)

Chadha's comments regarding inclusion as it exists in India are similar to experiences encountered internationally. Her advocacy for inclusion is based on the belief that schools isolating special education students deprive those children of opportunities for social interaction with their peers. Additionally, urban areas can provide necessary money and equipment for children with special needs whereas rural schools cannot. She believes inclusion in India needs to change in three directions: (1) movement toward school diversity, (2) movement from a teacher-centered approach to a student-centered approach, and (3) movement toward changing the view of a school as a provider of educational services to that of educational support.

Additionally, Baum and Wells (1990) in their article *Promoting Handicap Awareness in Preschool Children* write that "research suggests that the most opportune time to initiate planned instruction concerning handicapping conditions—particularly those that are more highly visible—is during the preschool and primary years" (p. 45).

Technology's Role in Classroom Inclusion

Adding to the success of inclusion is the use of technology, which can be integrated into the curriculum to facilitate learning objectives through a range of activities. Appropriate technology in the regular school classroom for special education students keeps those students involved in that classroom. Using technology in the form of adaptive input and output devices assists students with disabilities while keeping them in the least restrictive environment.

Students with mild mental handicaps, learning disabilities, or behavioral disorders such as hyperactivity or attention deficits are frequently instructionally integrated for academic subjects, especially at the middle or high school level. Sequential presentations, along with special organizational strategies, help these students succeed. Technology can aid both the regular education and special education student to stay on a task longer since it is visually more stimulating as well as motivating. An additional benefit is the feeling of being in control, which can increase self-concept, as discussed in Chapter 3.

Especially effective with students with disabilities are software tools such as word processing, databases, and spreadsheets. For students with emotional disabilities, the computer offers a personalized learning environment without complications of adult interactions or even peer interaction. Students with attention difficulties often appear to attend longer and more consistently to tasks presented on the computer (Center for Special Education Technology, 1990).

Initially, computer-assisted instruction (CAI) programs were developed for all students and were predominantly limited to drill and practice programs, tutorials, and simulations. As time went on, research focused on how technology could be applied to the "low-incident" populations of the hearing, visually, mentally, and physically disabled. Beginning in the early 1980s, the U.S. Department of Education's Office of Special Education Program funded work research in the use of technology for students with disabilities. The potential for CAI to raise academic achievement for children with mild and moderate disabilities is now viewed as positive (Woodward and Rieth, 1997).

Provenzo, Brett, and McCloskey (1999) explain how computers, adaptive computer interfaces, and specialized software are especially important to children with disabilities. They believe output devices such as monitors, printers, and speakers can be adapted for children with disabilities in order to encourage access. Adaptive input devices enable children with special needs to activate and send information: Keyboards can be modified, and alternative keyboards (usually larger in size) can provide access. Touch Windows, a touch-sensitive screen, is a direct way for students with disabilities to interact with the computer. Output devices such as monitors with enlarged text and graphics, printers producing large print or Braille, tactile devices produced using Braille, output hardware, and speakers are important for children with disabilities and also help meet the criteria mandated by the IDEA.

Assistive technology may appear in three places in the IEP: (1) in the annual goals and short-term objectives, (2) in the listing of supplementary aids and services necessary to maintain the student in the least restrictive setting, and (3) in the list of related services necessary for the student to benefit from his or her education.

When using assistive technology as part of the annual goals and short-term objectives of an IEP, the goal must be specific as to the role of assistance the technology will provide and how and why the technology will be used to accomplish this particular goal. It also must include which academic or social skill will be acquired.

As part of supplementary aids and services, assistive technology may be used to facilitate a student's ability to remain in the least restrictive environment by helping the student perform specific educational and social tasks. If assistive technology is necessary as a supplementary aid, its presence must support the student sufficiently to maintain the placement, and its absence would require the student's removal to a more restrictive setting. An example of this would be a student with multiple physical disabilities who could only make independent educational progress on his or her IEP goals in the regular classroom with the use of a computer and an augmentative communication device but could not make such progress in that setting without the devices.

Related services are mandated by the IDEA. Examples of these include transportation, speech pathology and audiology, psychological services, physical and occupational therapy, recreation, and social work. The federal law provides for almost all necessary developmental, corrective, or support services as may be required to assist a child with a disability to benefit from special education. The individual states have legislated additional related service requirements to include mobility training, training necessary for successful use of augmentative communication devices, and occupational therapy to include positioning in order to take advantage of assistive technology, computer keyboards, and communication boards (RESNA, 1999). Specific information with regard to technology for special education and how to access such technology is presented in Chapter 8.

Realities of Inclusion for Regular and Special Education Teachers

Despite the trend to meet the goals of the regular education initiative (REI) as well as full inclusion, one recent study found that regular education teachers generally do not support inclusion, nor do they believe they possess the competencies necessary to effectively instruct children with disabilities (Minke, Bear, Deemer, and Griffin, 1996). Furthermore, the study identified that many regular education teachers do not believe the regular classroom is the setting in which these students' needs can be adequately met. The attempts of regular education teachers to make adaptations in instruction were indicated as being few. They tended to be hesitant unless they were provided sufficient protected resources (instructional resources tagged solely to serve low-achieving students). Regular education teachers outside of a collaborative situation were most negative regarding inclusion. This study shows the importance of continued collaboration, protected resources, and careful selection of teachers in inclusive schools.

Teachers' Experiences with Inclusive Classrooms

Additional realities regarding inclusion for students with mild disabilities include:

- Continued inadequate allocation of resources, even when the role of special educators has been revised from one of direct service to one in which they provide assistance to the general educators; it is now the general educator who has the instructional responsibility for students with disabilities;
- The general education classroom is now confronted with the reality of teaching to the lowest achieving student; and
- How do educators make the idea of "inclusion" result in successful intended academic outcomes for students with mild disabilities as well as regular education students? (Deno, Foegen, Robinson, and Espin, 1996)

A variety of tools is now available to help educators and families make inclusive classrooms a success. Following are some specific techniques and tools useful in the planning of inclusion:

- Circle of Friends (also called Circle of Support) is a technique used to enlist the involvement and commitment of peers in developing and supporting effective inclusion.

- Coach is an assessment and planning tool designed to help educators identify family-centered priorities for their students, define the educational program components, and address these components in an inclusive setting.
- Maps (Making Action Plans) is a creative tool that inclusion facilitators can use to help individuals, organizations, and families move into the future.
- Path (Planning Alternative Tomorrows with Hope) is a creative tool used by inclusion facilitators to develop long- and short-range planning by encouraging people to think "backwards."

The two sides of inclusion are definite. Civil rights activists advocate for inclusion in order to decrease discriminatory treatment and segregated schooling. Others believe that inclusion can never meet the special needs of *all* students with disabilities. One thing is certain: Inclusion will continue to be an ongoing conversation involving students, teachers, related school personnel, families, and community leaders.

BRAIN RESEARCH

Our understanding of the brain's development and processes offers significant insight into approaches to early childhood education (ECE) and especially to early childhood special education (ECSE).

In the past, medical and educational professionals could only speculate about the functioning of the living human brain. However, in the early 1990s technologies were developed that now enable researchers to view brain circuitry in detail and monitor how, and where, the brain processes information. Magnetic resonance imaging (MRI) and the positron emission tomography (PET) scans record and measure the activity levels within the brain and have been used to monitor how the normal brain develops. These technologies have initiated an explosion in the field of brain research.

Three decades of research in child development corroborate brain research findings regarding the earliest years. We now have a better understanding of how nature and nurture impact the architectural shaping of the brain. Educational initiatives focusing on early intervention have developed and intensified in response to this new wealth of information.

Even before birth, brain cells make connections that plant the foundation for who we become as adults. These connections, or synapses, are created as a result of stimuli within that baby's environment. We are each born with 100 billion brain cells (neurons) that communicate with each other through synapses. Although the number of brain cells cannot later increase, it can decrease. Brain cells that go unused just wither away.

A key piece of the brain development puzzle is the fact that there are critical periods in brain plasticity when environment plays a major role working in tandem with biological factors. Synapses formed as a direct result of environmental stimuli cause the brain to develop rapidly. Repeated influences and experiences "hard wire" the neurocircuitry.

A child's earliest experiences are now believed to be extremely significant to brain development. Preterm infants are especially vulnerable to the environment because they enter the world with brains that have had less time to mature in the protected intrauterine environment (Shore, 1997).

Knowing what we now know about preterm development, nursing practices in neonatal intensive care units throughout the nation have been modified (Gilkerson and Als, 1995). By moving from "protocol and procedure-driven to relationship-based developmental care," researchers have found there to be a substantial improvement in preterm infants' potential for mental and physical well being. An additional positive outcome is the decrease in duration of hospital stays and financial expense.

Scientific advances in the field of neuroscience with respect to a child's first years have crucial implications for the development of policies and practices concerning early childhood. Current research supports redirecting our attention to provide more services to children from birth through the age of four. The education of children must begin long before they arrive at the doors of the kindergarten classroom. Florida's late governor Lawton Chiles informed participants at the Brain-Mind Connections Conference at the University of Florida that "education must start at gestation" (January 30, 1998).

"At-Risk" Children

The process of getting children ready for school begins long before they begin preschool. The 1992 report "Heart Start" dealt with the emotional foundations of school readiness and looked at the characteristics children develop in their first three years of life in preparation for school success. The report stated that too many preschools find themselves providing remedial support to three- and four-year-olds who are already delayed in their development. Heart Start cited seven characteristics a child needs to have in order to successfully learn once in school: confidence, intentionality, curiosity, communication, age-appropriate self-control, cooperativeness, and relatedness. For children lacking some, or all, of these characteristics, school becomes an "at-risk" situation. These children "tend to fall behind, become discouraged, resentful, perhaps disruptive, and, often, drop out" (Beatty, 1992).

Because toxins present within the mother move through the placenta, the exceptionally vulnerable fetal brain can be exposed to risks it may not be able to withstand. Prenatal cocaine exposure has been the subject of several research studies. Dixon and Bejar (1988) found that 41 percent of thirty-two infants prenatally exposed to cocaine suffered brain hemorrhage, cerebral infarction, and/or atrophy. Some prenatally exposed babies are born with a small head circumference that continues to chart small, which is "a significant predictor of poor development" (Griffith, 1992, pp. 30–34).

Alcohol use by the pregnant mother also creates an "at-risk" in utero environment for the baby. Fetal alcohol syndrome causes the child to develop a smaller brain as well as negatively impacting a child's motor coordination. Hyperactivity can also develop as a result of this syndrome (Healy, 1994).

Substance abuse by a parent places the unborn child at risk for a variety of negative outcomes. However, the environment the baby comes home to after leaving the hospital cannot be overlooked in the equation of the rapidly forming brain. Neonates become "caretaking victims" when parents lack the necessary skills and mental and emotional health to nurture them appropriately. If a parent is more concerned about nurturing a drug habit than nurturing the baby, serious implications exist for that baby. A chaotic and unpredictable environment can leave a permanent mark on the developing brain. Fear, anxiety, and neglect in young children can cause lifelong brain impairment. Impairment can take the form of emotional disturbances or learning problems. It is now known that "unpredictable, chaotic or traumatic experiences over-activate the neural pathways that control the fear response, causing children's brains to be organized for survival in a persistently threatening and violent world" (Perry, Pollard, Blakley, and Baker, 1995, pp. 271–291).

In *Ghosts from the Nursery,* Karr-Morse and Wiley (1997) state that "the majority of youthful offenders' records indicate that consistent patterns of antisocial behaviors are apparent by the time a child reaches four years of age. Toxic experiences such as neglect, abuse, family violence and substance abuse are being physically and emotionally absorbed by large numbers of our youngest babies."

Researchers now believe that children come into the world capable of learning any language. In essence, they are citizens of the world.

Neurons from the ear form vital connections in the auditory cortex as a result of the child hearing repeated sounds. By the time a baby reaches three months of age, the brain can decipher hundreds of spoken sounds. The auditory map is uniquely wired for the language spoken in the baby's environment by the time he or she is six months of age. "The critical period for mastering sound discrimination occurs early; even by six months the infant's brain is already pruning out sensitivity to sounds that are not heard in its environment. If the brain doesn't get good quality input and interactive practice with real people during these years, the child may have later difficulty with reading, spelling, and speaking clearly" (Healy, 1994, p. 75).

Dr. Stanley Greenspan has conducted extensive research in the area of autism as it relates to language. "Diagnosed between eighteen months and four years of age, these youngsters display a variety of bizarre and disturbing behavior—wandering aimlessly, compulsively flapping their arms, continually rubbing a spot on the carpet, repeatedly opening and closing a door, painstakingly marshaling small objects into rigidly straight lines—but almost no ability to respond to even the most basic attempts at communication" (Greenspan and Benderly, 1997).

Greenspan and his colleagues worked with over 200 children diagnosed with autistic spectrum disorder. It was found that by providing an intensive program that includes occupational and speech therapy as well as an interactive play component involving family members, early intervention could make a positive impact. "Working with these children, we found that the basic unit of intelligence is the connection between a feeling or desire and an action or symbol. When a gesture or bit of language is related in some way to the child's feelings or desires—even something as simple as the wish to go outside or to be given a ball—she can learn to use it appropriately and effectively" (Greenspan and Benderly, 1997). Greenspan and Benderly (1997) further report that out of approximately 200 of these students, they found that "between 58 percent and 73 percent have become warm, loving and communicative" (p. 310).

Research is rich with studies on the effects of quality early childhood programs on "at-risk" populations. The Carolina Abecedarian Project, the Yale Child Welfare Research Program, and the Perry Preschool Project all found that early intervention produced positive outcomes for children and families (Hamburg, 1994). Of these, the Abecedarian Project was found to have the greatest positive effect on young children who received child-focused, center-based services fifty weeks each year. In a recent article, Campbell and Ramey (1995) note additional evidence of the Abecedarian Project's merit.

Advocates of early childhood education have seized the opportunity neuroscience findings have provided and mobilized to disseminate this information to as wide an audience as possible. The Carnegie Corporation funded a project in fourteen states called the Starting Points Initiative, designed to train professionals to visit their communities and communicate the importance of quality caregiving and parenting during the first three years of life.

Sacks and Watnick (1998) share the Carnegie Corporation's 1194 findings that there is a "quiet crisis" in this country for children under three years old. Their study supports that many children in this age group have disabilities due to low birth weight, abuse, neglect, and difficulties encountered by teenage mothers. These children are at-risk for developmental delays additionally based on poverty and parent under-education. Disturbing statistics brought forth in their report include:

- One in four infants and toddlers under the age of three (nearly three million) live with families who have incomes below the federal poverty level;
- From 1987 to 1991, the number of children living in foster homes escalated by more than 50 percent—300,000 in 1987 to 460,000 in 1991;
- With growing economic pressures on both parents to join the work force, more than five million babies and toddlers are being taken care of by other adults;
- One in three victims of physical abuse are children under the age of one year;
- During 1990, approximately 90 percent of the children who died from neglect and abuse were less than five years old; 53 percent of these children were under one year of age;
- The major cause of death among babies and toddlers is accidental injury. (pp. 29–43)

Among the goals of early intervention services are to identify children who have disabilities or are at-risk for disabilities and meet criteria to have specialized services to maximize their potential for success, to include the family in order to ensure greater success of the child both in school and in the home, and to develop an individualized approach. Because parents of young children with special needs often require help themselves as well as help with other siblings, the services and support of organizations and community agencies (including clinics and transportation providers) have added to the overall success of early intervention. In a "normal" family, the child models much of what is going on around him. In families with young special needs children, frequently, the opposite is true—the child drives the family. The needs of such children can be so intense, as well as linked to sources outside the home, that the family finds itself operating around the needs of the special child. The interrelated structures outside the home must be coordinated in order to bring some type of normalcy to families with special-needs children. Strong communication and positive links between the intervening professionals and integrated service providers make the advocacy process more likely to succeed.

Controversy over Critical Learning Periods

The concept that parents have a window of opportunity regarding critical learning periods is disputed by John T. Bruer (1999) in *The Myth of the First Three Years,* who writes that "apart from eliminating gross neglect, neuroscience cannot currently tell us much about whether we can, let alone how to influence brain development during the early stage of exuberant synapse formation. If so, we should not be surprised that brain-based parenting advice is vague and contradictory" (p. 22).

Studies by Nelson and Bloom (as cited in Bruer, 1999) suggest that the brain continues to "reorganize itself in response to experience or injury throughout life" and that the one window of opportunity, as described by brain research advocates, is not accurate (pp. 649–657).

Advances in brain research have produced what has been called "brain-based education," which favors an active learning model engaging students in their own learning and instruction. According to Bruer (1999), support for this idea is based on a cognitive and constructionist model, rooted in thirty years of psychological research, easily found in any text on educational psychology but not developed from the biological sciences or pure sciences.

> For nearly a century, the science of the mind (psychology) developed independently from the science of the brain (neuroscience). Psychologists were interested in our mental functions . . . neuroscientists were interested in how the brain develops and functions. . . . Psychologists were interested in our mental software and neuroscientists were interested in our neural hardware. . . . In the past 15 years these theoretical barriers have fallen. Now scientists called cognitive neuroscientists are beginning to study how our neural hardware might run our mental software, how brain structures support mental functions. (Bruer, 1999, pp. 649–657)

Bruer and others believe this to be a very dangerous combination, as so much of the perceived "connection" is based on limited brain science research and is speculation.

The work of Dr. Harry Chugani is frequently quoted as a basis for brain research, brain-based studies, and education. According to Bruer's 1999 article, *In Search of . . . Brain Based Education,* "Chugani believes, along with some educators and early childhood advocates, that there is a biological window of opportunity when learning is easy, efficient, and easily retained. But there is no neuroscientific evidence to support this belief. And when there is no scientific evidence, there is no scientific fact" (pp. 649–657).

Obviously, scientific research on brain development needs to continue before we can conclude with conviction either way.

EARLY CHILDHOOD SPECIAL EDUCATION

Early childhood special education (ECSE) can be defined as an education setting in which specific interventions are set forth for young children at-risk for abnormal school development.

As Bowe (1995) explains, ECSE provides services for children under 6 years of age and their families, in response to disabilities or developmental delays in the children. ECSE joins Part H and Section 619 of Part B of the Individuals with Disabilities Education Act (p. 6).

To assure all young children an equal opportunity for success in school legislation, P.L. 99-457 was added through a federal amendment to already existing special education legislation (P.L. 94-142). The intent of this legislation was to provide states with specific funds to plan, develop and implement early intervention policies and programs for infants and toddlers who were handicapped, developmentally delayed, or at risk of handicaps or developmental delays and their families. A complete discussion of these laws follows in Chapter 2.

Numerous research studies have indicated the effectiveness of intervening on behalf of children during their early years. Conditions that may seriously impair a child's optimal development may be significantly reduced or improved if the right combinations of services are experienced as a form of intervention. A significant part of ECSE is the active participation of the family in decisionmaking, participation, and recipient services.

In a twenty-five-year longitudinal study of preschoolers, researchers followed forty families who had sought help from the Regional Intervention Program (RIP), a federally funded program, in Nashville,

Tennessee, and twenty-seven other areas (Regional Intervention Program, 2000). Each of these families looked for guidance due to displays of extreme behavior problems from their preschoolers. The researchers found that both the schools and the families had little chance of correcting antisocial behavior in their children after the age of nine. These antisocial behaviors often led to problems with the law, social rejection, and academic failure.

Through RIP, parents were trained in behavior modification skills such as monitoring their child's behavior, stating expectations and choices, rewarding appropriate behavior, and working with others to teach the child self-control and appropriate interaction behaviors. The study found that by the time the children reached elementary school, they were equal to their peers in responding positively to teacher requests, being appropriately engaged in structured and nonstructured activities, and reacting positively to teacher requests. A major finding of this study was that the earlier a child enrolled in RIP, the better the results. Because teacher surveys continuously point out that teachers believe they need more management and behavior management skills, this study has significant applications for early childhood special education. In addition, it supports the research supporting the need for early childhood intervention and the emphasis on early childhood special education programs as well as funding.

HEAD START

The Head Start programs of the 1960s gave regular educators their first opportunity to observe mass screening programs that had the potential for identifying and remedying behavioral and learning problems at an early age. The program's initial goals for early childhood education were to compensate for deficits in children's education and living environments. Disadvantaged children were to be provided with educational and environmental experiences to give them a "head start" for school. A subgroup of these children were the special needs children; to better serve their needs, Head Start developed an infrastructure and program that continues to support children with disabilities (Gearheart, Mullen, and Gearheart, 1993). It has created new opportunities through funding for Early Head Start programs to work with pregnant women and at-risk infants and toddlers. Another original Head Start principle that has continued is an emphasis on the central role of parents in the program; this has since become a significant element in preschool programs for children with disabilities.

The Division of Early Childhood (DEC) of the Council for Exceptional Children has urged Head Start to include in its agenda the following seven goals concerning special-needs individuals and special education (National Head Start Association, 2000):

1. Assure that all families of Head Start children, including those with disabilities, have the opportunity for full-day, full-year service;
2. Identify and publicize programs that have been effective in increasing access to and maintenance of comprehensive services for Head Start families of children with special needs;
3. Continue to encourage collaboration with community partners, including Early Intervention (IDEA, Part C), and ECSE (IDEA, Part B), and provide incentives to Head Start grantees for doing so;
4. Prepare every staff member to observe individual differences and support children with special needs, and follow up training with appropriate supervision and assistance;
5. Increase support of research tied to community-based practice, as well as dissemination of findings in language(s) from which staff and families can benefit;
6. Explore, as part of Head Start's increasing use of technology in the new century, the importance of and mechanisms for accessing assistive technology for Head Start children and families, to allow them full participation in learning opportunities;
7. Encourage employment of persons with disabilities in diverse roles in Early Head Start and Head Start services at all levels.

WHY SPECIAL EDUCATION TEACHERS?

According to the statutory requirements of IDEA 1997, the IEP decision-making team *must* include a regular education teacher if the special education child is participating in the regular education environment. That teacher must participate in the IEP process by assisting in the determination of positive behavioral interventions, supplementary aids, program modifications, and supports for school personnel to be provided for the child. If the regular education teacher is not comfortable with or adequately knowledgeable about these tasks, the leader of the multidisciplinary IEP team is required to assist the teacher so that he or she can be appropriately included.

Many teachers continually search for ways to bring information to various levels of comprehension and are constantly aware that the goal of language communication is the same for a child with special needs as for the normal child. Although the training of teachers focuses on academic or functional life skills, management skills and behavior modification skills must be woven into lessons in order to facilitate progress with special-needs students. Though individual lessons concern specific academic areas, hours of planning on how to get the material into small sequences, increasing frequently limited attention spans, and reinforcing the act of repetition for these children are a necessity.

The special-needs teacher, then, has to make the whole school receptive to the special-needs child. All the work done within the class to prepare that child to go into the mainstream of normal classes and activities can be undone by the normal classroom teacher's frown or body language or by another child's ridicule. Like any child, the special-needs child may experience the sting of pain each time he or she is ridiculed or criticized. Because the special-needs teacher is trained to help students develop their self-esteem, he or she can often help the student get beyond the pain to a place of happiness.

Children with special needs take time, individualized instruction, and specific instructional strategies set within annual goals based on their specific disability often using individualized remediation techniques. The regular classroom teacher has neither been trained nor prepared for these special educational structures. Due to the differing emphasis, unique curricula commonly used only in special education additionally need to be coordinated with special services provided along the way. All curricula must be adjusted and modified to match learner needs and abilities by the special education teacher (Meier, 1992). As stated before, general education teachers and special education teachers have very different professional knowledge structures and foundations. They identify strengths and weaknesses differently. "Special educators emphasize student strengths and needs that relate to curriculum and instruction, and general educators emphasize student strengths and needs related to social skills and behaviors. Traditionally special education teacher preparation programs have been grounded in behavioral theory whereas general education teacher preparation is grounded in cognitive or constructivist theory—a process orientation" (King-Sears and Carpenter, 1996, pp. 226–236).

The role of the special education teacher involves bearing the instructional responsibility similar to that of the regular education teacher; however, determining eligibility for services, which involves diagnosis; following IEP progress; and facilitating the participation in general education settings, when appropriate, are additional responsibilities. Along with collaboration with regular education teachers, the special education teacher works with the school psychologist in order to collaborate on prereferral observations and screening for possible special education placement.

In response to a survey in 1998 given by the Council for Exceptional Children (CEC) to its membership on special education teaching conditions, the greatest challenges facing effective teaching were: (1) paperwork, (2) class size, (3) conflicting role expectations (additional certifications added to special education courses already completed, by some states), (4) lack of collaboration with general education teachers, including lack of problem-solving opportunities with general education teachers, (5) lack of access to technology, (6) poorly trained paraeducators, and (7) lack of opportunity for professional development. The CEC is now holding regional meetings throughout the nation on special education teacher conditions and is working with other professional associations and parents to explore solutions.

According to Deiner (1993) the special education teacher and often the general education teacher in an inclusive setting must be able to specifically (1) program both for children with and without disabilities in one classroom, (2) hold individual conferences with parents about their children and cooperate with them to design an individual program, (3) conduct parent meetings to include the parents of all the children in their class, (4) participate in the early diagnosis of children with disabilities and be able to interpret the assessment and diagnostic reports coming from educational as well as noneducational sources, (5) write (with input from parents and other professionals) and implement IEPs for children over three years of age and individualized family service plans (IFSPs) for children below three years of age, (6) evaluate the child and the program itself to make changes and determine its effectiveness, (7) become the child's advocate when that child's needs are not being adequately met, and (8) be aware of legislation and litigation pertaining to teaching.

The philosophy of interdisciplinarity put into practice is the only way to bring special education and general education together. Additionally, cooperative consultation between the special education teacher and the regular education teacher is most likely to result in successful and positive decisionmaking.

Welch, Judge, Anderson, Bray, Child, and Franke (1990) describe prereferral consultation as a form of collaborative consultation. Prereferral consultation is a process that occurs before prescreening, an attempt to do very basic screening by communication of observations in order to identify children who are eligible for special services and placement. In the prereferral process, educators mutually identify a problem, consider a variety of possible interventions, and attempt and monitor such. This process is neither the regular or special education teacher advising the other. It can be two regular classroom teachers, two special education teachers, or a special and regular classroom teacher. One educator seeks support from a colleague in order to clarify and facilitate a situation.

Collaborative consultation is a method used to generate creative alternatives to traditional educational approaches for individual students. The educator develops a plan for selecting among resource and instructional alternatives to traditional pullout services. There are times during the day when the least intrusive form of assistance can be employed without taking the mildly disabled student out of the class. Through collaborative consultation, it is hoped that one of two things will occur: by collaboratively assessing current techniques and the effects on the student, a referral process might no longer be necessary; or this model might serve as additional verification that services different from those available in the regular education classroom are necessary (Donaldson and Christiansen, 1990).

The University of South Florida has responded to the need for reform, which can be applied to the regular and special education teacher roles. Its concept of change is based on five contextual phenomena: "(a) school reform which requires a rethinking of the system of which special education is a part; (b) the promotion of an inclusion policy at the national level; (c) the emergence of serious debate regarding the paradigms guiding traditional educational research; (d) decreasing resources available to support teacher education programs; and (e) increasing demands for well-educated and appropriately certified teachers" (Paul, Epanchin, Rosselli, and Duchnowski, 1996, pp. 310–322).

PARENTAL INVOLVEMENT AND THE NEED FOR PARENT EDUCATION

More attention is now being paid to *parental involvement* as a fundamental element in the academic success of all children. The field of early childhood now recognizes the important role parents play as the child's first and most important teacher. The National Education Goals Panel in 1998 established a set of goals that all persons involved in education and related health and social services were asked to achieve. Goal 8, "parental participation," states, "every school will promote partnerships that will increase parental involvement and participation in promoting the social, emotional, and academic growth of children" (The National Education Goals Panel, 1998, p. 36).

Building bridges between home and school becomes especially important in the case of exceptional student education. A parent of a child with a disability not only serves as caregiver but also takes a key role in the education, assessment, and advocacy of and for their child. This role thrusts a parent into a collaborative process that has potential to alienate rather than help. By providing this parent with the tools necessary to comprehend the legal and educational ramifications of professional collaboration and service delivery models, children will be the beneficiaries. Empowering parents can minimize family stress and provide critical resources for support. All members of a family are affected by a child with disabilities, and a full range of services and support is often needed. Parent education is a critical piece in helping a child with disabilities reach his or her full potential.

Today's statistics serve as a strong indication that families are faced with risk factors that can directly impact their children's academic success. The Children's Defense Fund (1999) published the following key facts about American children:

- ◦ 1 in 2 live in a single-parent family at some point in childhood;
- ◦ 1 in 3 will be poor at some point in his or her childhood;
- ◦ 1 in 3 is born to unmarried parents;
- ◦ 1 in 3 is behind a year or more in school;
- ◦ 1 in 4 is born poor;
- ◦ 1 in 4 lives with only one parent;
- ◦ 1 in 5 is born to a mother who did not graduate from high school;
- ◦ 1 in 8 never graduates from high school;
- ◦ 1 in 8 is born to a teenage mother;
- ◦ 1 in 12 has a disability;
- ◦ 1 in 25 is born to a mother who received late or no prenatal care.

For a significant segment of today's culturally diverse population, the stresses of disadvantage can place children in jeopardy. When multiple risk factors are compounded by the additional responsibility of caring for, and educating, a child with a disability, a family becomes exceptionally vulnerable. "The challenges faced by families exert a primary influence on their ability and desire to access services, and their resources for maintaining an active role with formal education and service delivery systems" (Hanson and Carta, 1996, p. 201).

Because of the intricacies of service delivery of exceptional education programs, the parents' role as advocate becomes particularly dynamic. Public Law 105-17, the Individuals with Disabilities Education

Act (IDEA) Amendments of 1997, builds upon Public Law 94-142 and Public Law 101-476 by further strengthening the rights of children with disabilities and their parents. These laws recognize and validate the key role parents play in the educational process of their children. This role is one that incorporates every aspect of a child's education including the process of evaluation, placement, monitoring of records, and management of behavioral issues.

IDEA 1997 also acknowledges parents' need to know to be significant. In order to empower parents, the following changes were implemented:

1. "Parent counseling and training" means that parents will receive support to help them acquire those skills necessary to implement their child's IEP or IFSP;
2. A new section has been added with regard to children with disabilities in public charter schools; their parents retain all rights under IDEA, and compliance with Part B of IDEA is required regardless of whether a public charter school receives Part B funds;
3. Parents may invite any individual "with knowledge or special expertise" to be on the IEP team;
4. Public agencies must inform parents relating to the participation of other individuals on the IEP team who have knowledge or special expertise about the child; and
5. Parents must be given a copy of their child's IEP without cost or having to request it.

We live in a nation of great diversity, and families' expectations for their children are sometimes deeply rooted in the value systems within their own cultures. Because of this, professionals cannot prescribe generic educational plans for individual children. There is a need for those practicing in the field of special education to "personalize" their professional relationships with their families. This requires those working with families to understand the family based on a *family systems theory,* which considers a family to be its own social system with its own particular needs and attributes (Turnbull and Turnbull, 1990). The underlying premise of this theory is that each family member's school experiences have an impact on the other members of the family because members are so closely interrelated.

Parents who are informed about early intervention can positively influence development in their young children. For older students, parents can serve as "the primary determinant of success in transition programs" (McNair and Rusch as cited in Turnbull and Turnbull, 1996, p. 3).

Whereas parent involvement in the educational planning process of children with disabilities dates back to 1975, the involvement of adolescents in their own planning is relatively new. "Research has shown that student involvement in educational planning is for the most part either nonexistent or passive" (Van Reusen and Bos as cited in Turnbull and Turnbull, 1996, p. 3). By educating adolescents so that they understand their own potential and capabilities, exceptional education professionals and parents are empowering their children to enter adulthood with self-determination.

The unique characteristics of family make it imperative that parents and children understand the legislation, requirements, and educational services available concerning special education. This is the only way to ensure that their children will have full access to a free and appropriate education.

REFERENCES

Baum, D., and C. Wells, 1990. "Promoting Handicap Awareness in Preschool Children." In *Annual Editions, Educating Exceptional Children*. 5th ed. Guilford, CT: Dushkin Publishing.

Beatty, N., ed., 1992. *Heart Start: The Emotional Foundations of School Readiness.* Executive Summary, Zero to Three. Arlington, VA: National Center for Clinical Infant Programs.

Bowe, F. G., 1995. *Birth to Five: Early Childhood Special Education.* New York: Delmar Publishers.

Brantlinger, E., 1997. "Using Ideology: Cases of Nonrecognition of the Politics of Research and Practice in Special Education." *Review of Educational Research* 67, no. 4: 425–459.

Bruer, J. T., 1999. "In Search of . . . Brain-Based Education." *Kappan* (May): 649–657.

———, 1999. *The Myth of the First Three Years.* New York: Free Press.

Buehler, C., and D. Dugas, 1979. *Directory of Learning Resources for Learning Disabilities.* Waterford, CT: Bureau of Business Practice.

Burnett, G., 1994. *Urban Teachers and Collaborative School-Linked Services.* ERIC Clearinghouse on Urban Education, New York: National Education Association, Washington, DC.

Campbell, T. A., and C. T. Ramey, 1995. "Cognitive and School Outcomes for High Risk African American Students at Middle Adolescence: Positive Effects of Early Intervention." *American Educational Research Journal* 32: 743–772.

Center for Special Education Technology, July 1990. *Tech Use Guide.* Reston, VA: Office of Special Education Programs, U.S. Department of Education.

Chadha, A., 1999. "The Inclusive Initiative in India." *Journal of the International Association of Special Education* 3, no. 1: 31–34.

Children's Defense Fund, 1999. *The State of America's Children.* Boston: Beacon Press.

Chiles, L., January 1998. Brain-Mind Connections Conference. Gainesville, FL: University of Florida.

Choate, J. S., 1993. *Successful Mainstreaming: Proven Ways to Detect and Correct Special Needs.* Boston: Allyn and Bacon.

Cline, S., and D. Schwartz, 1999. *Diverse Populations of Gifted Children.* Upper Saddle River, NJ: Merrill Publishers.

Davies, S., 1996. "The Tenth School." *Principal* 76, no. 2 (Nov.): 13–16.

Deiner, P. L., 1993. *Resources for Teaching Children with Disabilities.* Fort Worth, TX: Harcourt Brace Jovanich College Publishers.

Deno, S. L., A. Foegen, S. Robinson, and C. Espin, 1996. "Commentary: Facing the Realities of Inclusion for Students with Mild Disabilities." *The Journal of Special Education* 30, no. 3: 345–357.

Dixon, S. D., and R. Bejar, 1988. "Brain Lesions in Cocaine and Methamphetamine Exposed Neonates." *Pediatric Research* 23: 405.

Donaldson, R., and J. Christiansen, 1990. "Consultation and Collaboration: A Decision-Making Model." *Teaching Exceptional Children* 22, no. 2 (Winter): 225–228.

Dryfoos, J. G., 1994. *Full-Service Schools: A Revolution in Health and Social Services for Children, Youth, and Families.* San Francisco: Jossey-Bass.

Galis, S. A., and C. K. Tanner, 1995. *Inclusion in Elementary Schools.* Education Policy Analysis Archives, available on-line: http://olam.ed.asu.edu/epaa/v3n15.htm.

Gearheart, B., R. C. Mullen, and C. J. Gearheart, 1993. *Exceptional Individuals: An Introduction.* Pacific Grove, CA: Brooks/Cole Publishing.

Gearheart, C., and B. Gearheart, 1990. *Introduction to Special Education Assessment: Principles and Practices.* Denver: Love Publishing.

Gilkerson, L., and H. Als, 1995. "Developmentally Supportive Care in the Neonatal Intensive Care Unit." *Zero to Three* 15, no. 6: 34–35.

Greenspan, S., and B. Benderly, 1997. *The Growth of the Mind and the Endangered Origins of Intelligence.* Boston: Addison-Wesley.

Griffith, D., 1992. "Prenatal Exposure to Cocaine and Other Drugs: Developmental and Educational Prognoses." *Kappan* 74, no. 1: 30–34.

Hamburg, D. A., 1994. *Today's Children: Creating a Future for a Generation in Crisis.* New York: Time Books.

Hardman, M. L., C. J. Drew, M. W. Egan, and B. Wolf, 1990. *Human Exceptionality.* 3rd ed. Boston: Allyn and Bacon.

Healy, J., 1994. *Your Child's Growing Mind.* New York: Doubleday.

Karr-Morse, R., and M. Wiley, 1997. *Ghosts from the Nursery.* New York: Atlantic Monthly Press.

King-Sears, M., and S. L. Carpenter, 1996. "Empowering Teachers and Students with Instructional Choices in Inclusive Settings." *Remedial and Special Education* 17, no. 4: 226–236.

Lerner, J., 1993. *Learning Disabilities.* 6th ed. Boston: Houghton Mifflin.

Malmskog, S., and A. P. McDonnell, 1999. "Teacher-Mediated Facilitation of Engagement by Children with Developmental Delays in Inclusive Preschools." *Topics in Early Childhood Special Education* 19, no. 4: 213.

McAfee, O., and D. Leong, 1997. *Assessing and Guiding Young Children's Development and Learning.* 2nd ed. Boston: Allyn and Bacon.

Meier, F. E., 1992. *Competency-Based Instruction for Teachers of Students with Special Learning Needs.* Needham Heights, MA: Allyn and Bacon.

Minke, K. M., G. G. Bear, S. A. Deemer, and S. M. Griffin, 1996. "Teachers' Experiences with Inclusive Classrooms: Implications for Special Education Reform." *Journal of Special Education* 30, no. 2: 152–186.

National Association of State Boards of Education, 1992. "A Brief History of Special Education." *Winners All: A Call for Inclusive Schools.* Report of the National Association of State Boards of Education, Alexandria, VA.

National Education Goals Panel, 1998. *Promising Practices: Progress Toward the Goals, Lessons from the States.* Washington, DC: National Education Goals Panel.

National Head Start Association, 2000. "Report of the Head Start 2010 Advisory Panel." Alexandria, VA: National Head Start Association.

Paul, J., B. Epanchin, H. Rosselli, and A. Duchnowski, 1996. "The Transformation of Teacher Education and Special Education." *Remedial and Special Education* 17, no. 5: 310–322.

Perry, B. D., R. A. Pollard, T. L. Blakley, and W. L. Baker, 1995. "Childhood Trauma, the Neurobiology of Adaptation, and Use-Dependent Development of the Brain: How States Become Traits." *Infant Mental Health Journal* 16, no. 4: 271–291.

Provenzo, E. F., A. Brett, and G. N. McCloskey, 1999. *Computers, Curriculum, and Cultural Change.* Mahwah, NJ: Lawrence Erlbaum Associates.

Regional Intervention Program, 2000. *Twenty-five Year Study Finds Parents Can Deter Destructive Behavior.* Nashville, TN: Regional Intervention Program.

RESNA, 1999. *Spotlight on Technology.* Arlington, VA: Rehabilitation Engineering and Assistive Technology Society of North America (RESNA).

Sacks, A., and B. Watnick, 1999. "Brain Research: Implications for Early Intervention Theory, Research and Application." *Journal of the International Association of Special Education* 2, no. 1: 29–43.

Serraller, F. C., 1999. *Velazquez.* 2nd ed. Fundacion Amigos del Museo del Prado, Alianza Editorial, S. A. Madrid: Calle Juan Ignacio Luca de Lena.

Shore, R., 1997. *Rethinking the Brain: New Insights into Early Development.* New York: Families and Work Institute.

Shriner, J. G., 2000. "Legal Perspectives on School Outcomes for Students with Disabilities." *Journal of Special Education* 4, no. 33: 232–239.

Turnbull, A. P., and H. R. Turnbull, 1990. *Families, Professionals, and Exceptionality: A Special Partnership.* New York: Merrill/Macmillan.

———, 1996. "Helping Students Communicate in Planning Conferences: What Do Students with Disabilities Tell Us about the Importance of Family Involvement in the Transition from School to Adult Life?" *Exceptional Children* 62: 3.

Viola, S., 1997. "Redefining Assessment: Obtaining Information that Is Relevant to Curricular Interventions." *Journal of the International Association of Special Education* 1, no. 1: 61–67.

Welch, M., T. Judge, J. Anderson, J. Bray, B. Child, and L. Franke, 1990. "A Tool for Implementing Prereferral Consultation." *Teaching Exceptional Children* 22, no. 2 (Winter): 223–224.

Wolf, N., 1999. *Diego Velazquez, 1599–1660: The Face of Spain.* Cologne, Germany: Taschen Publishers.

Woodward, J., and H. Rieth, 1997. "A Historical Review of Technology Research in Special Education." *Review of Educational Research* 67, no. 4: 503–536.

Ysseldyke, J. E., and B. Algozzine, 1990. *Introduction to Special Education.* 2nd ed. Boston: Houghton Mifflin.

Chapter Two

•◆ Chronology

The following chronology presents in timeline fashion a review of the laws, court decisions, and related developments pertinent to the recognition and support of special education in the United States.

1791   The Tenth Amendment of the U.S. Constitution gives states jurisdiction over educational matters.

1840   Rhode Island becomes the first state to pass legislation for compulsory school attendance.

1855   The first kindergarten is established, in Watertown, Wisconsin.

1880s   Public concern regarding educational matters inspires the creation of the National Education Association (NEA) and the U.S. Office of Education. Public schools adapt an age-grade level system, categorizing students into grade levels according to chronological age. Differences between students placed in this system thus become very obvious.

1900s   The NEA endorses the revised Binet test of intelligence as being useful for predicting school achievement.

1916   Lewis Terman completes the design of the Stanford-Binet Intelligence Scale tests, which introduce the concept of intelligence quotient (IQ). This leads to the assumption that intelligence tests can predict school success or failure, which quickly becomes a significant factor in student stability placement.

1919   All states require compulsory school attendance.

        The White House Conference on Child Youth and Protection

stresses that "healthful school living is the most important aspect of education."

1946   The National School Lunch Act subsidizes school cafeteria facilities, placing emphasis on diet-related health of the school-age population.

1954   The U.S. Supreme Court's ruling on *Brown vs. the Board of Education* puts an end to "separate but equal" schools. This emphasis on the rights of a diverse population will serve as a basis for future rulings that children with handicaps cannot be excluded from school.

The Cooperative Research Act, one of the first federal laws relating to education, initiates cooperative research between the federal government and universities through funding of studies in critical issues in education. This serves as a beginning for professionals to recognize the need to study the education of handicapped students.

1958   The Education of the Mentally Retarded Children Act, P.L. 85-926, an amendment to the National Defense Education Act, becomes the first federal law addressing special education. It authorizes funding to train teachers and leadership personnel in the education of children who are considered mentally retarded. Overall, the National Defense Education Act serves to shift public attention from "healthful living" toward improved instruction in math, science, and foreign languages.

1961   The Special Education Act, P.L. 87-276, authorizes funds for training professionals to train teachers of the deaf.

1965   The Elementary and Secondary Education Act (ESEA), P.L. 89-10, provides a plan for rectifying the inequality of educational opportunity for economically underprivileged children by authorizing federal aid to improve the education of disadvantaged children, including students with disabilities. It results in the creation of the Head Start program for disadvantaged children and their families and will become the basis for future special education legislation.

1966   An amendment to Title VI of ESEA, P.L. 89-750, establishes the first federal grant program for children and youth with disabilities at the local school level. Additionally, it creates the Bureau of Education for the Handicapped and what later will become the National Council on Disabilities. Most important, it establishes equal status for programs for children with disabilities with the Bureau of Elementary and Secondary Education, the Bureau of Vocational Education, and the Bureau of Higher Education.

1967 *Hobson vs. Hansen* declares the tracking system, which uses standardized tests as a basis for special education placement, unconstitutional because it discriminates against black and poor children.

1968 Another ESEA amendment, P.L. 90-247, becomes the first special education legislation enacted at the federal level establishing a set of "discretionary programs" that provide support for special education services. Examples of this include regional resource centers, services for the deaf-blind, instructional media programs, and research in special education.

1970 The ruling in *Diana vs. State Board of Education of California* declares that children cannot be placed in special education on the basis of culturally biased tests or tests given in a language other than the child's native language.

The Education of the Handicapped Act (EHA) of 1970, P.L. 91-230, amends Title VI of P.L. 89-750, consolidating a number of separate federal grant programs into one authorization that becomes known as Part B, EHA.

1971 In *Wyatt vs. Stickney/Wyatt vs. Aderholt, Alabama,* the Court rules that individuals in state institutions have the right to appropriate treatment in those institutions.

1972 *Pennsylvania Association for Retarded Citizens (PARC) vs. Commonwealth* is a precedent setting case. PARC and thirteen children bring a class action suit against the Commonwealth of Pennsylvania for failure to provide its mentally retarded children with publicly supported education. The result is an agreement on the part of the Commonwealth of Pennsylvania to (1) not apply any law that would postpone, end, or deny mentally retarded children access to publicly supported education; and

(2) to identify all school age children with mental retardation and place them in a free public program of education and training appropriate to their disability.

In *Mills vs. Board of Education,* parents and guardians of seven District of Columbia children are awarded a court judgment against the district school board whereby all children with a disability, regardless of the severity, are entitled to receive a publicly supported education. Just as *Brown vs. the Board of Education* applied to race, the federal district court interprets the equal protection clause of the Fourteenth Amendment to apply to discrimination of students on the basis of disability. The impact of *Mills* is to reinforce legislation passed by forty-five states mandating the funding of special education.

1973   Section 504 of the Rehabilitation Act, P.L. 93-112, bars discrimination against the disabled in any federally funded program and specifically requires appropriate education services for disabled children. This is the first civil rights law specifically protecting the right of handicapped children; originally dealing with employment, it will be amended in 1974 (P.L. 93-516) to cover a broader array of services for the handicapped. It establishes nondiscrimination in employment, admission into institutions of higher learning, and access to public facilities.

1974   Education amendments passed this year contain two significant laws. The first makes provisions for education to all children with disabilities and reauthorizes all discretionary programs; the second is the Family Education Rights and Privacy Act (the Buckley amendment) giving parents and children under the age of eighteen, and students eighteen and over, the right to examine records in their personal files.

1975   The Education for All Handicapped Children Act, P.L. 94-142, mandates for all children with disabilities (1) a free and appropriate public education; (2) the right of due process; (3) education in the least restrictive environment; and (4) individualized educational programs. These four areas will serve as the nucleus of special education philosophy, documentation, and program development. Nowhere does this law state exactly how costs are to be considered. Whenever a service is necessary, cost consideration cannot allow a school district to escape its obligation to that child. Decisions concerning instructional matters remain at the discretion of state and local authorities.

1979   In *Central York District vs. Commonwealth of Pennsylvania Department of Education* the court rules that school districts must provide services for gifted and talented children whether or not advance guarantee of reimbursement from the state has been received.

The decision in *Larry P. vs. Riles,* a California case first brought to court in 1972, establishes that IQ test scores cannot be the sole basis for placing children in special classes.

1980   The ruling in *Armstrong vs. Kline, Pennsylvania,* establishes that some severely handicapped children have the right to schooling for twelve months instead of only the nine-month school year, if proof can be given that they will regress during the summer recess. The court also ruled that a state law requiring a nine-month school year violates P.L. 94-142 and Section 504 of the Vocational Rehabilitation Act.

1981   In regard to *Debra P. vs. Turlington,* the U.S. Court of Appeals for the Fifth Circuit Court holds that a diploma is a protected property right under the Fourteenth Amendment. If a state wishes to substantially change the requirements to earn a diploma, procedural due process requires that adequate notice of the change(s) be provided to students.

1982   In *Rowley vs. Hendrick Hudson School,* the issue of a free, appropriate public education (FAPE) reinforces school districts' provision of services permitting students with disabilities to benefit from instruction. Handed down by the U. S. Court of Appeals for the Second Circuit, this decision supports the philosophy behind IDEA, setting the standard for FAPE as more than simple access to education; instead, FAPE is viewed to consist of educational instruction assigned to meet the unique needs of a student with disabilities, supported by such services as needed to benefit from instruction. This law provides guidance for courts to use in deciding on a case-by-case basis whether a school has offered a FAPE to a student with disabilities.

1983   *Hall vs. Vance County Board of Education*—involves James Hall, a student with dyslexia who had been in the public schools for six years with no real grade improvement in his primary area of deficiency despite being consistently promoted. His parents enrolled James in a private school for the 1980–1981 school year and realized significant improvement in reading scores. Having determined that the IEP developed by Vance County, North Carolina, did not provide Hall with an appropriate education citing standardized education scores of sufficient gain, the presiding judge ruled to reward Hall's parents with reimbursement for the private school tuition.

In *Brookhart vs. Illinois State Board of Education,* a case involving a student receiving special education services, the circuit court rules that students with disabilities can be held to the same graduation standards as other students, but that their programs of instruction are not developed to meet the goal of passing the minimum competency test. The court also finds that students are entitled to sufficient time to prepare for a test (in this case the minimum competency test) and that accommodations are required as long as they do not modify the test to the point of altering its validity characteristics.

The Carl Perkins Vocational Act, P.L. 98-524, has as its focus the authorization of federal funds to support vocational education programs and offer access to those underserved in the past and who are special needs students, to include persons with a disability or who are disadvantaged or have limited English proficiency. Each of these groups is to henceforth receive equal access to recruitment, enrollment, and placement activities in vocational education, including specific courses of study, cooperative education, apprenticeship programs, and guidance and counseling services. Services have to be coordinated between public agencies, vocational education, special education, and state vocational rehabilitation services. These must all be consistent with objectives specified in the IEP.

1984   The case *Burlington School Committee vs. Department of Education* again affirms the meaning of IDEA whereby public schools may be required to pay for private school placements when an appropriate education is not provided by the school district.

In *Cleburne vs. Cleburne Living Center, Texas,* the U.S. Supreme Court rules unanimously that communities cannot use a discriminatory zoning ordinance to prevent establishment of group homes for persons with mental retardation.

1985   In *Burlington vs. Department of Education for the Commonwealth of Massachusetts,* the Supreme Court addresses IEPs and what they should include. The Court rules that the free, appropriate public education (FAPE) mandated by IDEA is designed for the specific needs of the child through the IEP, which is a "comprehensive statement of the educational needs of a handicapped child and the specially designed instruction and related services to be employed to meet those needs."

An EHA amendment, P.L. 99-457, mandates services for preschoolers with disabilities and establishes the Part H program to help states develop and provide systems for early intervention to include infants and toddlers from birth through age three. This is a landmark success for proponents of early intervention. The law provides for an individualized family service plan for each qualifying family.

1986   The Handicapped Children's Protection Act, P.L. 99-372, provides for reasonable attorney's fees and costs to parents and guardians who prevail in administrative hearings or court where there is a dispute with the school system concerning their child's right to a free and appropriate education.

1988   *Honig vs. Doe* again reaffirms IDEA with regard to excluding a student from school in that if a student's behavior is related to his or her disability, that student cannot be denied education.

The case *Lachman vs. State Board of Education* (852 F2d 290, Seventh Circuit) concerns parents who want their deaf child mainstreamed in a neighborhood school in contrast to the opinion of their school district, which believes that half days in a self-contained hearing-impaired classroom are appropriate. The court applies the Rowley rule to determine if the state has met federal standards in providing a free, appropriate education. The court rules in support of mainstreaming but determines that educational methods are the responsibility of the state and local education agencies and that parents have no right to dictate specific program or methodology to the school.

Martinez vs. School Board of Hillsboro County, Florida (861 F2d 1502 Eleventh Circuit) concerns a trainable mentally handicapped (TMH) AIDS-infected child who is not toilet trained, whose saliva contained blood, and who had skin lesions and was thus excluded from classroom placement. Whereas the trial court found "a remote theoretical possibility" of disease transmission, the district court finds the child presented no significant risk to exclude her from the TMH classroom. The court determines that "reasonable medical judgments" are required to determine the level of risk for children with a communicable disease. The parents win their case—AIDS cases cannot be excluded from public school.

1989   In *Timothy W. vs. Rochester School District,* a case from New Hampshire that is taken to the U.S. Appeals Court, a literal interpretation of P.L. 94-142 is upheld, requiring that all handicapped children be provided with a free, appropriate public education. The three-judge appeals court overturns the decision of the district court judge who had ruled that the local school district was not obligated to educate a thirteen-year-old boy with multiple and severe disabilities because he could not "benefit" from special education.

U.S. governors meet in Charlottesville, Virginia, and commit themselves to a nationwide effort to reform education around a core set of six goals for improving the education system. These goals, with the addition of two more, will be formalized into law in 1994 in the Goals 2000: Educate America Act.

The ruling in *Lascari vs. Board of Education of the Ramapo Indian Hills Regional High School District* (New Jersey) states that the required public-school IEP is intended to guide teachers and to ensure that the child receives the necessary education; without an adequately drafted IEP it would basically be impossible to measure a child's progress, which is necessary to determine changes to be made to the next IEP. The court rules that the IEP in this case is incapable of review because it is based on teacher subjectivity, thereby denying the child's parents the opportunity to help shape their child's education and hindering the child's ability to receive the education to which he is entitled.

1990   The Individuals with Disabilities Education Act (IDEA), P.L.
101-476, originally realized as an amendment to the Education of the Handicapped Act, reauthorizes and expands discretionary programs and mandates transition services and assistive technology services to be included in the IEP, adding autism and traumatic brain injury to those categories for special education programs and services.

The Americans with Disabilities Act (ADA), P.L. 101-336, is passed. ADA is based on the Rehabilitation Act of 1973, which guarantees equal opportunities for individuals with disabilities in employment, public accommodation, and transportation. Included in this act are persons with HIV infection, diabetics who without insulin would lapse into a coma, former cancer patients, persons erroneously classified as having a disability (for example, a psychiatric disorder), recovering alcoholics and drug addicts, and those with a back condition. Accessibility requirements for employers with over twenty-five employees will begin in 1992, and for employers with over fifteen employees will begin in 1994. Public services affected by the ADA include public transportation and telecommunications, which must make changes to telephone services offered to the general public with respect to interstate and intrastate as well as TT/TDD users. As defined by the act, *public accommodations* include private entities that affect commerce, among them restaurants, theaters, hotels, shopping malls, retail stores, museums, libraries, parks, private schools, day care centers, and similar places of accommodation, all of which may not discriminate on the basis of disability. Physical barriers must be removed, new construction must be made accessible, alterations to existing facilities must be made for travel paths and such, and new buses and similar vehicles must be accessible. ADA does not require modifications that would alter the nature of the service provided by the public accommodation; for example, a physician who does not treat that disability on a regular basis will not be required to add that service.

1991   In *French vs. Omaha Public Schools,* the court determines that the IEP at a Nebraska public school was appropriate when it analyzed the goals and objectives and the inclusion of very specific test data, including percentile ranks and grade equivalent scores used to describe the child's present levels of performance.

1992　In *Greer vs. Rome City School District* (Georgia), the Eleventh Circuit Court rules in favor of parents who objected to the placement of their daughter in a self-contained special education classroom. Administrators at the child's school had determined that the services needed to keep the child in the regular education classroom were too costly. The court's opinion states that all options must be considered before removing a child from the regular classroom.

1993　The Third District Court rules in *Oberti vs. Board of Education of the Borough of Clementon School District* (California) in favor of a placement for a special-needs child that was more inclusive than that provided by a self-contained placement. The court bases its decision on the fact that the whole range of supplemental aids and services must be considered to make a regular education setting successful.

1994　The Improving America's Schools Act (IASA) extends for five years the authorization of appropriations for programs under the Elementary and Secondary Education Act of 1965 and requires that districts and schools receiving federal Title I funds implement a standards-based accountability system to include multiple sources of assessment data. All children, including students with disabilities, are to be included in assessment from which achievement results can be disaggregated for several groups including "special education status."

　　　The Safe and Drug-Free Schools and Communities Act (SDFSCA), Title IV of the Improving America's Schools Act of 1994, authorizes the U.S. Secretary of Education to make grants to states to prevent school violence and to deter the use of illegal drugs and alcohol. This affects special education in terms of early intervention and rehabilitation in that the SDFSCA provides federal assistance to governors, state and local educational agencies, institutions of higher education, and nonprofit entities for (1) grants to local education agencies (LEAs) and educational service agencies to establish, operate, and improve local programs of school drug and violence prevention, early intervention, rehabilitation referral, and education in elementary and secondary schools; (2) grants to public and private community based agencies and organizations for programs of drug and violence prevention, early intervention, rehabilitation referral, and education; and (3) development, training, technical assistance, and coordination activities.

The Gun-Free Schools Act (GFSA) requires every state receiving federal aid for elementary and secondary education to enact a law requiring a local educational agency (LEA) to expel from school for at least one year any student who brings a gun to school. Educational services must continue for students with disabilities who are properly expelled, although services may be continued in another setting. If the student's action in bringing a firearm to school is related to his or her disability, the student may not be expelled but may instead be suspended for up to ten days. The LEA may also seek a court order to remove a student who is considered dangerous.

In *Sacramento City Unified School District vs. Holland,* the Ninth Circuit Court upholds the decision of the lower court, which decided in favor of the parents of a California child who had been placed half-time in a special education classroom and half-time in a regular education classroom; considering the nonacademic benefits of the regular classroom to be significant, the circuit court rules that the child should be placed in the regular classroom full-time.

The Goals 2000: Educate America Act, P.L. 103-227, based on eight goals formulated by U.S. governors for improving the national education system, is signed into law. The eight goals are:

Goal 1: Ready to Learn—By the year 2000, all children in the United States will start school ready to learn.

Goal 2: School Completion—By the year 2000, the high school graduation rate will increase to at least 90 percent.

Goal 3: Student Achievement and Citizenship—By the year 2000, all students will leave grades 4, 8, and 12 having demonstrated competency over challenging subject matter, including English, mathematics, science, foreign languages, civics and government, economics, arts, history, and geography. Every school in the United States will ensure that all students learn to use their minds well, so they may be prepared for responsible citizenship, further learning, and productive employment in the economy.

Goal 4: Teacher Education and Professional Development—By the year 2000, the nation's teaching force will have access to programs for the continued improvement of their professional skills and the opportunity to acquire the knowledge and skills needed to instruct and prepare all students in the United States for the next century.

Goal 5: Mathematics and Science—By the year 2000, students in the United States will be first in the world in mathematics and science achievement.

Goal 6: Adult Literacy and Lifelong Learning—By the year 2000, every adult in the United States will be literate and will possess the knowledge and skills necessary to compete in a global economy and exercise the rights and responsibilities of citizenship.

Goal 7: Safe, Disciplined, and Alcohol- and Drug-Free Schools—By the year 2000, every school in the United States will be free of drugs, violence, and the unauthorized presence of firearms and alcohol and will offer a disciplined environment conducive to learning.

Goal 8: Parental participation—By the year 2000, every school in the United States will promote partnerships that will increase parental involvement and participation in promoting the social, emotional, and academic growth of children.

1996   The Ninth Circuit Court affirms in *County of San Diego vs. California Special Education Hearing Office* that a county cannot challenge a student's classification as seriously emotionally disturbed on the ground that state law gives school districts the sole authority to make such eligibility decisions.

Wall vs. Mattituck-Cutchogue School District concerns parents of an elementary student with learning disabilities who bring action against a school district in New York requesting their child be taught reading using the Orton-Gillingham instructional procedure. The student, who was educated in a public school's self-contained special education classroom, was unilaterally placed in a private school that used the reading procedure. At an earlier hearing, the parents did not challenge the appropriateness of the IEP; rather, they contested the school district's failure to offer the Orton-Gillingham program. The hearing officer found that the school district's program was appropriate, and the parents appealed to federal district court. The court, finding that the student has made progress in the school district's program, affirms the ruling for the school district.

The judge for *Evans vs. Board of Education of Rhinebeck Center School District* (New York) overturns earlier administrative rulings and awards the Evans family reimbursement for tuition at a private school because the IEP failed to identify deficit areas, was based on outdated information, and did not adequately set forth strategies for evaluating progress.

1997   In *Logue vs. Shawnee Mission Public School Unified School District,* the federal district court that hears the case determines that Kansas does not have a higher standard of appropriateness than the IDEA. The court indicates that since the measure in question parallels the Supreme Court's standard in *Rowley,* there is no evidence to indicate that the state legislature intended to bind itself to a higher duty.

Another IDEA amendment, P.L. 105-17, applies to the nation's 5.8 million children with disabilities and enhances what children with disabilities learn versus what is expected in the regular classroom, in short decreeing that children with disabilities have the right to be educated, or included, in the regular classroom. It differs from the previous IDEA amendment, P.L.101-476, in that it protects the rights of students and families by having them become more involved in general curriculum, eligibility, and placement, and requires on the part of the schools more accountability for results. Additionally, this amendment guarantees that general education teachers will be included in teams that develop mandated IEPs for disabled students when the student is in a general classroom. Students in special education were being excluded from many state and district assessments, which leads to exclusion from curriculum planning.

Eligibility for alternate assessments are to be made with students with significant support needs. For example, per the 1997 IDEA amendment, if the child's disability has not changed over a three-year period, that child should not be forced into unnecessary reassessment. Participation in the regular program is to be promoted as much as possible with modifications and adaptations to include adaptive and assistive technology. Disciplinary rules and instructions in terms of behaviors are to be part of the individualized education program if the child's behavior impedes learning. It is a requirement of the IEP to include a behavioral management plan and information on a child's past violent behavior. Parental responsibility in working with the schools is emphasized; parents are to be involved in eligibility and placement decisions, and the new emphasis is to be able to attain high-quality education rather than just access to education. The significance of early intervention is reiterated, and the funding formula for federal assistance under IDEA is changed to include poverty factors.

The following definitions and explanations of terms are included in the 1997 IDEA amendment in order to make explicit and clear for parents and educators the legal rights added under this amendment:

"Attention deficit disorder" and "attention deficit hyperactivity disorder" have been added as conditions that could render a child eligible under the "other health impairment" category. (See 300.7(c)(9).)

The statement "helping parents to acquire the necessary skills that will allow them to support the implementation of their child's IEP or IFSP" has been added to the definition of "parent counseling and training." (See 300.24(b)(7).)

"Travel training" has been added to the definition of "special education" and defined to mean "Providing instruction, as appropriate, to children with significant cognitive disabilities and any other children who require this instruction, to enable them to (i) develop an awareness of the environment in which they live; and (ii) learn the skills necessary to move effectively and safely from place to place within that environment (e.g., in school, in the home, at work, and in the community)." (See 300.26(b)(4).)

A new section 300.312, Developmental Delay, has been added, which makes it clear that children with disabilities in public charter schools and their parents retain all rights under this part, and that compliance with Part B is required regardless of whether a public charter school receives Part B funds.

A new section 300.313, Children Experiencing Developmental Delays, has been added to (1) specify the conditions that states and LEAs must follow in using the term, and (2) clarify that a state or LEA that elects to use "developmental delay" also may use one or more of the disability categories for any child who has been determined (through the IDEA evaluation procedures) to have a disability and need special education. Thus, if a child has an identified disability (e.g., deafness), it would be appropriate to use the term with that child even if the state or LEA is using "developmental delay" for other children aged three through nine. The regulations also make clear that a state may adopt a common definition of "developmental delay" under Parts B and C of the act.

1998   The Assistive Technology Act offers block grants to states for public education and advocacy related to assistive technology products and services. In addition, the law authorizes a new micro loan program to encourage the development and purchase of accessible technology-related products and services.

1999   The proposed Gifted and Talented Students Education Act, also called the Educational Excellence for All Children's Act, would provide funding to states based on population. It reauthorizes ESEA (1994) and Goals 2000: Educate America Act. The funds could be used at state discretion for any of four activities: personnel preparation, technical assistance, innovative programs and services, and emerging technologies including distance learning. This proposed education bill is presently in committee.

2000   The Class Size Reduction Act, P.L.106-113, Section 310, is a government initiative to help schools improve student learning by hiring additional qualified teachers so that children, especially those in early elementary grades, can attend smaller classes. Beginning July 3, 2000, the Department of Education sends class-size reduction funds to all states, the District of Columbia, Puerto Rico, the outlying areas, and the Bureau of Indian Affairs. The amount of each allocation is based on Title I or Title II of the ESEA, whichever would result in the larger amount for the state or entity.

Chapter Three

⊷ Special Education Curriculum

Curriculum can be viewed as anything that occurs in the education program during the school day. This can begin the moment a student leaves home to begin the school experience and last until the time he or she returns home. More specifically, curriculum can be viewed as a composition of vision and structure. *Vision* for a curriculum is frequently what we see as important for people to experience in order to learn. How we view the people for whom a curriculum is developed and the environment in which we anticipate they live becomes the basis of the plan for the vision. The plan we develop for this to happen takes place within a specific *structure.* That specific structure is the way the organization of the information is implemented. bō´ĭng

Once the vision and philosophy of what we want special education students to gain within the educational experience are clear, the development of curriculum becomes direct and purposeful. From knowledge and understanding obtained, skills and applications can be developed.

Eisner (as cited in Florida Department of Education, 1994) explains that *curriculum* comes from the Latin word "currere," meaning "the course to be run." Additionally, *curriculum* has been conceived of as all the experiences a child has during the school day; this includes the quality of the experiences, not just the lessons. A curriculum cannot ignore individual differences. Whatever the philosophy behind curriculum, the consequences of the concept are greater than solely educational; they influence people in a variety of ways. The development of skills is parallel to that of attitudes and values. The classroom actually becomes a social environment that serves as a microcosm for the social experiences to be experienced by each person. ᵗⁱⁱᵍⁿ´quim·

According to Fogarty (as cited in Florida Department of Education, 1994) *integrating* the curriculum helps teachers make connections between new experiences and prior knowledge. "Innovative teaching models call for integrated, cross disciplinary instruction. As teachers begin to mix and match subject-matter using creative combinations, the restructuring process is actually generated from the inside out" (p. 259). In a traditional model, there are separate and distinct disciplines. In an integrated curriculum, relating ideas and concepts within and across disciplines gives a different emphasis. By tying thoughts, social skills, topics, and technology across disciplines, commonalities emerge.

The concept of the integrated curriculum is especially significant when viewing the academic and specific needs of the special education child. A curriculum that is developed for someone needing remediation of either the material or an area of the brain, that focuses on training all thought processes, and that utilizes more tools and technology allows the special education student to operate the same part of the thought process as the rest of the group.

Although the content of a curriculum is important, the *process* of curriculum development is equally important. When the process of curriculum development for at-risk and handicapped children is based on the concept of individual differences due to intellectual, cognitive, and physical disabilities, the strategies and activities can be planned more thoughtfully. In all probability, they will have more successful outcomes. Interventionists and curriculum planners need to be very aware of this.

When dealing with young children to develop annual goals and objectives, which drive curriculum development, the presence of a family member is mandatory. Additionally, it is important that specific health professionals or allied health professionals be present in such planning. Strategies developed as part of the curriculum will be more meaningful if that professional is part of the team. Whether the health professional or a resource person is providing the therapy or recommended procedure, at least the team will be knowledgeable of the best practice. A consultation model may be the best way to implement these specific responsibilities (Bricker, 1989).

CURRICULUM DEVELOPMENT INVOLVES A MULTIDISCIPLINARY TEAM

In addition to the special education teacher and the regular education teacher, related service personnel are involved in both the IEP and curriculum development, helping to create a multidisciplinary team. They include:

Social Worker/Visiting Teacher. The school social worker/visiting teacher may

- serve as liaison between student, family, community agencies, and the schools;
- coordinate social services for the student and the family;

- consult with families to assist them in child-rearing practices;
- contact social and medical agencies regarding referrals from the school; and
- assist in the return of the students to regular class placement.

Speech-Language Pathologist. The speech-language pathologist may
- provide speech and language assessments;
- provide speech and language therapy;
- interpret test information;
- provide in-service training for special education and basic education teachers;
- provide parent training; and
- assist in the development and implementation of an appropriate individual educational plan.

Psychologist. The school psychologist may
- conduct formal observations and testing;
- interpret test information;
- supervise evaluation procedures;
- consult directly with teachers, other school personnel, and parents; and
- provide in-service training on behavior management techniques.

Behavior Specialist. The behavior specialist may
- provide technical expertise to address complex student behavior issues;
- assist school staff in development, implementation, and education of student behavior management plans; and
- provide technical expertise to assist parents in addressing complex student behavioral issues.

Guidance Counselor. The school guidance counselor may
- participate in screening, referral, and placement procedures;
- observe and participate in behavioral management strategies;
- consult with teachers with regard to specific interaction techniques designed to assist the student; and
- provide guidance and support to students who have specialized needs.

Vocational Rehabilitation (VR) Counselor. The VR counselor may
- determine specific strengths, weaknesses, needs, and interests of the individual as related to job placement;
- assist in appropriate job placement according to the individual's profile;

➡ provide for vocational training (whether on or off the job);

➡ provide for follow-up and job-related counseling; and

➡ participate in a support team of educational, career counseling, vocational, and job-training personnel.

School Nurse. The school nurse may

➡ facilitate referrals for medical and/or social services for students;

➡ serve as a consultant on matters related to student development, especially in the physical and social areas;

➡ serve as liaison between community agencies, family, and the school;

➡ provide screening for hearing, vision, or other health areas as indicated in the school health services plan.

Health Professionals (may include community nurses, pediatricians, psychiatrists, and neurologists). Health professionals may

➡ provide for the student's physical well-being;

➡ make referrals, as appropriate, to other health professionals;

➡ assist in coordination of health services between educational specialists and other medical personnel;

➡ communicate to the educational personnel the specific medical needs of the student;

➡ provide information related to medication for the student;

➡ provide assistance in implementing the school medical program; and

➡ provide specific diagnostic information.

Occupational Therapist. The occupational therapist may

➡ provide expertise in areas of motor development; positioning; adapting the environment; gross motor skills; posture; ambulation; cardiorespiratory functioning; joint mobility; muscle strengths; fine motor, perceptual-motor, and sensorimotor skills; sensory integration; and environmental and equipment adaptations to increase participation in functional daily activities;

➡ assist the student to achieve the goals and objectives on the IEP;

➡ integrate therapeutic practices noted above into the student's education program; and

➡ assist the student in integrating into and participating in normalized school, home, and community environments.

Physical Therapist. The physical therapist may

➡ provide expertise in the areas of motor development, positioning, adapting the environment, gross motor skills, posture, ambulation, cardiorespiratory functioning, joint mobility, and muscle strength;

➼ assist the student in achieving the goals and objectives on the IEP;

➼ integrate therapeutic practices noted above into the student's educational program; and

➼ assist the student in integrating into and participating in normalized school, home, and community environments.

CURRICULUM-BASED ASSESSMENT AND EVALUATION APPROACH

Measurement tools linking assessment with curriculum are frequently called curriculum-based assessment (CBA). It is important to note that focusing on the assessment or evaluation takes away from the focus of the curriculum upon which that specific form of assessment is based.

Curriculums are usually based on certain developmental norms and patterns. Provisions for handicapped children must be very specific because these are not norms and patterns specifically developed for them. Developmentally arranged patterns are very general guidelines for a very different population. Children using augmentative communications systems especially cannot adhere to these. All this considered, developmental theory and research provides a general guideline. Curriculum goals have been broadened to include competencies that cut across all developmental and curriculum domains to include problem solving, creative thinking, and reasoning. Each emphasizes that at-risk children, as well as regular education children, need to be able to apply what they need to situations in the real world. Curriculum goals and objectives can be assessed on a broad basis as well as a specific basis. By having assessment based on specified curriculum goals and objectives, a greater understanding of results compared to expected outcomes can be achieved. A general assessment can be ascertained with specific assessments based on disability and level, compatible with goals and objectives in the IEP. This will provide a basis for comparison as well as a guide for planning additional experiences, if necessary (McAfee and Leong, 1990).

The curriculum can also be responsive to children's strengths and needs as determined by the assessment so that modifications can be made. Thus CBA becomes a circular plan—thought is given to the development, assessments are made, and new strategies are created based on those assessments to help achieve curriculum goals or to reevaluate those goals.

If students are assessed based on the curriculum they experience, and curriculum is developed based on individual goals and objectives developed for each child, the circle may become complete. Performance assessment will be based on what was initially determined to meet the special needs of the individual. Feedback based on the performance of the special needs child will have meaning, and new curricula goals can be developed. Additionally, successes and failures in both teaching and learning can more easily be determined. Clear goals, monitoring of progress, and revising of materials offer an alternative way to assess curricula success, in contrast to a narrow curriculum focusing on information to be covered in order to fit the demands of testing and accountability.

Lambert and McCombs (1998) point out that standardized achievement tests do not offer options for assessing what children have learned in a complex era when diverse curricula are being developed. These tests demonstrate only one way children learn and do not properly demonstrate what children with special needs or children from different cultures know. Alternate forms of assessment need to be given equal weight in the assessment process. In *How Students Learn: Reforming Schools through Learner-Centered Education,* Lambert and McCombs identify effective curricula as those that

- attend to affect and mood as well as cognition and thinking in all learning activities and experiences, thereby engaging the learner;
- include assessments from students, peers, and teachers to check for student understanding of the subject matter, including implications and applications of knowledge;
- have an affective and cognitive richness that helps students generate positive thoughts and feelings of excitement, interest, and stimulation;
- help students engage in higher-order thinking and practice metacognitive strategies, including reflective self-awareness and goal setting;
- help students to be more aware of their own psychological functioning and how it relates to their own learning;
- include authentic tasks (relevant to the real world) and assessments that help students integrate information and performance across subject matter disciplines while allowing students to choose levels of difficulty for challenge or novelty;
- are developmentally appropriate to the unique intellectual, emotional, physical, and social characteristics of the individual;

•• incorporate meaningful materials and activities relevant to different cultural groups;

•• help students to increase awareness and understanding of how thought processes operate to produce separate, self-confirming realities so that they can better understand different individuals, as well as different social, cultural, and religious groups;

•• encourage students to see positive qualities in all groups of learners, regardless of race, sex, culture, language, physical ability, or other individual differences; and

•• include activities that promote empathy and understanding, respect for individual differences, and valuing of different perspectives, including materials from a multicultural perspective.

INCLUDING THE AFFECTIVE DOMAIN

Along with the concept of a meaningful integrated curriculum is the desire to develop the *affective domain*—that is, emotion—through the experiences of the special education student. Group experiences always affect the development of the child in terms of interpersonal relationships. Because people are put together physically does not mean that they are a successful group. When someone is uncomfortable, he or she is not going to participate and often feels threatened, which can lead to inappropriate interaction, a breakdown in communication, inappropriate attention-getting behaviors, and conflict.

There is a distinction between *social skills*—specific behaviors that a person uses to perform competently on social tasks—and *social competence*—an evaluative term based on a person's adequate performance on social tasks. Social skills are *behaviors*, and social competence represents *judgments* about those behaviors. Because social competence deficits are used to identify children as emotionally disturbed or having behavioral disorders, fostering social skills among learning-disabled children is an important part of school success. Teachers react to more than academic success when identifying at-risk children. Those who exhibit behaviors different from model behavioral profiles and who are also mildly handicapped frequently are referred for testing. Additionally, children with mild disabilities (LD, MMR, BD, ADHD) are frequently rejected by peers in general education classrooms. Self-concept and self-esteem and their place in the affective domain can be addressed by becoming part of the curriculum. Failing to include the affective domain serves only to alienate the special needs student more and increase the likelihood of school failure (Gresham and MacMillan, 1997).

Simply taking time, or including in the daily curriculum, an explanation of an appropriate climate for living within a group can be the difference between successful and unsuccessful educational experiences. To omit the affective domain of any area of study leaves out an important piece of total development. Sharing experiences, providing for rules for common courtesy, empathy toward others, collective decisionmaking, values clarification, conflict resolution, and other steps toward the collective productivity of experiences can enhance the learning situation.

When teachers create conditions that foster an atmosphere of trust, the student becomes more secure with the teacher as the guide through the curriculum. This creates a more positive emotional environment for the special needs student. Specific teaching techniques to encourage development of the affective domain include modeling—imitating observed behavior; role-playing and simulation—acting out and trying social behavior without consequences; counseling—working with an adult on a specific skill; and values clarification strategies—activities used to examine choices, make decisions, and acquire self-knowledge. These strategies can be especially useful with special education students who may have several layers of acceptance issues.

ENCOURAGING A MORE PEACEFUL ENVIRONMENT

Students with disabilities find themselves subjected to a variety of unpleasant situations during the day, both outside and inside the school building. Not only are students who are rationally or culturally different subjected to cultural violence, but concern in this area for the special needs student and its contribution to low self-esteem is significant.

A teacher trained in this sensitive area will more probably (1) model such behavior and (2) include cultural sensitive experiences in the curriculum in order to create a less violent classroom and more peaceful, safe place. In the curriculum, structured reflections on experiences and classroom situations provide the opportunity to think critically about human relationships. The act of cooperative teaching and cooperative learning as part of the curriculum will enhance cooperation as opposed to competition. The classroom will set the scene for a more global application of peace education.

Within the curriculum, academic experiences can be offered through specific instructional strategies in order to create a philosophy of peace and acceptance in an educational setting. This can have enormous impact on the special needs child when experiencing a mainstreamed or particularly an inclusive setting. For the young child the act of sharing and caring can be a strategy; for the young adult, tools such as abstract reasoning to achieve higher-level conflict resolution can be employed. It appears that it is to the advantage of those involved in curriculum development for both regular and special education students to include experiences encompassing the cognitive as well as the affective domain. In other words, when academic experiences and accompanying goals and objectives are developed, some form of the affective domain encompassing communication involving values and socioemotional development needs to be included. An example of balancing both domains, cognitive and affective, might be to present historical and geographic *factual experiences* regarding both sides of a war (the cognitive domain) and to include *pictures of families* of both sides of the war (the affective domain), then discuss implications of the lack of conflict resolution and peace.

Violence in the curriculum goes beyond the traditionally physical violent act and can extend to verbal, visual, or physical acts intended to demean or harm another individual. If not addressed, bullying of a physically challenged student or use of racial epithets, for example, can occur on a daily basis. By using concepts such as conflict resolution, curricula can contain elements to prevent this type of physical and non-physical violence. Kopka (1997) identifies specific violence prevention curricula involving the following fourteen educational strategies:

(1) *Afrocentric curricula* aim to prevent violence through an awareness of African and African-American roots. They are designed to instill a sense of cultural identity and pride.

(2) *Aggression reduction/anger management curricula* convey the message that anger is a normal human emotion. They explore healthy and unhealthy ways to express and channel anger.

(3) *Conflict resolution curricula* help develop empathy; impulse control; and skills in communication, problem solving, and anger management.

(4) *Crime prevention/law-related education curricula* teach students how to reduce their chances of becoming victims of crime and encourage them to develop school and community projects to reduce crime.

(5) *Gang prevention/reduction curricula* build awareness of the consequences of gang membership among youth who are not yet gang members.

(6) *Handgun violence prevention curricula* alert students to the

risk posed by handguns and help them recognize and avoid potentially dangerous situations.

(7) *Life skills training curricula* teach a range of social skills that students need for healthy development, such as problem-solving skills, decisionmaking skills, and strategies for resisting peer pressure or media influences.

(8) *Peace education curricula* look at violence prevention interpersonally and within and among societies as a whole.

(9) *Peer mediation programs* involve about fifteen to twenty hours of training for students and teachers. Afterward students identify and mediate conflicts that occur in the school.

(10) *Prejudice reduction/cultural awareness curricula* attempt to overcome stereotypes and prejudices that foster violence.

(11) *Promoting cooperation* is an education approach that emphasizes cooperative learning in which students achieve academic success through dependence on and accountability to each other.

(12) *Role model curricula* help students learn lessons in nonviolent behavior by exploring the lives of exceptional historical or contemporary figures.

(13) *Self-esteem development curricula* aim to raise students' self-esteem with the underlying assumption that doing so can raise academic performance and reduce violence.

(14) *Teen-dating violence/family violence/sexual assault curricula* address the increased incidents of domestic violence in recent years.

Continued support for students with disabilities who are victims of harassment is evidenced by the July 26, 2000, joint letter from the Office of Civil Rights and the Office of Special Education. Sent to principals, superintendents, and university presidents, this letter concerned the harassment of students with disabilities based on their particular disability. The letter asked administrators to advise related professionals to (1) develop greater awareness of this issue, (2) remind interested persons of the legal/educational responsibilities of institutions to prevent and respond to disability harassment, and (3) suggest measures that school officials should take to address the issue.

It is significant to understand that the curriculum in special education has to include the areas of exceptionalities as opposed to age or grade. In an inclusive curriculum/classroom, peer tutoring, special education consultants, and centers aid the regular classroom teacher throughout the educational experience.

MULTIPLE INTELLIGENCE AND ITS
IMPACT ON THE CURRICULUM

Influencing the development of curriculum are the beliefs that (1) the only limits to our intelligence are limits we set; (2) we can become more intelligent by increasing the activity of perception and knowing by working on higher levels of thought; (3) there are many ways we know, understand, and learn about our world beyond what the IQ tests measure; and (4) when there is a challenge, all of our "intelligences" work together in an integrated way. These beliefs considered together form the multiple intelligence theory first posited by Howard Gardner.

Gardner (1991) presents seven "intelligences," or distinct ways individuals learn and live within reality: (1) *verbal/linguistic intelligence,* responsible for the production of language and complex possibilities such as poetry, humor, grammar, and abstract reasoning; (2) *logical-mathematical intelligence,* scientific thinking or deductive reasoning, the capacity to recognize patterns, work with abstract symbols, and discern relationships; (3) *visual/spatial intelligence,* including visual arts (painting, drawing, and sculpture), navigation (map-making and architecture), visualization of objects from different perspectives and angles (e.g., chess playing), all which use the sense of sight to include the ability to form images and pictures in the mind; (4) *bodily/kinesthetic intelligence,* the ability to use the body to express emotion (dance and body language), participate in sports, and create a new product (devise and invention); (5) *musical/rhythmic intelligence,* recognition and use of rhythmic and tonal pattern sensitivity to sounds from the environment (human voice and musical instruments); (6) *interpersonal intelligence,* the ability to work cooperatively in a group as well as the ability to communicate verbally and nonverbally with others (and thereby notice distinctions such as moods, temperament, motivation, and intentions); and (7) *intrapersonal intelligence,* knowledge of the internal aspects of the self such as feelings, emotional responses, thinking processes (metacognition), and self-reflection. This is one's ability to transcend the self, the capacity to experience wholeness and unity and to discern patterns of our connection with the large order of things.

Gardner maintains that we use many different skills to solve a problem, and that those skills assist in the acquisition of new knowledge (Morrison, 1993). His theory of multiple intelligences can guide educators in designing curriculum and instruction that appeals to more than a single dimension of intelligence (Oliva, 1997). The theory has many implications for curriculum models and how teachers view and teach children.

The curriculum is the one place these multiple ways to learn can come together and serve as a basis from which instructional strategies can be developed. Curriculum strategies that involve the separate intelligences will awaken more intellectual potential because they use more senses and have different areas of the brain working together.

The following example gives the view of a student who demonstrates spatial, bodily-kinesthetic, and intrapersonal intelligences and how he can be helped to develop his linguistic intelligence.

> Trevor (12 years old) is a seventh grader who is just as proud of his collection of doodles and pictures as he is of his good grades (in math). Many of his drawings are done during school in classes that are lecture-based or "just plain boring," as Trevor puts it. Others are a result of long hours of detailed work on sketches and designs. While his classmates make simple book covers, Trevor creates covers with intricate and complex geometrical designs or cartoon characters. Trevor is drawn to classrooms that are picture rich. Slides, mobiles, photos, overhead transparencies, and other visuals that reinforce the lesson make all the difference in his motivation and understanding. He is easily frustrated by an overdose of words, whether he's reading, writing, or listening to them. His frustration about long writing assignments quickly changes to excitement, however, when he is encouraged to include visuals. Trevor's teacher can identify Trevor's reports without his name because they always have one picture on the front, one on the back, and several throughout.
>
> Trevor spends most of his free time putting together and painting models. He loves math class this year because, as he says, the teacher "keeps us really busy when we learn. We move around to different centers and use manipulatives."
>
> Trevor is definitely not a social butterfly. He has a small group of close friends and is happy to spend time alone. His mental and physical well-being are very important to him, as is his academic achievement. (Gipe, 1998, p. 23)

Based on this description of Trevor's learning skills and preferences, the best curriculum for Trevor would make use of his spatial talents, as well as his bodily-kinesthetic and intrapersonal intelligences. This type of child is one who is in almost every classroom, in every school, in every district. Reaching the Trevors of our schools, and providing a curriculum model that encourages them to succeed, is one of the great challenges of educators today.

Different types of intelligence are highly valued in individual cultures, and educators should be aware of this. For example, linguistic and mathematical intelligences are considered supreme among most Americans whereas spatial intelligence is most valued among Eskimo peoples, because knowledge and awareness of even slight differences in ice surfaces are significant to survival skills.

According to Gipe (1998) multiple intelligence theory is not the same concept as *learning styles.* Proponents of learning styles suggest that the learner approaches different contents (language, numbers, music, etc.) in the same way (global, analytical, or impulsive, reflective). Multiple intelligence theory supports the possibility that a learner may have more than one learning style. It is appropriate that curriculum models include the expansion of instructional methods that link learning to as many intelligences as possible. For example, in teaching a concept in social studies, the teacher can encourage the students to read about it (linguistic), draw it (spatial), build a model of it (bodily-kinesthetic), find music that complements it (musical), relate it to a personal feeling (intrapersonal), involve critical thinking (logical-mathematical), and work in cooperative groups (interpersonal). In this way, curriculum models will incorporate the theory of multiple intelligence and possibly assist educators in meeting the needs of all children. One of the most significant thoughts of using multiple intelligences is that educators can increase the self-esteem of youngsters in the classroom. In a kindergarten classroom in Colorado, a teacher discusses the different kinds of "smarts" with her five-year-olds. While pointing to a poster with pictures and symbols depicting the multiple intelligences, she discusses with the children that they are all smart in different ways. With choices of body-smart, people-smart, music-smart, picture-smart, word-smart, and number-smart, the children learn right from the beginning of their kindergarten curriculum that they each have individualized approaches to intelligence (Collins, 1998).

Gardner based his initial list of multiple intelligences on research in neurological, developmental, and cognitive psychology, as well as on anthropology. He believes that the various intelligences can be shown in areas of the brain, and that child prodigies are an example of the evidence of their existence. He has theorized about an eighth intelligence, "the naturalist" (sensitivity to the ecological environment), and a "half" intelligence, "the moralist" (sensitivity to ethical concerns), which serves to remind us that the concept of multiple intelligence is open to further speculation (Meyer, 1997; Checkley, 1997).

Some researchers feel that Gardner is just giving hope to parents and educators. Many researchers want to see further investigation into Gardner's theory. One study (Merrefield, 1997) found great success in including the multiple intelligence concepts with disabled preschool-ers. Teaching with multiple intelligences in mind has been found to keep the lessons interesting, the assessment varied, and the strategies diverse (Emig, 1997).

CURRICULUM FOR BOTH GENERAL EDUCATION AND SPECIAL EDUCATION

Frequently, general education teachers have curriculum that is already set up for them by curriculum specialists. Examples of such curricula are:

(1) Grade-Level Curricula—which is specific content and related skills particular to a specific grade level. This is important be-cause what is taught in one grade is contingent upon what is taught in the grade before it.
(2) Core Curricula—the basic areas of reading, writing, and arithmetic upon which further learning depends. Support areas such as social studies, science, and spelling revolve around the basic accomplishments of a core curriculum.
(3) Subject-Area Curricula—these are also content-area curric-ula, which differ throughout the states. For example, the sub-ject area of social studies differs for New Jersey and Okla-homa as the specific content changes.
(4) Competency-based Curricula—involves setting competen-cies or proficiencies before a student can progress to the next level of learning. Part of this is competency-based testing, where the student must demonstrate an acceptable level of skill in competencies required before moving on or actually passing the material.

The special educator needs to be familiar with these in order to ensure successful student transfer, placement, or possibly inclusion. A large majority of mildly handicapped students spend part of the day in the regular classroom setting. Special education teachers and regular education teachers work together on curricular information and devel-opment in order to make this happen. It is important for the special ed-ucator to see where in the regular curriculum the student has difficulty, gets lost, or cannot intellectually progress. The special education teacher needs to be familiar with curricula developed for children with special needs, for the individual child, and how to adjust such curricu-lum. Examples of this:

(1) A Parallel Curriculum reflects, or parallels, the basic information and skills of the regular curriculum and focuses on shorter assignments, fewer objectives, untimed tests, alternative testing models, and breaking concepts into smaller steps.
(2) Community-based Curricula set competencies for areas not able to be achieved in the classroom itself, such as basic experiences, for example, looking right and left before crossing a street, negotiating intersections, and trips downtown.
(3) Life Management Curricula involve areas necessary for independent living, such as grooming, communicating, traveling, and using a telephone.
(4) Specialized Curricula are developed for the individual special needs person. For example, some students need experience in social skills behaviors, career education, and vocational programming.
(5) Functional Curricula is a field unto itself with tremendous impact on the special needs population. It transcends the specific information that these children need to master with the reality of practical living. The curriculum helps children function appropriately in their own environment.

The fact remains, however, that with some special students, the individual challenge of the disabilities dictate that some specific instructional methodology be included into whatever curricular approach is advocated. For example, historically, the mentally handicapped were presented with a slower version of the regular education curriculum and set of experiences. Other than that, the most common educational placement for the mentally handicapped was the self-contained classroom. More recently, a functional curriculum has been developed to help these students acquire everyday skills that will help in everyday living—functioning within the community as well as at the workplace. "A functional curriculum approach is a way of delivering instructional content that focuses on the concepts and skills needed by all students with disabilities in the area of personal-social, daily living and occupational adjustment. What is considered a functional curriculum for any one student would be the content (concepts and skills) included in that student's curriculum or course of study that targets his or her future needs" (Clark, as cited in Florida Department of Education, 1994, p. 348).

The conflict arises between how this type of curriculum is to be viewed and provided for in an inclusive setting. To look at this as an *approach* as opposed to a specific order of curriculum makes possible the view that regardless of the environment in which this is delivered, the responsibility is on the regular classroom teacher and the special education consultant to comply with the goals and objectives of the individualized educational plan as mandated by IDEA. If the regular educational plan is on a more vigorous academic emphasis, how can a functional curriculum be delivered in an inclusive setting? The hope is that the desire to provide responsible adults in a more thoughtful society will allow both emphases to work together. The bonus of having disabled students interact more effectively with their nondisabled peers becomes a normal outcome of implementation of the functional curriculum within the normal classroom setting. Additionally, the goals and objectives of a functional curriculum are important for many of the regular education students as well as other challenged students operating within the inclusive classroom. This may provide enough diversity within the curriculum as well as within the social interaction of the classroom. If schools are to be concerned with addressing student diversity, then diversity needs to be addressed in the curriculum.

When dealing with students with severe handicaps, such emphasis on functional curricula is especially important. To wit:

> Today, most educators of individuals with severe handicaps consider it important to be familiar with the normal sequences of child development, but they recognize that their students often do not acquire skills in the same way that nonhandicapped students do and that developmental guides should not be the only basis for determining teacher procedures. For example, a 16-year-old student who is just learning to feed and toilet himself should not be taught in exactly the same way or with the same materials as a nonhandicapped 2-year-old child who is just learning to feed and toilet himself. The past experiences, present environments, and future prospects of the two individuals are, of course, quite different, even though their ability to perform certain skills may be similar. (Heward and Orlansky, 1992, p. 433)

COMMUNITY-BASED INSTRUCTION AND CURRICULUM

Decisions regarding appropriate curriculum and delivery models of instruction for the developmentally disabled are not, as explained earlier, based on developmental milestones. Such students have more difficulty generalizing from one instructional environment to another; therefore, targeting specific skills is more appropriate. The philosophy of a curriculum based on instruction within the real community is to use the classroom environment only as a beginning for simulation and infuse it with community-based instruction (CBI) in order to achieve applications of skills to actual adult life.

The special needs of students with moderate and severe disabilities are best met through direct instruction where they live, work, and play. The direct association between IEP objectives and skills required in order to function independently is essential and as often as possible needs to parallel the work environment. Local offices of the U.S. Department of Labor, Wage and Hour Division, need to be contacted to verify compliance with current labor laws. Part of this curriculum development may be the process of supported employment, a placement and training model for students who cannot succeed without intensive supportive individual on-the-job training with a job coach or employment specialist. The ultimate goal is for the intensive coaching to decrease so that the curriculum provides for decreased but continued monitoring (Department of Education/Vocational Programs, 1993).

Different from the previous exceptionality but equally important if we are to deliver appropriate services to all children is the curriculum developed for the gifted. Just as we prepare special education consultants and need to prepare regular education teachers for dealing with the mentally and developmentally disabled, the same rights apply to those children who are assessed to be gifted and talented. Controversy arises here in that often parents and teachers believe these children have been given more by nature or nurture to begin with and that others need educational funding more. This, however, is not the prevailing law, which funds the gifted and talented through IDEA as well as through the recently passed Educational Excellence for All Children's Act (1999, described in Chapter 2).

Concepts regarding high-order thinking can be accomplished in myriad settings, be they special classes, honors classes, resource rooms, or enrichment and acceleration programs. Models for teaching to the gifted include Bloom's Taxonomy of Educational Objectives, Renzulli's Enrichment Triad Model, Bett's Autonomous Learning Model, Clark's Integrative Education Model, and Maker's Integrated Curriculum Model.

Based on the amendments to the original P.L. 94-142, IDEA 1990, and IDEA 1997, the area of transition of young adults and the inclusion of specific plans for the continuation of services of these 14- to 21-year-olds into the workplace requires specific curriculum planning in the form of goals and objectives.

The strongest transition models appear to be those that include a functional secondary school curriculum that provides work experience. The law now requires an individualized educational plan stating the transition from school to work process. The coordination of this plan between the school vocational planner, the community, and an employer is a team approach that works best using a functional curriculum as previously described. Heward and Orlansky (1992) stress the importance of a continual curriculum beginning in the elementary years focusing on the functional curriculum. They stress that

> Development of career awareness should begin in the elementary years for children with severe disabilities. This does not mean, of course, that six-year-old children must be placed on job sites for training. For example, elementary students might sample different types of jobs through classroom responsibilities such as watering plants, cleaning chalkboards or taking messages to the office. Young children with disabilities might also visit community work sites where adults with disabilities are employed. . . . Middle school children should spend time at actual job sites, with an increased amount of in-school instruction devoted to the development of associated work skills, such as being on time, staying on task. . . . Secondary school should spend an increasing amount of time receiving instruction at actual job sites. (P. 637)

Ultimately, curriculums need to provide for the type of residential choices available to these children, be they state residential facilities, group homes, foster homes, or apartment living. The ultimate goal is to open the doors to a more productive life as part of the greater community.

DISCIPLINE AS PART OF THE CURRICULUM

IDEA 1990 provided for school personnel to remove a child to an interim alternative educational placement for up to forty-five days if that child brought a gun to school or a school function. Since the IDEA 1997 amendments became effective, the following disciplinary measures have applied to disabled and special-needs students:

> ➻ Removal of the child for up to ten school days at a time: The regulations clarify that school personnel may remove a child with a disability for up to ten consecutive school days and allow for additional removals of up to ten school days for sep-

arate acts of misconduct, as long as the removals do not constitute a pattern.

❥ Providing services during periods of disciplinary removal: Schools do not need to provide services during the first ten school days in a school year that a child is removed. During any subsequent removal that is for ten school days or less, the school must provide services to the extent determined necessary to enable the child to appropriately progress in the general curriculum and appropriately advance toward achieving the goals of his or her IEP. In cases involving removals for ten school days or less, school personnel, in consultation with the child's special education teacher, make the service determination. During any long-term removal for behavior that is not a manifestation of a child's disability, schools must provide services to the extent determined necessary to enable the child to appropriately progress in the general curriculum and appropriately advance toward achieving the goals of his or her IEP. In cases involving removals for behavior that is not a manifestation of the child's disability, the child's IEP team makes the service determination.

❥ Conducting behavioral assessments and developing behavioral interventions: Meetings of a child's IEP team to develop a behavioral assessment plan, or (if the child has one) to review the child's behavioral intervention plan, are only required when the child has first been removed from his or her current placement for more than ten school days in a school year, and when commencing a removal that constitutes a change in placement. If other subsequent removals occur, the IEP team members must review the child's behavioral intervention plan and its implementation to determine if modifications are necessary; they need only meet if one or more team members believes that modifications are necessary.

❥ Change of placement; manifestation determinations: The regulations provide that change of placement occurs if a child is removed for more than ten consecutive school days or is subjected to a series of removals that constitute a pattern because they cumulate to more than ten school days in a school year, and because of factors such as the length of each removal, the total amount of time the child is removed, and the proximity of the removals to one another. Manifestation determinations are only required if the school is implementing a removal that constitutes a change of placement.

Additionally, the 1997 amendments expanded the authority of school personnel regarding the removal of a child who brings a gun to school to also apply to *all* dangerous weapons and to *knowing possession* of illegal drugs or the sale or solicitation of the sale of controlled substances, and they added a new ability of appropriate school personnel to request a hearing officer to remove a child for up to forty-five days if keeping the child in his or her current placement is substantially likely to result in injury to the child or to others.

The 1997 amendments also require appropriate school personnel to assess a child's troubling behavior and develop positive behavioral interventions to address that behavior and to describe how to determine whether the behavior is a manifestation of the child's disabilities.

EARLY CHILDHOOD SPECIAL EDUCATION CURRICULUM

Curriculums for early childhood special education (ECSE) programs became a part of the responsibility of the U.S. Department of Education when P.L. 99-457 and IDEA 1990 mandated that family-focused intervention services had to be spelled out and provided for in an individualized family service plan. This interdisciplinary approach with screening, assessment, and specific programs led to a focus on curricular development. Appropriate curricula for children from birth to age five in both homes and centers need to be based on goals and objectives. Most early childhood special education programs have a developmentally based curriculum, which means that each child can be measured against a normal developmental standard. Focus can include remediation, basic process skills, developmental tasks, psychological concepts, and preacademic skills. Essential to the success of early intervention is an interdisciplinary team of parent(s), teachers, and various ECSE specialists.

The following materials are commonly found in the ECSE curriculum:

Language Arts/Reading

•◆ Steck-Vaughn Reading Comprehension Skills Series
Complements and supplements reading, phonics, and language arts programs; uses short, high-interest stories for low-level readers.
•◆ Steck-Vaughn Phonics
A holistic and multisensory instruction approach.

➽ Steck-Vaughn Sight Word Comprehensive

Sight word program incorporating interesting topics and motivating activities.

➽ Steck-Vaughn Spelling

Integrates reading, writing, and language arts in a holistic approach.

➽ DLM Dolch Reading and Vocabulary

High-interest, low-reading-level paperback readers emphasizing sight word vocabulary.

➽ DLM Cove Reading Program

Workbooks in a thorough, sequenced program reinforcing decoding skills.

➽ DLM Survival Words Program

Low-reading-level readers with abundant structure and repetition reinforcing reading in context.

➽ Project Read

A multisensory reading program to teach and reinforce decoding and phonetic skills.

➽ Merrill Linguistic Readers

Low-level reading series reinforcing decoding and comprehension skills using the linguistic approach.

➽ Strategies Intervention Model (SIM)

Includes teacher's manual for strategies with regard to word identification, sentence writing, paraphrasing, paragraph writing, first-letter mnemonics, and error monitoring.

➽ Balance Materials/Curriculum

Blends precision teaching, direct instruction, and whole language instruction; addresses all academic areas with emphasis on reading and language arts areas.

➽ LinguiSystems No Glamour Grammar

Teaches "no-frills" grammar through structures practice of verbal and written skills.

➽ Moving Up in Grammar

A low-reading-level grammar skills kit.

➽ SRA/Distar

Builds upon skills previously learned and introduces new skills continuously using a systematic, direct instruction approach to teach reading, spelling, writing, math, science, social studies, and reasoning and thinking skills through a variety of curricula. Individual programs are Distar Language, SRA Reading Mastery Series, SRA Corrective Reading Program, SRA Expressive Writing, SRA Your World of Facts, SRA Cursive Writing, SRA Spelling Mastery, and SRA Reading, Writing and Thinking Skills.

Mathematics

➥ Steck-Vaughn Mastering Math

A developmental program for low reading levels with sufficient practice, review, and assessment included.

➥ Steck-Vaughn Succeeding in Mathematics

Consistent step-by-step approach using practical applications at low reading levels. Provides frequent practice and review.

➥ DLM Math Problem-Solving Kits

An extensive program to develop and reinforce story problem skills on a low reading level.

➥ DLM Mathematics Big Box Kits

Comprehensive hands-on math centers providing instruction, reinforcement, and practice with manipulatives. Specific kits include Math Big Box, Math Manipulative Big Box, Time Big Box, and Money Big Box.

➥ DLM Moneywise

Comprehensive, developmentally sequenced instruction and practice in money concepts; includes manipulatives.

➥ Creative Publications Mathematics Their Way

An activity-centered math program to build and reinforce math skills.

➥ Creative Publications Hands-On

Concrete, sequenced activities using a variety of manipulatives.

➥ Creative Publications Base Ten Block Program

Teaches and reinforces the base ten number system and place value skills using concrete problem-solving activities with manipulatives.

➥ Creative Publications WorkMat Math Story Problems Series

Teaches logical thinking by interpreting problems with manipulatives.

➥ Mathematics for Daily Use

Math skills for everyday function are presented through visual means to assist students with low reading levels and/or motivation.

➥ Project Math

Especially for students with learning and/or behavior problems; skills are presented at four different mental age levels.

➥ Distar Math

Systematic, direct instruction approach to teaching math by building upon skills previously learned while introducing new skills.

➥ Innovative Learning Concepts, Inc., Touch Math

A multisensory method of teaching basis counting and computation skills by counting sequentially.

Science/ Social Studies

•• Steck-Vaughn The Wonders of Science Series
Complete science program presenting content in brief, high-interest, low-level readings.
•• Steck-Vaughn Health and You
Comprehensive health program with controlled vocabulary at low reading levels.

Career-Vocational Skills

•• Community-Based Instruction
Teach students the necessary skills for functioning within a community, including lessons in daily living and social/personal and career-occupational skills. Among the individual programs are Donn Brolin's Life Center Career Education (LCCE), Attainment Company's Stepping Out, and community-referenced curriculum guides by local school districts or BEES.
•• Clearinghouse/Information Center.
SRA Reading, Writing and Math for Independence.

CURRICULUM ACCOMMODATES DUAL EXCEPTIONALITIES

As discussed in Chapter 1, children with dual exceptionalities present unique curricular challenges. An environment taking into consideration both the gifts of the child and the disability while offering stronger emotional support tends to result in greater success. Developing a curriculum that offers remediation for the disability while at the same time focusing on the child's intellectual strengths may take time but will offer an enriched environment as well as higher self-esteem. According to Whitmore and Maker (1985) more gains are seen when intervention focuses on the gift rather than on the disability. Providing an environment through specific strategies in the curriculum for the gifted/learning disabled child can produce unusual productivity. For example, is a tedious book report any greater a documentation of acquired information than a student's production of a video focusing on what the message of the book was? Children with learning disabilities can produce more creative and probably more meaningful documentation when allowed to use their creative abilities. If a student has difficulties with handwriting, will learning to use a computer to record his or her thoughts and plans not serve the same purpose? Finding alternate ways to receive and document information does not make a curriculum less challenging but does encourage success. Technology provides organization, management, and access and is an integral part of curriculum development for many children with special needs but especially for gifted children with inconsistent abilities.

INCLUSION IN THE CURRICULUM

The scope of curriculum has changed over the years, yet some similarities have remained. One of the changes is in the inclusion of special needs students in general education classrooms, and how that affects the curriculum. Including students with disabilities in the regular education program is the "right thing to do and is the presumption of the special education law" (Schaffner and Buswell, 1998). When most of us attended school, the special education students were separated and away from us, in their own classes. Schaffner and Buswell (1998) believe that this may cause some perplexing fearfulness in the educators of today, who did not interact with special education students as youngsters. Whether we buy into that belief or not, the fact is, the "least restrictive environment" provision of the Reauthorization Act (IDEA, 1997) states, "To the maximum extent appropriate, children with disabilities are educated with children who are not disabled, and special classes, separate schooling, or other removal of children with disabilities from the regular educational environment occurs only when the nature of severity of the disability of a child is such that education in regular classes with the use of supplementary aids cannot be achieved satisfactorily" (Section 612(a)(5)). The general educational classroom must be the first placement considered. Therefore, in attempting to benefit special needs students and give them the best possible education, many students are now being educated in the least restrictive environment of the regular class, with a continuum of support available.

There is some debate of what *inclusion* actually means (see Dyal, Flynt, and Bennet-Walker, 1996). According to the Grapevine-Colleyville ISD Inclusion Task Force Report of 1997, inclusion is "a collaborative process among students, parents, and educators which enables students with and without disabilities to learn together in the same class to the greatest extent possible utilizing appropriate support services" (p. 1). As a report prepared for the Florida Department of Education (Stetson and Associates, 1998) notes, there are students who will succeed in school no matter what educators do, there are students who will fall through the cracks, and there are students who will not succeed in

school unless something different is done. Inclusion is a possible answer to the problem that the highest dropout groups of students are
those who fall between the cracks and those who did not succeed in
school because something different was not done. In an inclusion setting, everyone is part of the solution. It includes collaboration and trust
and a passion for learning and growing. There is a focus on the academic success of *every* student, not just some of them. Supporters believe that *inclusion* is just another word for "good teaching." As special
education is a service, not a place, the general education setting may be
appropriate for many students. How does this affect the curriculum of
the general education class?

Curricula need to be adapted for all students, not just for students with identified disabilities. Adaptations of the standard curriculum can benefit "students all along the continuum, from students with
disabilities to students 'at risk,' to students who need enriched curricular options . . . adaptation increases the likelihood of success for more
learners" (Ebeling, Deschenes, and Sprague, 1994, p. 68). Curriculum
can be altered without compromising it in terms of content or accountability. Classrooms have always had students who learn at different
rates, who have more background knowledge, who have varying abilities. Good teachers have always automatically and intuitively adapted
the curriculum and instruction to meet the needs of each student. An
inclusive curriculum that involves collaboration with colleagues makes
this task even easier, enabling the educators to facilitate changes and
adaptations (Snyder, 1999; Tapasak and Walther-Thomas, 1999; Tichenor, Heins, and Piechura-Couture, 1998).

Deschenes, Ebeling, and Sprague (1994) note a variety of instructional approaches to curricula that accommodate a wide range of learners:

- cooperative learning structures
- multidimensional student grouping
- thematic, integrated approaches
- multilevel instruction
- class projects
- outcomes-based instruction
- applied learning stations
- student presentation and projects
- role playing, skits, and plays
- peer supports
- community volunteers
- multimedia presentations
- concrete experiential learning activities

- community-referenced and community-based projects
- short-term skill-based grouping
- assignment menus and contracted grades
- community-based instruction
- portfolio or "authentic" assessments

Utilization of the above strategies in a curriculum allows all students the opportunity to participate and succeed. *Reciprocal teaching* is another strategy that has been successful in various classrooms (Lederer, 2000). In reciprocal teaching, the teacher and student take turns assuming the role of leader of the conversation. The purpose is to facilitate the group experience between teacher and student as well as to increase understanding of the meaning of the instructive activity.

Beliefs about students and learning form the foundation from which a curriculum is developed. According to Onosko and Jorgensen (in Jorgensen, Fisher, and Roach, 1997) these beliefs include: (1) All students can think and learn; (2) All students have value and unique gifts to offer their school; (3) Diversity within a school community should be embraced and celebrated; (4) All students differ in the ways they most effectively learn and express their understandings; (5) All students learn best when they are actively and collaboratively building knowledge with their classmates and their teacher; (6) All students learn best when studying interesting and challenging topics that they find personally meaningful; and (7) Effective teaching for students with disabilities is substantively the same as effective teaching for all students.

All students—with or without disabilities—"need to learn three types of skills: (1) dispositions and habits of mind, such as inquisitiveness, diligence, collaboration, work habits, tolerance, and critical thinking; (2) content area knowledge, in science, social studies, language arts, computers, the arts, etc.; and (3) basic academic skills such as reading, writing, and mathematics" (Sizer, 1992, and U.S. Department of Labor, 1991, in Jorgensen, Fisher, and Roach, 1997). These three types of skills should be included in the curriculum of general education classes as well as in various types of inclusive settings.

Collaboration and teaming, problem solving, and using strategies in the classroom to accommodate a diverse group of learners are common approaches in quality inclusive curriculum (McGregor, Halvorsen, Fisher, Pumpian, Bhaerman, and Salisbury, 1998; Tichenor, Heins, and Piechura-Couture, 1998). These approaches help educators guide and support the efforts of teaching and learning, including success for all students.

REFERENCES

Bricker, D., 1989. *Early Intervention for At-Risk and Handicapped Infants, Toddlers, and Preschool Children.* 2nd ed. Palo Alto, CA: Scott, Foresman & Co.

Checkley, K., 1997. "The First Seven . . . and the Eighth: A Conversation with Howard Gardner." *Educational Leadership* 55: 8–13.

Collins, J., 1998. "Seven Kinds of Smart." *Time* 152, no. 16: 94–96.

Department of Education/Vocational Programs, 1993. *Career Development Resource Guide for Students with Disabilities.* Tallahassee, FL: Department of Education/Vocational Programs.

Deschenes, C., D. Ebeling, and J. Sprague, 1994. *Adapting Curriculum and Instruction in Inclusive Classrooms: A Teacher's Desk Reference.* Minneapolis: The Center for School and Community Integration Institute for the Study of Developmental Disabilities.

Dyal, A., S. Flynt, and D. Bennett-Walker, 1996. "Schools and Inclusion: Principals' Perceptions." *The Clearinghouse* 70: 32–35.

Ebeling, D., C. Deschenes, C., and J. Sprague, 1994. *Adapting Curriculum and Instruction in Inclusive Classrooms: Staff Development Kit.* Minneapolis: The Center for School and Community Integration Institute for the Study of Developmental Disabilities.

Emig, V., 1997. "A Multiple Intelligences Inventory." *Educational Leadership* 55: 47–50.

Florida Department of Education, 1994. *Specialized Curriculum for Exceptional Students: Florida Alternatives, Module 3.* Tallahassee: Florida Department of Education.

Gardner, H., 1991. "Intelligence in Seven Phases." Paper presented at the Centennial of Education at Harvard. Precis published in the *Harvard Graduate School Alumni Bulletin* 36, no. 1: 18–19.

Gipe, J. P., 1998. *Multiple Paths to Literacy: Corrective Reading Techniques for Classroom Teachers.* 4th ed. New York: Merrill Publishing.

Grapevine-Colleyville ISD Inclusion Task Force Report, 1997. Grapevine, TX: Grapevine-Colleyville School District.

Gresham, F. M., and D. L. MacMillan, 1997. "Social Competence and Affective Characteristics of Students with Mild Disabilities." *Review of Educational Research* 67, no. 4: 377–415.

Heward, W. L., and M. D. Orlansky, 1992. *Exceptional Children.* 4th ed. New York: Macmillan.

Jorgensen, C., D. Fisher, and V. Roach, 1997. "Curriculum and Its Impact on Inclusion and the Achievement of Students with Disabilities." *Policy Research Practice: Issue Brief—Consortium on Inclusive Schooling Practices.* Pittsburgh: Allegheny University of the Health Sciences.

Kopka, D. L., 1997. *School Violence: A Reference Handbook.* Santa Barbara, CA: ABC-CLIO.

Lambert, N. M., and B. L. McCombs (eds.), 1998. *How Students Learn: Reforming Schools through Learner-Centered Education.* Washington, DC: American Psychological Association.

Lederer, J., 2000. "Reciprocal Teaching of Social Studies in Inclusive Elementary Classrooms." *Journal of Learning Disabilities* 33, no. 1: 91–106.

McAfee, O., and D. Leong, 1990. *Assessing and Guiding Young Children's Development and Learning.* 2nd ed. Boston: Allyn and Bacon.

McGregor, G., A. Halvorsen, D. Fisher, I. Pumpian, B. Bhaerman, and C. Salisbury, 1998. "Professional Development for All Personnel in Inclusive Schools." *Policy Research Practice: Issue Brief—Consortium on Inclusive Schooling Practices.* Pittsburgh: Allegheny University of the Health Sciences.

Meyer, M., 1997. "The Greening of Learning: Using the Eighth Intelligence." *Educational Leadership* 55: 32–34.

Morrison, G., 1993. *Contemporary Curriculum K–8.* Boston: Allyn and Bacon.

Oliva, P., 1997. *Developing the Curriculum.* 4th ed. New York: Longman.

Schaffner, C. B., and B. Buswell, 1998. *Opening Doors: Strategies for Including All Students in Regular Education.* Colorado Springs, CO: PEAK Parent Center, Inc.

Snyder, R., 1999. "Inclusion: A Qualitative Study of In-service General Education Teachers' Attitudes and Concerns." *Education* 120, no. 1: 173–180.

Stetson and Associates, 1998. *A Step by Step Approach for Inclusive Schools: Together Is Better!* Tallahassee: Florida Department of Education and the Florida Inclusion Network.

Tapasak, R., and C. Walther-Thomas, 1999. "Evaluation of a First-Year Inclusion Program: Student Perceptions and Classroom Performance." *Remedial and Special Education* 20, no. 4: 216–225.

Tichenor, M., B. Heins, and K. Piechura-Couture, 1998. "Putting Principles into Practice: Parent Perceptions of a Co-taught Inclusive Classroom." *Education* 118, no. 3: 471–477.

Whitmore, J., and J. Maker, 1985. *Intellectual Giftedness among Disabled Persons.* Rockville, MD: Aspen Press.

Chapter Four

⚫➤ Special Education Programs and the Law

Whereas policy- and lawmakers view results of regular education programs based on formalized testing and evaluation of large groups of children, special education programs focus on *individual* student assessment. Development of special education programs is based on the laws passed to create educational opportunities, and how those laws have developed and changed. In special education, educators spend a great deal of time on the goals and objectives identified in the IEP.

The successful delivery of services provided by several laws, including the Vocational Rehabilitation Act of 1973 and IDEA 1990, depends on how the local and state agencies choose to fulfill the laws' intentions. Neither the Vocational Rehabilitation Act nor IDEA have resulted in absolute equal opportunity and inclusion of all individuals with disabilities.

Although the federal government sets laws, if state and local governments do not agree with those laws, they will not implement them, resulting in lost opportunities. An example is the Head Start federal program, which includes a provision for the early education of young children who live in poverty. Beginning in 1972, Head Start was required to set aside 10 percent of its monies/opportunities to be available for children with disabilities. This was seen as such an important and positive step that in 1975, the Education for All Handicapped Children Act (P.L. 94-142, now known as IDEA) was passed, requiring all states applying for and receiving funding under that act to ensure a free, appropriate public education (FAPE) for all children with disabilities between six and eighteen years of age. This mandate of services is referred to as a "zero reject" policy. What is important to note is that for children ages birth through five and eighteen through twenty-one, FAPE was at *state discretion*. The federal government offered financial aid to implement its vision, and state and local governments had the right to choose not to participate. Under IDEA, state governments apply for the federal funds for state and local initiatives and must implement the mandates—even, if necessary, changing the state law.

When IDEA was amended in 1986 (see Chapter 2), two important early childhood special education policies were established: States had to ensure services to children age 3–5 years (applying the "zero reject" policy down to age three), and a new program (Part C) for newborns through two-year-olds (the Infants and Toddlers Intervention Program) was developed. Therefore, in 1986, ECSE took a new place within the field of special education and related services.

These new policies highlighted the balance of power set forth in the U.S. Constitution: The federal government made a statement by making the necessary funds available for these programs, and each state was left to decide whether to apply for the funds, knowing that accepting the funds required compliance with significant federal procedures and rights.

The federal government also has been instrumental in supporting and funding research and development. The Handicapped Children's Early Education Program (HCEEP) was established in 1968 and for thirty years has funded research and development (R&D) efforts that have resulted in tests, curriculum, and models of delivery service used today. Additionally, the Personnel Development Program under IDEA has provided funds for training personnel since the 1950s. States and localities seldom see their role as supporting R&D efforts; they leave this to the federal government. Instead, they focus on providing services to the citizens of their state and enacting laws to ensure access to services rather than quality of services. Through the use of federally supported research demonstrating the importance of early intervention, the states implemented early intervention policies—so that by 1994 the number of infants and toddlers receiving services had increased almost threefold, and preschool-age children receiving services had increased by over 100,000. The balance of power between federal and state has tipped in favor of children and families (Smith, 2000).

SECTION 504 OF THE VOCATIONAL REHABILITATION ACT AND IDEA COMPARED

Identifying the similarities and differences between Section 504 of the Vocational Rehabilitation Act of 1973 and IDEA will help the reader understand the difficulties lawmakers as well as advocates encounter in having just one group of laws on which they can rely. Originally enacted to "level the playing field," Section 504 applies to all persons with disabilities regardless of age.

Whereas IDEA is more remedial, often requiring the provision of services and programs in addition to those available to persons without disabilities, Section 504 is meant to preclude hurdles to participation, whether physical (steps to preventing a person in a wheelchair from accessing a building) or programmatic (excluding a child with AIDS from a classroom). Additionally, while IDEA requires more of schools for children with disabilities, it also provides routes to funding. Section 504 does not provide for financial support of its recommendations.

The definition of a disability under Section 504 is much broader than the definition under IDEA. Section 504 is less discriminatory in that it protects all persons with a disability who have a physical or mental impairment limiting one or more of life activities, and have a record of this impairment.

The Americans with Disabilities Act (ADA) of 1990 has its roots in Section 504. Whereas Section 504 applies only to organizations receiving funding from the federal government, ADA applies to a broader spectrum. Also, Section 504 is broader than IDEA with regard to a "free and appropriate public education." IDEA defines FAPE to include special education and related services, whereas Section 504 includes the provision of special or regular education and related services. IDEA focuses on the unique educational needs of the student; Section 504 compares the education of students with or without disabilities.

Child Find originated under Section 504, which puts the responsibility for identifying and locating children with disabilities on the school. The schools in turn must designate some agency to identify and locate every qualified child in the school's jurisdiction who is not receiving a public education and its related services. Public elementary and secondary schools must develop standards and procedures for evaluating and placing students who are believed to have a disability needing special education and or related services. Because the definitions under Section 504 are broader than IDEA, even if there is no reason that a student is in need of special education under an IEP, a district's procedures and staff training may require an evaluation. These evaluations must have (1) reliable and valid evaluation measures, (2) administration by trained personnel, and (3) evaluations assessing specific educational needs. Unlike IDEA, Section 504 does not mandate a multidisciplinary team, and parents do not have to be included.

Section 504 covers preschool and adult programs as well as elementary and secondary education, requiring equal and accessible transportation, architecture, educational programs, and nonacademic services. Graduation and textbook standards may not be discriminatory, nor may evaluation systems. Different treatment is justified only if it is necessary to provide services to persons with disabilities that are as effective as those provided to others.

Section 504 guarantees an appropriate special education as well as accessibility to regular education programs. It requires that all handicapped children be provided a free, appropriate public education in the least restrictive environment. A handicapped person under Section 504 is (1) any person who has physical or mental impairment that substantially limits one or more major life activities, (2) has a record of such impairment, or (3) is regarded as having such an impairment. This definition differs from that found in IDEA, which defines specific disabling conditions. Because of this difference, some individuals who are not qualified for special education under IDEA may be qualified for special services under Section 504.

Like IDEA, Section 504 requires identification, evaluation, provision of appropriate services, notification of parents, an individualized accommodation plan, and procedural safeguards. These activities must be performed in accordance with Section 504 regulations, which have some requirements that differ from those of IDEA.

Because Section 504 comes under the Office of Civil Rights within the U.S. Department of Education (DOE), students with disabilities have been granted additional support with regard to transportation and facilities. Transportation schedules must not cause students with disabilities to spend appreciably more time on buses than students without disabilities, and arrival and departure times must not reduce the length of the school day. With regard to facilities, room sizes must be adequate to accommodate the educational, physical, and medical needs of the students. Classes for students with disabilities should not be held in storage rooms, partitioned offices, or other inappropriate locations. Teachers of students with disabilities must be provided adequate support and supplies to give their students an education equal to that of nondisabled students (ERIC Clearinghouse on Handicapped and Gifted Children, 1992).

FUNDING AND OPPOSITION

Funding provided to programs developed in IDEA 1990 and the amendments of 1997 has proven to be enormous when compared to the cost of educating the regular education student. In March 2000, the Supreme Court declared that school districts should additionally pay the costs of nursing care during the school day for disabled persons, which could cost as much as $15,000 annually, per pupil. The increase in the number of special education students is approximately 3 percent each year. To keep up with this, 23,000 more special education teachers will be needed. These factors alone present enormous implications for universities and state and local governments.

Opponents to special education believe these programs and expenditures are taking money away from school construction, books, and teacher salaries. Opponents also believe that vague wording in IDEA produced frivolous lawsuits.

Proponents for special education counter with the thought that the lack of funding and programs based on such funding so far has caused many special education problems and challenges to increase; for example, learning disabled students account for one-half of the special education students, and early identification is equally critical. Additionally, school districts must continuously collect meaningful data to document student progress toward IEP goals, thus documenting program validity. Data needs to be collected throughout instruction so that student progress is continually monitored, which can support the decisions as to whether or not a program or instruction is continued (Yell and Drasgow, 2000).

Both political parties support increased spending for special education. The Republican Party recently went on record in support of an increase in the funding level to the legal maximum, and the Democratic Party has responded with support for the largest increase in funding for education ever.

Progress is continually being made from the laws that were passed to legislative and congressional effort being put forth now with regard to the special education movement. According to a progress report on National Disability Policy, IDEA is becoming an achievement of bipartisan compromise. Parts of the 1997 IDEA amendments provided for disciplinary action and payment of attorneys' fees to parents (described in Chapter 2). A nine-month study of the effect of federal special education protections on the ability of schools to maintain discipline is currently being planned by the U.S. General Accounting Office. Advocates for special education work to keep these areas of provision alive.

CHARTER SCHOOLS AND CHILDREN
WITH SPECIAL NEEDS

Charter schools are based on a specific philosophy and *charter,* or contract, about what objectives the school wants to meet. The charter is held accountable for academic and operational results. Some parents of special-needs children believe charter schools provide less bureaucracy and can more easily meet their childrens' needs.

Charter schools sometimes can provide a lower student-teacher ratio, and they may be more open to adopting a variety of instructional techniques—in part because they are at liberty to exhibit more autonomy, which may lead to a more individualized program. The programs available at the charter school may provide what the parents believe are significant to their child's academic and social development. A charter school may also provide simply the opportunity for a fresh start. McKinney (1996) explains that few of the twenty-five states that have passed charter school legislation have resolved whether the charter schools are separate school districts or part of the regular school district. If they are, in fact, legally autonomous school districts, they act as the local education agencies (LEAs), which are required under IDEA to provide a free, appropriate public education. If a charter school accepts special education children as part of the general population being served according to the charter or contract—and therefore receives funding for these children— it is required to follow the regulations set forth by Section 504 of the Rehabilitation Act of 1973 and the Americans with Disabilities Act (ADA). All public school districts, including charter schools wholly funded by the state, are bound by Section 504, which prohibits discrimination on the basis of disability by any agency that receives federal financial assistance.

What happens if a charter school's administration believes it cannot meet the needs of special education students? *Charter Schools: A Reference Handbook* (Weil, 2000) offers several reasons why some charter schools eliminate students with specific needs. Primary among them is cost. As Secretary of Education Richard W. Riley commented, it is often more expensive to educate a child who is disabled or emotionally troubled (p. 128). Many charter schools therefore determine to improve their bottom line by leaving the education of students with special needs to the regular public schools.

It is important to note that parents who choose charter schools give up some of their individual rights under IDEA, as the charter school selected may not have as many specific resources on site to meet the special needs of the child. However, parents may choose the charter school experience in order to receive what they believe are better educational services. This has implications for future planning, programs, and funding allocations (Lange and Lehr, 2000).

TECHNOLOGY PROGRAMS BASED ON THE LAW

The Department of Education has since 1991 funded projects at the state level to promote systems change and advocacy activities enhancing access of children and adults with disabilities to assistive technology devices and services. These projects were originally authorized under the section Technology Related Assistance in IDEA. In October 1998, Congress passed the Assistive Technology Act (see Chapter 2). Disability advocates continue to lobby for more access and training, including use of the Internet at public libraries. The latter has revolutionary potential for individuals with special needs because of the extraordinary potential to empower them in education, employment, and civic activities (National Council on Disability, 1999).

PROGRAMS FOR AT-RISK INFANTS AND TODDLERS

The Department of Education's twenty-first annual report on the implementation of IDEA acknowledges a sharp rise in the number of children two years old or younger who are receiving special education services. Between 1988 and 1997, that number soared from 34,270 to 197,376. A majority of these children—55 percent—received services in their home. Children from birth to age two are also receiving services in early-intervention classrooms and outpatient service facilities.

The rise in the number of infants and toddlers receiving special education services can be attributed to better identification practices over that ten-year period. This is especially due to the fact that the 1997 revision of IDEA added a category for the developmentally delayed, giving more flexibility to define needs based on academics and more for young children (Galley, 2000).

It is important to note that when IDEA was adopted in 1975, lawmakers decided that the federal government should pick up 40 percent of the additional costs associated with the law's requirements. Congress has never come close to that goal, though spending for IDEA rose by 66 percent in the five years since the Republicans took control of Congress. But federal aid still amounts to an estimated 13 percent of the total state and local costs for special education, according to the Department of Education. For the fiscal year 2000, Congress allocated $5.75 billion for state grants under IDEA; most of that money, about $5 billion, went to educate students ages 6–21; the rest went to early childhood and preschool programs.

Again, there are bipartisan efforts to continue the support. A new grassroots group from Concord, New Hampshire, the National Campaign to Fully Fund IDEA, is attempting to collect a million signatures of support to bring to Washington in the year 2001. The Council for Exceptional Children (CEC) has recommended spending nearly $7 billion on

IDEA, Part B, along with an additional $1 billion for early childhood and preschool programs. The National School Boards Association is requesting that Congress approve an additional $2.2 billion a year for the next ten years. Additionally significant is that two representatives, Matthew G. Martinez (D-Calif.) and Bill Gooding (R-Penn.), have introduced legislation to authorize an appropriation of an additional $2 billion each year until 2010, at which time the federal government's contribution would meet its 40 percent mark—the original goal of 1975 (Sack, 2000).

POLICY VERSUS PROGRAM IMPLEMENTATION

As Garrett, Thorp, Behrman, and Denham (1998) point out, when the vision of policymakers is turned into specific services and actions, policy implementation takes place. It is here where the decision maker's ideas become real for the intended beneficiaries of the policy. With regard to Part H of IDEA 1990 (reauthorized in 1997 as Part C of IDEA), the policy becomes actuality when (1) an early intervention system is put in place, and (2) when infants, toddlers, and their families receive appropriate services. Practicality comes in when modifications are made by the implements. Each agency applies its own version of the legislation and is affected by the knowledge of the implementers and availability of resources. When Congress passed Part H of IDEA, "appropriate intervention services" were to include multidisciplinary, interagency coordination; the funding was never intended to be solely the responsibility of the federal government. Congress required each state to develop an interagency coordinating council (ICC) to assist state agencies in developing and implementing the early intervention system, with parents of young children with special needs composing one fifth of each state's ICC membership.

Garrett, Thorp, Behrman, and Denham (1998) also discuss a study employing in-depth interviews with local interagency coordinating councils, observations, review of materials, and additional interviews at two expanded data collection sites; results demonstrated that policy intentions and implementation frequently differ. In this case the early childhood intervention legislation had both positive and negative effects. Local impact in areas of family-centered activities and service coordination, improved Child Find, and referral for services, funding, networking, and developmental outcomes were very positive. However, negotiating system bureaucracies, increased paperwork, reduction in at-risk services, increased financial responsibility for parents, and budget impacts from nonreimbursable services were noted drawbacks.

Early childhood intervention is one of the few special education legislations of IDEA, which requires much coordination on the part of funding that does not predominately come from the federal government. The program is so significant in the hearts and minds of special education policymakers and practitioners that the local application and effort from advocates of the law's success will not fade.

SPECIAL EDUCATION AS IT IS IMPACTED BY GOAL 1 OF GOALS 2000

As a response to Goal 1 of The Goals 2000: Educate America Act (see Chapter 2), a position statement by the Division for Early Childhood, a part of the CEC, was drafted. Goal 1 states: "By the year 2000, all children in the United States will start school ready to learn." The CEC decided to define and explain the implications of this federal act for children with disabilities, children placed at-risk for school failure, children of poverty, children who are non-English speaking, and children with gifts and talents.

The Division of Early Childhood's statement posits that to reach Goal 1, it is imperative to have healthy and competent parents, wanted and healthy babies, decent housing, and adequate nutrition. Its interpretation additionally offered that quality early education and childcare is a birthright for all children, and, therefore, services to support this concept must be comprehensive, coordinated, and focused on individual family and child needs. Additionally, the division wrote, it is inappropriate to screen children into or out of early education programs that give them a legitimate opportunity to learn. Finally, early educators must be schooled in and encouraged to use developmentally appropriate curricula, materials, and procedures to maximize a child's growth and development.

REFERENCES

ERIC Clearinghouse on Handicapped and Gifted Children, 1992. Section 504: The Rehabilitation Act of 1973 and the Americans with Disabilities Act of 1990. Reston, VA: The Council for Exceptional Children, Office of Educational Research and Improvement, U.S. Department of Education.

Galley, M., 2000. "Report Charts Growth in Special Education." *Education Week* 19, no. 32: 35.

Garrett, J. N., E. K. Thorp, M. M. Behrmann, and S. A. Denham, 1998. "The Impact of Early Intervention Legislation: Local Perceptions." *Topics in Early Childhood Special Education* 18: 183–190.

Lange, C. M., and C. A. Lehr, 2000. "Charter Schools and Students with Disabilities: Parent Perceptions of Reasons for Transfer and Satisfaction with Services." *Remedial and Special Education* 21, no. 3: 141–151.

McKinney, J. R., 1996. "A New Barrier for Children with Disabilities." *Educational Leadership* 54 (October): 22–25.

National Council on Disability, 1999. *National Disability Policy: A Progress Report.* Washington, DC: National Council on Disability.

Sack, J., 2000. "Congress Poised to Increase Funding for Special Education." *Education Weekly* 19, no. 31: 39.

Smith, B., 2000. "The Federal Role in Early Childhood Special Education Policy in the Next Century: The Responsibility of the Individual." *Topics in Early Childhood Special Education* 20, no.1 (Spring): 10.

Sung, E., 2000. "At What Cost Special Education?" *The Policy News & Information Service,* VoxCap Network, http://www.policy.com/news/dbrief/farc480. asp.

Weil, D., 2000. *Charter Schools: A Reference Handbook.* Santa Barbara, CA: ABC-CLIO Publishers.

Wurtz, E., 1999. *Promising Practices: Progress Toward the Goals 1999.* Washington, DC: National Education Goals Panel.

Yell, M. L., and E. Drasgow, 2000. "Litigating a Free Appropriate Public Education: The Lovaas Hearings and Cases." *Journal of Special Education* 33, no. 4: 205–214.

Chapter Five

⚫✦ Special Education and Advocacy

Chapters 2 and 4 identified the development of specific laws and their applications to the field of special education. This chapter takes the laws to their next level: advocacy.

THE SCHOOL AS ADVOCATE

Because education in the public schools is mandatory for all children, schools are the great equalizer. They are the one place in the United States where we can be certain that the rights of all children are protected and appropriate placements are implemented.

Throughout our country's history, schools have functioned as an advocate for immigrant populations and lower socioeconomic groups—a ladder up which countless individuals have climbed to reach opportunity and security. Generally speaking, our public schools allow all children to achieve personal and academic success through merit and hard work rather than by elitism.

By advocating the rights, privileges, and needs of children with disabilities and exceptionalities; by including the challenged in the mainstream; and by providing services that help special children fit in, our schools may make accessible to them all the wonders available to normal children. Following are specific examples of how schools may advocate for a child to receive appropriate services:

- ✦ The regular education teacher makes a referral to the school psychologist (or that school's designated person) based on the regular education teacher's observations that the child cannot learn in the regular education classroom.
- ✦ The regular education teacher contacts the special education teacher for that special education teacher to come into the regular education classroom and observe the child for con-

cerns that the regular education teacher has expressed.

- The regular education teacher contacts the parents with concerns to obtain their input, or if it might be more expedient, based on the regulations of that school district, have the parents request the referral for special education services.
- The staffing specialist, a person designated by the school district to coordinate all efforts, presents the special needs of the child in order to obtain either appropriate placement or appropriate services.
- A person is designated at the school district level to look beyond special services authorized by the school district toward national programs or services available for the most appropriate education.
- A person is designated by the school district to connect the parents of the special needs child with any of the appropriate organizations, associations, agencies, or services listed in Chapter 7.

DEVELOPMENT OF ADVOCACY GROUPS

The civil rights movement of the 1950s and 1960s drew attention to social injustices experienced by minorities, the poor, and women. The first advocacy groups for the disabled grew out of the protests and legal actions of that time. Advocates for persons with disabilities worked tirelessly to obtain access to rights for these individuals, as well as the funding, programs, and facilities that go with them. Litigation and legislation were the major tools used to access educational programs as well. The same parents who had complained to school boards and community representatives for years now discovered that the lawsuit was a more effective tool. These parents formed groups of advocates that could influence the voting for or against congressional and other political leaders. Most of the successful outcomes of individual court cases and appropriate administration of the federal and state laws concerning special education can be attributed to advocates, be they parents or other professionals in the field.

Legislators usually do not just decide that special needs children and adults require laws to ensure their rights. Parents, committees from advocacy groups, or representatives from professional groups with related interests are almost always the initiators, supporters, and organizers of proposed legislation. In their book *Mental Retardation,* Patton, Beirne-Smith, and Payne (1990) describe four types of advocacy:

➼ Systems advocacy: Advocacy by an independent collective of citizens in order to: (1) represent the rights and interests of groups of people with similar needs, and (2) pursue human service system quality and progressive change.

➼ Legal advocacy: Advocacy by attorneys at law in order to represent individuals or groups of individuals in the litigation or legal negotiations process.

➼ Self-advocacy: Advocacy by individuals whose rights are at-risk of being violated or diminished in order to represent one's own rights and interests as well as to speak on one's own behalf.

➼ Citizen advocacy: Advocacy by a mature, competent, volunteer citizen in order to represent, as if they were his or her own, the rights and interests of another citizen.

In any of the above types of advocacy, the concept remains the same; citizens are coming together to create, first, *awareness* of social policy regarding rights of the individual, and, second, *legislation* to make the policy a reality in order to eliminate barriers of access. Organizations such as those listed in Chapter 7 help make certain that persons with disabilities exercise their rights as individuals as well as a group.

Among the advocates for persons with disabilities and special needs have been many unheralded parents whose names are lost to history. In 1921, the National Society for Crippled Children, organized by parents, became the first national advocacy group for children with disabilities. As in most early organizations of this sort, medical professionals played a major role in providing organizational impetus. Physical and medical needs (as opposed to educational needs) were the original emphasis of such groups, though they eventually began to focus efforts on improving education for children with special needs (Gearheart, Mullein, and Gearheart, 1993). Two parent groups, the National Association for Retarded Children (NARC), which later became the National Association for Retarded Citizens, and the United Cerebral Palsy Association (UCP) strongly influenced early federal legislation and encouraged even those who were not parents of children with disabilities to support their cause.

PARENT ADVOCACY

Parents working alone and as members of organized lobbying forces—such as the Association for Children with Learning Disabilities, which began to influence legislation in the 1960s—have long been the grassroots of all support for children with disabilities. When in the 1970s it became obvious that federally mandated services and federal financial support were needed, parents and other primary caregivers banded together to revolutionize special education through the passage of P.L. 94-142, the Education for All Handicapped Children Act. Today, parents continue to be the foremost advocate for their children's educational needs. After all, who can speak more effectively about the abilities and obstacles to their children's emotional and academic success than an involved and loving parent?

Peterson (1987) offers the following as rationale for parental involvement in securing rights and opportunities for their special-needs children:

(1) Parents (or their substitutes) are the key teachers, socializing agents, and caregivers for children during their early years.
(2) Parents can be effective intervention agents and teachers of their own children.
(3) Parents are in a particularly strategic position to enhance or negate the potential benefits of educational programs.
(4) Involvement offers a mechanism for helping parents build a positive perspective about their child.
(5) Intervention works best when parents and professionals are working toward common goals for their children and when all are applying compatible strategies.
(6) Involvement of parents in planning and implementing special services for a young child is a parental right.
(7) Involvement brings parents into contact with a great variety of resources that can help them in their parenting roles.

POPULAR CULTURE AND ADVOCACY

In recent years, fictional characters in books, in movies, and on the stage have brought international attention to persons with special needs. Either the individual's advocate or the person him- or herself is featured. Such portrayals often result in (1) the disabled person or disabled group getting looked upon with more respect and (2) an increase in the funding for programs that serve members of the disabled group. Although negatives and inaccuracies are certain in the presentation of some portrayals, on the whole, they have served to increase awareness and understanding of special-needs audiences.

The films *Mask, Rain Man, Children of a Lesser God,* and *The Mir-*

acle Worker all brought special-needs individuals to the center of public attention, and all four received Academy Awards. *David and Lisa,* the story of two special education students attending a residential school for emotionally disturbed adolescents, is a cult classic among black-and-white films. The popularity of these films suggests a wide acceptance of their message and portrayals.

In *Mask,* the main character, Rocky Dennis (played by Eric Stoltz), is afflicted with craniodiaphysealdysplasia, a physical disorder that affects development of a part, system, or region of the body, in this case the head, face and clavicle; Rocky's specific affliction is commonly called lionitis. The film

> presents Rocky Dennis as a high functioning adolescent. A great deal of his strong self-esteem is attributed to his advocate mother [played by Cher] and supportive friends, who, as members of a motorcycle gang, are social outcasts. It is the depth of the love of the significant adult, the mother, that draws the viewer to support her advocacy for her son. The strength of her determination becomes clear when she confronts the principal of a local school to which Rocky has been assigned. The principal wants to place Rocky in a special, separate school for handicapped students, simply because of the way he looks. Rocky's mother insists that he stay, and proceeds to explain Rocky's rights and to display appropriate documentation, including his last report card, demonstrating that he has been in the top fifth of his class. This experience demonstrates the ongoing struggle over school placements for Rocky. The principal demonstrates the desire of the school to hide, rather than mainstream, the exceptional student. (Farber, Provenzo, and Holm, 1994, p. 193).

A similar situation to the one found in *Mask* can be assessed in *Rain Man.* The main character, Raymond (played by Dustin Hoffman), has an advocate younger brother, Charles (played by Tom Cruise), just as Rocky in *Mask* had his mother. Raymond is autistic and so exhibits severe disturbances "characterized by bizarre behavior, developmental delays, and extreme isolation" (Meyen, 1990, p. 514). Here, too, the advocate supplies the force that changes the situation for the special needs person. The film simplifies and distorts autism, asking informed viewers to suspend their understanding of the autistic person's need for a quiet, undisturbed routine when Raymond spends time with Charlie in a Las Vegas casino. Another scene, however, deals quite realistically with the act of touching, a very difficult experience for the autistic. As Farber, Provenzo, and Holm (1994) note in their analysis of *Rain Man,*

> If there is to be success, the full picture of reality must be taken into account. If not, the fantasy, and whatever positive effects it may have in generating heightened awareness and support for the autistic, must be weighed against the impact of any misconceptions and disappointments that result from the film's tendency to simplify and distort what is known. (P. 196)

In *Children of a Lesser God,* the main character, Sarah (played by then-newcomer Marlee Matlin), and the advocate, her teacher (played by William Hurt), draw the public's attention to the issue of educational achievement for the deaf and the hearing impaired.

In this film, the teacher takes his students in a school for the deaf to new heights of experience by teaching them to dance to music vibrations felt through large speakers. After some conflict between Sarah and her teacher, Sarah eventually becomes her own advocate. Even the controversial issue of total communication, an approach involving all forms of communication—speech, signing, and fingerspelling—is presented in the movie.

The Miracle Worker is the well-known film version of the story of young Helen Keller, blind and deaf, who achieves some normalcy in life through the efforts of teacher/advocate Annie Sullivan. Helen (played by Patty Duke) is at first angry and resentful of her new teacher but eventually comes to accept Annie (played by Anne Bancroft), who first reaches Helen in the pivotal water pump scene. Viewers learn that Helen is far from being mentally disturbed and is, in fact, a brilliant and inquisitive child who just needed the right advocate to help her achieve her potential.

David and Lisa is the story of two special education students at a residential school for emotionally disturbed adolescents. David (played by Keir Dullea) is severely emotionally disturbed and believes that touch can kill; he is arrogant and difficult and seems incapable of developing interpersonal relationships. Lisa (played by Janet Margolin) communicates through rhyme, exhibits wide mood swings, and has a personality disorder that manifests in the persona of "Muriel." The significant advocate in the film is their psychiatrist (played by Howard DeSilva).

Through the development of the relationship between David and Lisa and the intervention of the advocate, David teaches Lisa to speak without rhyme, and she encourages him to allow touching. The film proposes that emotional disturbance can be overcome through advocacy and support, appropriate placement, and good psychiatric care.

Of course, this is not always the case in the real world—disorders don't just melt away, and the "right" advocate is not always miraculously found. But the film wins credit for its realistic portrayal of special-needs individuals.

ADVOCACY AND POLITICS

As South Dakota governor Bill Janklow stated in his 1999 State of the State address, "It's so politically easy and convenient to talk about kids and children and use them for rhetoric" (Sconyers and Levy, 1999, p. 22).

The National Association of Child Advocates examined the responses of Governor Janklow and thirty-five other governors elected in November 1998 in order to determine whether they were incorporating campaign promises to children in their policy decisions. The association specifically considered how the governors followed through on children's health insurance, Head Start, childcare subsidies, and programs for at-risk youth and others. It found that "Analyzed by region, candidates in the West most frequently supported children's issues (67%) while candidates in the East supported them the least (54%). By party, Democrats showed stronger support than Republicans (79% verses 58 %) did. The positive information was that there was a follow-through rate of almost 80% of the increased funding for at-risk youth" (Sconyers and Levy, 1999, p. 22). The success rate of advocates and their organizations in influencing policy at the state level is thus considerable.

REFERENCES

Gearheart, B., R. Mullein, and C. Gearheart, 1993. *Exceptional Individuals and Introduction.* Belmont, CA: Brooks/Cole Publishing.

Farber, P., E. Provenzo, and G. Holm (eds.), 1994. *Schooling in the Light of Popular Culture.* Albany, NY: State University of New York Press.

Meyen, E. L., 1990. *Exceptional Children in Today's Schools.* Denver: Love Publishing.

Patton, J. R., M. Beirne-Smith, and J. S. Payne, 1990. *Mental Retardation.* Columbus, OH: Merrill Publishing.

Peterson, N. L., 1987. *Early Intervention for Handicapped and At-risk Children.* Denver: Love Publishing.

Sconyers, N., and T. Levy, 1999. *Promises to Children.* State Government News, The Council of State Governments, Lexington, KY: The Council of State Governments.

Chapter Six

⦿ Politics and the Special Education Challenge

THE DEVELOPMENT OF TEACHER UNIONS AND THEIR IMPACT ON SPECIAL EDUCATION

Concerned about the neglect of parents in the training of their children, the Puritans of the Massachusetts Bay Colony, a religious society, proposed and supported the Massachusetts Law of 1642, which called for an investigation of the ability of children to read and understand the principles of religion and the laws of society. In 1647 the Old Deluder Satan Laws passed, requiring communities in Massachusetts Colony to establish and support schools. At that time in the American Colonies, there were no licensing or professional standards to be met.

In the early 1800s, most Americans lived in farm communities with one-room schools and a single teacher. By the mid-1800s a reform movement called "the common school movement" attempted to bring schools under state control, teaching a common body of knowledge to children from different social and economic backgrounds. The first teacher organizations and teacher unions were organized around this time.

In 1857 ten state teacher associations met with the objective of upgrading teaching to a profession. They called their combined organization the National Teachers' Association. Years later, when it merged with the National Association of School Superintendents, the two organizations became the National Education Association (NEA). Because the NEA was dominated by superintendents and college professors, teachers themselves had little influence on issues and advocacy.

It was left to two women, Margaret Haley and Catherine Goggin, working tirelessly for the benefit of classroom teachers, to form the Chicago Teacher's Federation (CTF) in 1897, the forerunner of the American Federation of Teachers (AFT). In 1902 the CTF formed an alliance with the Chicago Federation of Labor that resulted in heightened antagonism against the Chicago Board of Education. The board had voted not to increase teachers' salaries and required teachers to sign yellow-dog contracts, which prevented them from joining a union (if they did, they would be discharged).

By 1917 the NEA had become an association pledging professionalism encompassing education training and scientific inquiry. In April 1916, the CTF regrouped in order to organize the American Federation of Teachers, an organization that had minimal impact up to World War II.

Major differences between AFT and the NEA were evident from the beginning. AFT was a teachers union organized and lead by teachers, whereas the NEA membership was largely school administrators, including school district representatives. Although by the 1960s NEA membership was mostly composed of teachers, administrators still led the organization, resulting in adversarial bargaining when conflicts arose. It wasn't until fairly recently that teachers and administrators came to respect each other's rights and roles and cooperate for the good of their students.

In recent years, school districts and unions have worked together to establish conditions conducive for the success of special education programs. Both groups recognize that federal laws for programs and practices related to special education require the teachers unions to advocate and districts to provide appropriations so that special education teachers are able to effectively do their jobs. Proof of this are the special certifications developed by most state departments of education in areas such as learning disabilities; mental, physical, and visual handicaps; hearing impairments; and giftedness.

State departments of education, school districts, and teachers unions have demonstrated that special education teachers and the population they teach have definite and important needs. To include teachers in decisionmaking is one of the missions of teachers unions. This ability is essential if, for example, inclusion of special education students in regular education classrooms is to come about successfully. Other good examples of this are special education programs serving students with various disabilities that "years ago, the public schools did not attempt to serve" (Streshly and DeMitchell, 1994, p. 32).

In education there is a flow from politics to economics to collective bargaining. Education advocacy groups have supported the political debates regarding the setting of values for education. These values support special education and are evident in the laws that have been passed to protect children with special needs. Collective bargaining ensures that the advocate's initial work gets into the special programs the politics support. The distribution of funds is something teachers unions have kept a close eye on.

The unions have specifically made issues important for the equal education of special needs students part of their political agenda. For example, both the NEA and AFT have stated that charter schools (discussed in Chapter 4) must be open to all students, including those with special needs. This was part of a conscious effort to not allow charter schools to create a multitiered choice system discriminating against some students (Weil, 2000).

Teachers unions have developed collaborative relationships with local universities to help teachers gain more academic background in their fields as well as meet requirements of the Department of Education. A new partnership, the United Teachers of Dade (UTD) in Miami-Dade County, Florida (an affiliate of the American Federation of Teachers), has forged a pioneering relationship with a national university, the Union Institute, based in Cincinnati, Ohio, in order to develop an innovative model designed to make learning more accessible and available to teachers and other related school personnel. Its aim is to provide the most highly educated people possible to work with our most treasured resource—our children. The National Education Goals Panel in its publication *Promising Practices: Progress Toward the Goals 1998* proposed important educational goals for the year 2000, among them "the nation's teaching force will have access to programs for the continued improvement of their professional skills and the opportunity to acquire the knowledge and skills needed to instruct and prepare all Americans for the next century." One objective of this goal was that "Partnerships will be established, whenever possible, among local education agencies, institutions of higher education, parents, and local labor, business and professional associations to provide and support programs for the professional development of educators" (National Education Goals Panel, 1998). The partnership between the Union Institute and UTD is an ideal example of an educational institution and a labor association joining forces to support professional education for teachers.

Recently the NEA and AFT locals have come together to develop TURN, the Teachers Union Reform Network, headed by Roger Erskine of the Seattle, Washington, NEA and Adam Urbanski of the Rochester, New York, AFT. These joint union/association leaders have committed to helping to bring to the forefront educational reform issues such as quality teaching, pay for performance, evaluation, and parental involvement.

One of the goals of TURN's mission statement is to "promote in public education and in the union democratic dynamics, fairness and due process for all" (Urbanski, 1998). This is parallel to the goals of IDEA, which identified that due process for special-needs children is essential. The goals of TURN appear to be consistent with the goals of the federal government and special education advocates.

Teachers unions organize around school reform as well as salary benefits, and a report by the AFT calls for stricter requirements for new teachers with regard to standardized tests, higher grades, and more student teaching experiences. The efforts by teacher associations and unions to influence policy are continual.

Specifically, in resolutions set forth by the AFT at the 1994 national convention in Anaheim, California, support was unconditionally given for major issues related to special education. With regard to inclusion, a concept with no legal mandate or consistent definition, the AFT recognized (1) a working definition of inclusion to be "the placement of all students with disabilities in general education classrooms without regard to the nature or severity of the students' disabilities, their ability to behave and function appropriately in the classroom, or the educational benefits they can derive"; (2) that two years before the twentieth anniversary of the passage of the Education for All Handicapped Children Act (P.L. 94-142), Congress's continuing cynicism with funding the mandates of the law at under 10 percent instead of the 40 percent promised compromised schools' ability to provide appropriate services to children with disabilities; and (3) that there is a high percentage of minority children in some classes for students with disabilities, and inclusion is viewed by some advocates as the only means of getting minority children out of some of these placements.

Convention attendees discussed eleven other issues regarding children with special needs and passed seven resolutions, including:

(1) The AFT will continue to seek high national achievement standards for all education, applicable to all students, disabled and nondisabled alike.
(2) The AFT opposes inclusion based on placing all students with disabilities in general education classroom regardless of disability, their ability to behave or function appropriately.
(3) The AFT opposes administrative practices placing too many students with disabilities in the general education classroom, often without services, and changing IEPs in order to do this.
(4) The AFT seeks alliances with organizations supporting alternative placements and the educational placement of students with disabilities in the LRE (American Federation of Teachers, 1994).

It is important to note that the AFT represents *all* teachers, many more regular education than special education. In trying to make the educational experience in the regular education classroom the highest academically, and by recognizing the needs of the regular education teacher and restating the desire to support both students with and without disabilities, the AFT is supporting all of its membership.

Another demonstration of AFT support for special education is its Educational Research and Dissemination (ERD) Program, which disseminates research to help promote effective teaching and learning with a variety of courses related to special education. Additionally, AFT is involved with the Association of Service Providers Implementing IDEA Reforms in Education (ASPIRE) partnership. ASPIRE develops materials to support special education teachers as well as regular education teachers.

EARLY INFLUENCE OF POLITICS ON SPECIAL EDUCATION PROGRAMS FOR YOUNG CHILDREN

The first U.S. preschools were affiliated with colleges and universities, who developed them in an effort to find better ways to care for children. Garwood (1983) points out that federal legislation under the Works Progress Administration Program of the 1930s and the Lanham Act during World War II was instrumental in providing funds for the spread of preschools beyond the university community. Thus began the traditional nursery school.

During the so-called War on Poverty in the 1960s, the young economically disadvantaged child became a focus of discussion. Many believed that if the disadvantaged child had the same advantages middle-class children had, especially in the early years, the educational achievement of the disadvantaged child would increase. Thus evolved the *enriched curriculum* exemplified by the Bank Street Program and the Erickson Institute Program. Both the cognitive and affective domains were promoted, with development of language as well as a positive self-image of paramount importance. In an enrichment model, structure is low, flexibility is high, and there are no lists of measurable objectives; developing one's own choice of activities and projects is stressed.

Another model of curriculum evolving from 1960s political philosophy was the direct instruction curriculum of Carl Bereiter and Sigfried Engelmann, in which the desire to increase the linguistic and cognitive levels of disadvantaged children was so imperative that a highly structured direct teaching system was developed. Aligned with the theories of B. F. Skinner, the curriculum's results appeared dramatic and quick. Garwood (1983) describes the Bereiter and Engelmann theory that "disadvantaged children have a severe language deficit in thinking about and describing experiences . . . . The teacher was the key to this instructional model focusing initially on language" (p. 415). From this model developed the Distar curriculum, which follows all the initial premises but added reading and arithmetic. All curriculum goals and objectives are in measurable terms, instructed in groups with children responding orally in unison.

The politics of this time was to raise the level of education of the disadvantaged because the social consciousness of the country was high. The flame of this desire, as evidenced by the laws being enacted for special education beginning in the 1960s, has continued to the present through hundreds of federally funded, state funded, and community supported programs.

POLITICAL CHANGES AFFECTING THE EDUCATION OF DISABLED CHILDREN

Secretary of Education Richard W. Riley, in a 2000 speech before the House Education and Welfare Committee, indicated that "because three-quarters of all children with disabilities spend over half their time in regular classrooms, many of the broader educational programs benefiting all children will also help students with disabilities."

Changes in society that affect aspects of daily life produce actions and reactions by political and educational leaders. This has certainly been the case concerning the recent trend in students bringing weapons to school. The original Individuals with Disabilities Education Act stated that disabled students who carry guns to school could be removed for more than ten days without parental consent or court approval. In 1997 Congress approved changes that gave schools the power to suspend for up to forty-five days disabled students who bring guns or other weapons to school. Additionally, the 1997 revision streamlined the procedure for removing dangerous students from the classroom by allowing placement decisions to be made by a hearing officer rather than a judge. A loophole allowing (1) students to claim disability status after committing a crime, and (2) the school district to call police without penalty when disabled students commit crimes has since been closed.

Also affecting special education students is the Class Size Reduction Program, enacted in 2000, which seeks to help schools improve student learning by providing reduction funds to hire additional qualified teachers so that classes contain no more than a nationwide average of eighteen pupils. A guidance memo for the program specifies that if a special education class has more than eighteen students, the local education agency (LEA) may use the reduction funds to achieve a reduced class size. Since mainstreaming and inclusion are important to special education, LEAs may also use these funds to pay professional development costs for regular education classroom teachers to help educate them to the needs of special education children. LEAs may also use these funds to hire special education teachers to team-teach with regular education teachers when needed.

Another political act allocating funds to create programs for special education students is the Reading Excellence Acts (REA) Program. On July 26, 2000, the Secretary of Education announced the award of $198.4 million in grants to help improve the reading skills of prekindergarten through third-grade children. The funds will help nine states and Washington, D.C., use scientifically based research to improve the reading skills of up to one million elementary school students, particularly at-risk students during the critical grades of kindergarten through grade three. One of the key purposes of REA is to provide early intervention to children who are at-risk of inappropriately being identified as having special needs.

Political support for special education has continued in the form of federal mandates to accommodate students with disabilities, as evidenced by the greater number of critical issues being addressed and funding being allocated through the Americans with Disabilities Act, the Individuals with Disabilities Education Act, Section 504 of Title V of the Rehabilitation Act, and advisory guidelines from the U.S. Architectural and Transportation Barriers Compliance Board.

Further evidence of political support for special education and the rights of the disabled is found in the Consortium on Inclusive Schooling Practices, a collaborative effort to build the capacity of state and local education agencies serving children and youth with and without disabilities in school and community settings. It is a five-year project funded by the U.S. Department of Education/Office of Special Education Programs to aid states participating in the Allegheny University program. (Participating states are California, Missouri, and New Mexico, in conjunction with the National Association of State Board of Education.)

Here's how the consortium works: Policies and practices within the participant states are first audited, and the results are communicated to policymakers. This allows monitoring of the policy objectives and reveals which are being accomplished and which need to be changed. If individual schools need to develop more inclusive educational experiences, consortium staff will provide training and technical assistance. Additionally, the consortium facilitates conferences, workshops, and forums on critical issues throughout the participating states. By linking key personnel at the state and local level of the target state, the groups can be directly involved in policy and implementation issues.

Within the institution of the school itself, special education is dependent on politics at the national, state, and local levels: It is the politics of the nation that enacts laws that ultimately determine who is included or excluded in the schools; the state budget determines what basic or enrichment programs can be allotted; and the local educational settings are responsible for developing and presenting the curriculum content. The selection of knowledge included in a curriculum is often a political act. Political ideology directs social and political action, which manifests itself in school philosophy and, ultimately, in what is taught. English (1992) states that "curriculum construction goes on in schools within the unspoken and dominant education ideology, the dominant political ideology that serves as 'hidden' screens for the actual process of writing the acceptable work plans in schools" (p. 30). The political agenda directly affects practical educational aspects of the special education child.

REFERENCES

American Federation of Teachers, 1994. Resolution on Inclusion of Students with Disabilities. National convention. Anaheim, CA. Available at http://www.aft.org/about/resolutions/1994/inclusion.html.

English, F. W., 1992. *Deciding What to Teach and Test.* Thousand Oaks, CA: Corwin Press.

Garwood, S. G., 1983. *Educating Young Handicapped Children.* Rockville, MD: Aspen Publications.

National Education Goals Panel, 1998. *Promising Practices: Progress Toward the Goals.* Washington, DC: National Education Goals Panel.

Riley, R. W., 2000. "Remarks as Prepared for Delivery by U.S. Secretary of Education Richard W. Riley." Washington, D.C.: House Education and Workforce Committee Testimony.

Streshly, W. A., and T. A. DeMitchell, 1994. *Teacher Unions and TQE: Building Quality Labor Relations.* Thousand Oaks, CA: Corwin Press.

Urbanski, A., 1998. "Turning Unions Around." *Contemporary Education* 69, no. 4: 186–190.

Weil, D., 2000. *Charter Schools: A Reference Handbook.* Santa Barbara, CA: ABC-CLIO Publishers.

Chapter Seven

☙ Organizations, Associations, and Government Agencies

NATIONAL CONTACTS

Alexander Graham Bell Association for the Deaf (AG Bell)
3417 Volta Place NW
Washington, DC 20007-2778
(202) 337-5220 (Voice)
(202) 337-5221 (TTY)
Fax: (202) 337-8314
Web site: http://www.agbell.org/

Founded in 1890 by Alexander Graham Bell as an information provider and support network, AG Bell is the largest organization in the United States focused on the needs of hearing impaired children who use auditory approaches to communicate. AG Bell offers a variety of member-oriented programs, financial aid, publications, software, audiovisual materials, and other information on hearing impairment, with an auditory-oral emphasis.

American Amputee Foundation (AAF)
P.O. Box 250218
Hillcrest Station
Little Rock, AR 72225
(501) 666-2523
Fax: (501) 666-8367
Web site: http://www.healthfinder.gov/text/orgs/hr2429.htm

The American Amputee Foundation (AAF) began in 1975 as a national information clearinghouse and referral center serving primarily am-. putees and their families. AAF offers a variety of services, including help with insurance claims, financial aid for prosthetic devices, counseling services, information concerning support groups, and self-help publications.

American Association of People with Disabilities (AAPD)

1819 H Street NW, Suite 330
Washington, DC 20006
(202) 457-0046
(800) 840-8844
Web site: http://www.aapd.com/

The AAPD is a nonprofit, nonpartisan membership organization that promotes the goal of full inclusion of people with disabilities in American society. This newly organized association promises to bring about "the next step in the evolution of the disability rights movement"—economic clout and power through numbers, with unity, leadership, and impact.

√American Association of the Deaf-Blind (AADB)

814 Thayer Avenue
Silver Springs, MD 20910
(800) 735-2258 (Voice)
(301) 588-6545 (TTY)
Fax: (301) 588-8705
Web site: http://www.tr.wou.edu/dblink/aadb.htm

The AADB is a consumer advocacy organization for people who have combined hearing and vision impairments. It is open to all persons who are deaf-blind as well as to individuals directly concerned with their well being, including spouses, children, friends, and health care professionals.

√American Association on Mental Retardation (AAMR)

444 North Capitol Street NW, Suite 846
Washington, DC 20001
(202) 387-1968
(800) 424-3688
Fax: (202) 387-2193
Web site: http://www.aamr.org/index.shtml

This organization provides leadership in the field of mental retardation. The AAMR is the oldest and largest interdisciplinary organization of professionals (and others) concerned about mental retardation and related disabilities.

American Council of the Blind (ACB)

1155 15th Street NW, Suite 1004
Washington, DC 20005

(202) 467-5081
(800) 424-8666
Fax: (202) 467-5085
Web site: http://www.acb.org/

The ACB is the nation's leading membership organization of blind and visually impaired people. It strives to improve the well-being of all blind and visually impaired people by offering educational and rehabilitation facilities and opportunities, and it cooperates with public and private institutions and organizations concerned with blind services. The organization also publishes *The Braille Forum,* a free monthly magazine.

American Council on Education
One Dupont Circle NW
Washington, DC 20036
(202) 939-9300
Fax: (202) 833-4760
Web site: http://www.acenet.edu/contact.html

This is a national coordinating higher education association dedicated to equal educational opportunities and a strong higher education system.

American Disability Association (ADA)
2201 Sixth Avenue S
Birmingham, AL 35233
(205) 328-9090
Fax: (205) 251-7417
Web site: http://www.adanet.org/

This organization serves as an informational and resource center for Americans with diverse disabilities. It provides an international distributed computer network serving the interests of people with disabilities.

American Epilepsy Society
342 North Main Street
West Hartford, CT 06117-2507
(860) 586-7505
Fax: (860) 586-7550
Web site: http://www.aesnet.org/

The society promotes research and education for professionals dedicated to the prevention, treatment, and cure of epilepsy.

American Federation of Teachers
555 New Jersey Avenue NW
Washington, DC 20001
(202) 879-4400
Web site: http://www.aft.org/contact.html

This teachers union strives to attain a quality public education for all citizens and efficient and effective delivery of public services. It also has a goal to secure adequate health care for every American, especially children.

American Foundation for the Blind (AFB)
11 Penn Plaza, Suite 300
New York, NY 10001
(212) 502-7661
(212) 502-7662 (TDD)
(800) 232-5463
Fax: (212) 502-7777
Web site: http://www.afb.org/default.asp

A nonprofit organization founded in 1921, AFB is a resource for people who are blind or visually impaired, the organizations that serve them, and the general public. It publishes books, pamphlets, videos, and periodicals about blindness for professionals and consumers through AFB Press.

American Heart Association (AHA)
National Center
7272 Greenville Avenue
Dallas, TX 75231
(800) 242-8721
Fax: (214) 369-3685
Web site: http://www.americanheart.org

The American Heart Association (AHA) is a not-for-profit, voluntary health organization funded by private contributions. Its mission is to reduce disability and death from cardiovascular diseases and stroke. The AHA provides reliable information to the American public on prevention and treatment of heart disease and stroke.

American Lung Association (ALA)
1740 Broadway
New York, NY 10019
(800) LUNG-USA (586-4872)

Web site: http://www.lungusa.org/history/

Founded in 1904 to fight tuberculosis, the ALA today fights lung disease in all its forms. It offers a variety of programs and strategies for fighting lung disease as well as a wide variety of printed informational materials, public service announcements, news releases, and conferences.

American Paralysis Association and the
Christopher Reeve Paralysis Foundation
500 Morris Avenue
Springfield, NJ 07081
(800) 225-0292
Fax: (973) 912-9433
Web site: http://www.apacure.com/

This organization encourages and supports research to develop effective treatments and a cure for paralysis caused by spinal cord injury and other central nervous system disorders. The foundation also allocates a portion of its resources to grants that improve the quality of life for people with disabilities.

American Red Cross
431 18th Street NW
Washington, DC 20006
(202) 639-3520
Web site: http://www.redcross.org/

The American Red Cross is a humanitarian organization that provides relief to victims of disasters and helps people prevent, prepare for, and respond to emergencies.

✓**American Society for Deaf Children (ASDC)**
National Office
P.O. Box 3355
Gettysburg, PA 17325
(800) 942-2732 (Hotline)
(717) 334-7922 (Business Voice/TTY)
Fax: (717) 334-8808
Web site: http://www.deafchildren.org/

The ASDC is an organization of parents and families that advocates for deaf or hard-of-hearing children's total quality participation in education, the family, and the community. Staff handle inquiries on a variety of topics related to raising children who are deaf or hard of hearing.

✓American Speech-Language-Hearing Foundation

10801 Rockville Pike
Rockville, MD 20852
(301) 897-7341
Web site: http://www.ashfoundation.org/about.htm

The foundation is a charitable research and education organization that helps ensure the gift of communication for 42 million Americans with communication disorders.

American Spinal Injury Association (ASIA)

345 East Superior Street, Room 1436
Chicago, IL 60611
(312) 238-1242
Fax: (312) 238-0869
Web site: http://www.asia-spinalinjury.org/

ASIA is composed of professionals who have contributed to the field of spinal cord injury. The group promotes and establishes standards of excellence for all aspects of health care of individuals with spinal cord injury from onset through life and facilitates communication between members and other physicians, other health care professionals, researchers, and consumers.

✓The Annie E. Casey Foundation

701 Saint Paul Street
Baltimore, MD 21202
(410) 547-6600
Fax: (410) 547-6624
Web site: http://www.aecf.org/

The Casey Foundation is a private charitable organization dedicated to helping build better futures for disadvantaged children in the United States.

✓The Arc of the United States

1010 Wayne Avenue, Suite 650
Silver Spring, MD 20910
(301) 565-3842
Fax: (301) 565-5342
Web site: http://www.thearc.org/about.htm

The nation's leading national organization on mental retardation, the Arc provides organizational support to affiliated chapters and represents its membership on advocacy and programmatic issues pertaining to mental retardation.

Autism Society of America
7910 Woodmont Avenue, Suite 300
Bethesda, MD 20814-3015
(301) 657-0881
(800) 328-8476, ext. 150
Fax: (301) 657-0869
Web site: http://www.autism-society.org/

The society serves the needs of individuals with autism and their families through advocacy, education, public awareness, and research.

Avenues, a National Support Group for Arthrogryposis Multiplex Congenita
P.O. Box 5192
Sonora, CA 95370
(209) 928-3688
Web site: http://www.sonnet.com/avenues/

Avenues is a nonprofit information and support group for individuals and families affected by arthrogryposis multiplex congenita, a neuromuscular disease leading to multiple joint contractures at birth.

Blind Children's Fund
4740 Okemos Road
Okemos, MI 48864
(517) 347-1357
Fax: (517) 347-1459
Web site: http://www.blindchildrensfund.org/BCFCover.html

The fund is a nonprofit organization providing parents and professionals with information, materials, and resources that help them successfully teach and nurture infants and children who are blind or visually or multi-impaired.

Centers for Disease Control (CDC) National AIDS Hotline
American Society Health Association
P.O. Box 13827
Research Triangle Park, NC 27709
(800) 342-2437
Web site: http://www.ashastd.org/

The National AIDS Hotline operates under contract with the Centers for Disease Control and Prevention. Information concerning prevention, risk, testing, treatment, and other HIV/AIDS-related concerns is available.

✓ **Center for the Study of Autism**
P.O. Box 4538
Salem, OR 97302
Web site: http://www.autism.org/

The center provides information about autism to parents and professionals, and conducts research on the efficacy of various therapeutic interventions.

Child Welfare League of America (CWLA)
440 First Street NW, Third Floor
Washington, DC 20001-2085
(202) 638-2952
Fax: (202) 638-4004
Web site: http://www.cwla.org/

The CWLA is the oldest and largest nonprofit organization dedicated to developing and promoting policies and programs to protect America's children and strengthen America's families.

✓**Children and Adults with**
Attention-Deficit/Hyperactivity Disorder (CHADD)
8181 Professional Place, Suite 201
Landover, MD 20785
(301) 306-7070
(800) 233-4050
Fax: (301) 306-7070
Web site: http://www.chadd.org/

CHADD is an advocacy group dedicated to improving the lives of people with attention-deficit/hyperactivity disorder through education, advocacy, and support. Information concerning AD/HD, conferences, and educational materials is available.

Children's Brain Tumor Foundation
20312 Watkins Meadow Drive
Germantown, MD 20876
(301) 515-2900
Web site: http://www.childhoodbraintumor.org/

The foundation raises funds for scientific research on brain tumors and provides public awareness of this most devastating disease; it seeks to improve prognosis and the quality of life for those that are affected.

Clearinghouse on Disability Information
Office of Special Education and Rehabilitation Services
U.S. Department of Education
Switzer Building, Room 3132
330 C Street SW
Washington, DC 20202
(202) 205-8241
Fax: (202) 401-2608
Web site: http://www.healthfinder.gov/text/orgs/hr0035.htm

The clearinghouse provides information, research, and documents in response to inquiries concerning disabilities. The data is used by disabled individuals and their families, schools and universities, teachers and school administrators, and organizations that have persons with disabilities as clients.

Compassionate Friends
P.O. Box 3696
Oak Brook, IL 60522
(630) 990-0010
Fax: (630) 990-0246
Web site: http://www.compassionatefriends.org/

Compassionate Friends is a nonprofit, self-help support organization that assists families in the positive resolution of grief following the death of a child.

The Council for Exceptional Children (CEC)
1920 Association Drive
Reston, VA 20191-1589
(703) 620-3660
888-CEC-SPED
Fax: (703) 264-9494
Web site: http://www.cec.sped.org/

CEC is the largest international professional organization dedicated to improving educational outcomes for individuals with exceptionalities, students with disabilities, and the gifted. The council advocates for governmental policies, sets professional standards, provides professional development, and helps professionals obtain conditions and resources necessary for effective professional practice.

Division of Mental Retardation and Developmental Disabilities

105 Fairgrounds Road, P.O. Box 1098
Rolla, MO 65402
(573) 368-2200
Fax: (573) 368-2206
Web site: http://www.modmh.state.mo.us/index.htm

Serving a population that has developmental disabilities such as mental retardation, cerebral palsy, head injuries, autism, epilepsy, and certain learning disabilities, the division works to improve their lives through programs and services to enable them to live independently and productively.

Education Commission of the States

707 17th Street, Suite 2700
Denver, CO 80202-3427
(303) 299-3600
Fax: (303) 296-8332
Web site: http://www.ecs.org/

This organization provides information concerning early childhood education. It provides helpful information about educational initiatives and direction as to other policy and informational sites.

Educational Resources Information Center (ERIC)

The Council for Exceptional Children (CEC)
1920 Association Drive
Reston, VA 20191
(800) 328-0272
Web site: http://ericec.org/abouterc.htm

The ERIC Clearinghouse on Disabilities and Gifted Education (ERIC EC) is a nationwide information network sponsored by the U.S. Department of Education. The center gathers and provides professional literature, information, and resources on the education and development of individuals of all ages who have disabilities and/or who are gifted.

Epilepsy Foundation of America

4351 Garden City Drive
Landover, MD 20785
(800) 332-1000
(301) 459-3700
Fax: (301) 577-4941
Web site: http://www.efa.org/aboutus/index.html

The Epilepsy Foundation is a charitable organization dedicated to the welfare of individuals with epilepsy and their families. It works with children and adults who are affected by seizures and provides education, advocacy, and service.

Equal Employment Opportunity Commission (EEOC)
1801 L Street NW
Washington, DC 20507
(202) 663-4900
(800) 669-4000
Web site: http://www.eeoc.gov/

The EEOC enforces the principal federal statutes prohibiting employment discrimination.

✓**Federal Communications Commission (FCC)**
445 12th Street SW
Washington, DC 20554
(202) 418-0190
Web site: http://www.fcc.gov/cib/dro/

The FCC maintains a Disabilities Rights Office, which has an obligation to ensure that telecommunications are accessible and usable to the 54 million Americans with disabilities. Information concerning closed captioning and video description, hearing aid compatibility, and general answers to questions that the public may have about the FCC Disabilities Issues Task Force (DITF) are provided.

✓**Federal Resource Center (FRC) for Special Education**
Academy for Educational Development
1825 Connecticut Avenue NW
Washington, DC 20009
(202) 884-8215
Fax: (202) 884-8443
Web site: http://www.dssc.org/frc/about.htm

The FRC supports a nationwide technical assistance network to respond to the needs of students with disabilities, especially students from underrepresented populations.

Federation for Children with Special Needs
1135 Tremont Street, Suite 420
Boston, MA 02120
(617) 236-7210

(800) 331-0688
Fax: (617) 572-2094
Web site: http://www.fcsn.org/

The federation is a center for parents and parent organizations to work together on behalf of children with special needs and their families.

Institute on Community Integration
102 Pattee Hall
150 Pillsbury Drive SE
Minneapolis, MN 55455
(612) 624-9344
Fax: (612) 624-9344
Web site: http://ici.umn.edu/default.html

The Institute on Community Integration is a University Affiliated Program committed to improving the quality and community orientation of professional services and social supports available to individuals with disabilities and their families. It publishes numerous newsletters, resource guides, technical reports, and brochures.

Learning Disabilities Association of America
4156 Library Road
Pittsburgh, PA 15234
(412) 341-1515
Fax: (412) 344-0224
Web site: http://www.ldanatl.org/

This nonprofit organization works to advance the education and general welfare of children and adults of normal or potentially normal intelligence who manifest disabilities of a perceptual, conceptual, or coordinative nature.

Muscular Dystrophy Association—USA
3300 East Sunrise Drive
Tucson, AZ 85718
(800) 572-1717
Fax: (602) 529-5300
Web site: http://www.mdausa.org/

This association is a source for news and information about neuromuscular disease, research, and services for adults and children with neuromuscular diseases and their families. Publications are available on issues such as treatments, therapies, diagnosis, and daily living.

National Amputation Foundation (NAF)
38-40 Church Street
Malverne, NY 11565
(516) 887-3600
Fax: (516) 887-3667
Web site: http://www.nationalamputation.org

This organization's membership is made of amputee volunteers who offer their support to fellow amputees and their families. The NAF provides legal counsel, vocational guidance and placement, psychological aid, and training in the use of prosthetic devices. It publishes a bimonthly newsletter and a variety of pamphlets.

National Association for Gifted Children (NAGC)
1707 L Street NW, Suite 550
Washington, DC 20036
(202) 785-4268
Web site: http://www.nagc.org/toc.htm

The NAGC is an organization of parents, educators, other professionals, and community leaders to address the unique needs of children and youth with demonstrated gifts and talents. It also supports children who may be able to develop their talent potential with appropriate educational experiences. NAGC engages in research and development, staff development, advocacy, communication, and collaboration with other organizations and agencies that strive to improve the quality of education for all students.

National Association for the Education of Young Children (NAEYC)
1509 16th Street NW
Washington, DC 20036
(202) 232-877
(800) 424-2460
Fax: (202) 328-1846
Web site: http://www.naeyc.org/

The NAEYC consolidates the efforts of individuals and groups working to achieve healthy development and constructive education for all young children. It devotes primary attention to assuring the provision of high-quality early childhood programs for young children.

National Association for Visually Handicapped
22 West 21st Street, Sixth Floor
New York, NY 10010

(212) 889-3141
Fax: (212) 727-2931
Web site: http://www.navh.org/mission.html

This association works with millions of people worldwide dealing with difficulties of vision impairment. Its goal is to provide the finest non-profit independent health agency solely dedicated to serving the visually impaired.

✓National Association of Developmental Disabilities Council

1234 Massachusetts Avenue NW, Suite 103
Washington, DC 20005
(202) 347-1234
Fax: (202) 347-4023
Web site: http://www.igc.apc.org/NADDC/

The council promotes national policies that enable individuals with developmental disabilities the opportunity to make choices regarding the quality of their lives and to be included in the community.

National Brain Tumor Foundation

785 Market Street, Suite 1600
San Francisco, CA 94102
(800) 934-2873
Fax: (415) 284-0209
Web site: http://www.braintumor.org/about/intro.asp

This not-for-profit health organization is dedicated to providing information and support for brain tumor patients, family members, and healthcare professionals while supporting innovative research into better treatment options and a cure for brain tumors.

✓National Center for Learning Disabilities (NCLD)

381 Park Avenue South, Suite 1420
New York, NY 10016
(212) 545-7510
(888) 575-7373 (Referral Service)
Fax: (212) 545-9665
Web site: http://www.ncld.org/

The NCLD provides advocacy, resources, and referral services for children and adults with learning disabilities. The center develops and supports innovative educational programs, seminars, and workshops; conducts public awareness campaigns; and works for more effective policies and legislation to help individuals with learning disabilities.

National Down Syndrome Congress
7000 Peachtree-Dunwoody Road NE
Lake Ridge 400 Office Park Building No. 5, Suite 100
Atlanta, GA 30328
(770) 604-9500
(800) 232-NDSC
Web site: http://www.ndsccenter.org/index3.htm

This organization provides leadership in all areas of concern related to persons with Down Syndrome and their families.

✓**National Early Childhood Technical Assistance System (NECTAS)**
Frank Porter Graham Child Development Center
University of North Carolina at Chapel Hill
137 East Franklin Street, Suite 500
Chapel Hill, NC 27514
(919) 962-2001
Web site: http://www.nectas.unc.edu/about/staff.html

NECTAS provides information and resources about the Individuals with Disabilities Education Act (IDEA) and programs and projects funded under IDEA.

National Educational Service
1252 Loesch Road
Bloomington, IN 47401
(812) 336-7700
(800) 733-6786
Fax: (812) 336-7790
Web site: http://www.nesonline.com/about/about.html

The National Educational Service provides tested and proven resources to help those who work with youth create safe and caring schools, agencies, and communities.

✓**National Head Start Association**
1651 Prince Street
Alexandria, VA 22314
(703) 739-0875
Fax: (703) 739-0878
Web site: http://www.nhsa.org/

This is a private, not-for-profit membership organization representing the Head Start programs. It works to improve the quality of Head Start's comprehensive services for America's children and families.

National Hydrocephalus Foundation (NHF)
1670 Green Oak Circle
Lawrenceville, GA 30243
(770) 995-9570
Fax: (770) 995-8982
Web site: http://www.healthfinder.gov/text/orgs/HR2212.htm

The NHF seeks to remove stigma from individuals with hydrocephalus and improve their lives. To that end, it collects and disseminates information about hydrocephalus, counsels parents on specific problems encountered as a result of hydrocephalus in their children, and works to obtain health insurance covering this disease. It also has created a consumer pressure group to get government funding for research.

National Information Clearinghouse on Children Who Are Deaf-Blind
U.S. Department of Education
400 Maryland Avenue SW
Washington, DC 20202
(800) USA-LEARN (872-5327)
(800) 438-9376
Web site: http://www.tr.wosc.osshe.edu/dblink/

This information center is supported by the U.S. Department of Education, Office of Special Education Programs. The center provides links to publications as well as state resources concerning children who are deaf-blind.

National Organization for Rare Disorders (NORD)
P.O. Box 8923
New Fairfield, CT 06812
(800) 999-6673
Fax: (203) 746-6927
Web site: http://www.rarediseases.org/

NORD offers programs and services for the patient community, the public, physicians, support groups, researchers, and medically related companies. The organization also offers programs that provide assistance to people who need specific prescription drugs but cannot afford them.

National Organization of Parents of Blind Children
1800 Johnson Street
Baltimore, MD 21230
(410) 659-9314
Fax: (410) 685-5653
Web site: http://www.nfb.org/brochure.htm

This is a support group of parents and friends of blind children who wish to reach out to each other to give vital encouragement and share information.

√**National Organization on Fetal Alcohol Syndrome**
216 G Street NE
Washington, DC 20002
(202) 785-4585
Fax: (202) 466-6456
Web site: http://www.nofas.org/

This nonprofit organization is dedicated to eliminating birth defects caused by alcohol consumption during pregnancy and improving the quality of life for those individuals and families affected by fetal alcohol syndrome.

√**National Parent Information Network (NPIN)**
ERIC Clearinghouse on Elementary and Early Childhood Education
University of Illinois at Urbana-Champaign
Children's Research Center
51 Gerty Drive
Champaign, IL 61820
(800) 583-4135
Fax: (217) 333-3767
Web site: http://www.npin.org/

NPIN is a project of the ERIC system, which is administered by the National Library of Education in the U.S. Department of Education. Its goal is to provide access to research-based information about the process of parenting and about family involvement in education.

√**The National Parent Network on Disabilities (NPND)**
1130 17th Street NW, Suite 400
Washington, DC 20036
(202) 463-2299
Fax: (202) 463-9403
Web site: http://www.npnd.org/

The NPND is a parent network dedicated to providing a national voice for families of children, youth, and adults with disabilities.

National Pediatric and Family HIV Resource Center
University of Medicine and Dentistry of New Jersey
30 Bergen Street ADMC No. 4
Newark, NJ 07103
(973) 972-0410, (800) 362-0071
Fax: (973) 972-0399
Web site: http://www.pedhivaids.org/

This nonprofit center serves professionals who care for children, adolescents, and families with HIV infections and AIDS. It offers education, consultation, technical assistance, and training for health and social service professionals.

National School Age Care Alliance (NSACA)
1137 Washington Street
Boston, MA 02124
(617) 298-5012
Fax: (617) 298-5022
Web site: http://www.nsaca.org/

Representing an array of public, private, and community-based providers of after-school programs, the NSACA promotes national standards of quality school-age care for children and youth 5–14 years old, grants accreditation to programs meeting the standards, and connects people who work with school-age children and youth in a variety of agencies and settings.

Office of Special Education Programs
U.S. Department of Education
400 Maryland Avenue SW
Washington, DC 20202
(800) USA-LEARN
Web site: http://www.ed.gov/offices/OSERS/OSEP/

The Office of Special Education Programs is a component of the Office of Special Education and Rehabilitative Services, which is one of the principal components of the U.S. Department of Education. This organization focuses on the free, appropriate public education of children and youth with disabilities from birth through age twenty-one.

Osteogenesis Imperfecta Foundation
804 West Diamond Avenue, Suite 210
Gaithersburg, MD 20878
(301) 947-0083
(800) 981-2663
Fax: (301) 947-0456
Web site: http://www.oif.org/tier1/contact.htm

This organization is dedicated to helping people cope with problems associated with osteogenesis imperfecta (OI) and to improve the quality of life for individuals affected by OI through research to find a cure, education, awareness, and mutual support. It provides funding for research and hosts support groups in twenty-one states.

Phoenix Society for Burn Survivors
2153 Wealthy Street SE, Suite 215
East Grand Rapids, MI 49506
(800) 888-BURN (2876)
Web site: http://www.phoenix-society.org/

This nonprofit organization provides peer support, education, collaboration, and advocacy for individuals affected by burn injuries.

Spina Bifida Association of America
4590 MacArthur Boulevard NW, Suite 250
Washington, DC 20007
(800) 621-3141
Fax: (202) 944-3285
Web site: http://www.sbaa.org/
This association is charged with promoting the prevention of spina bifida and is dedicated to enhancing the lives of all affected. It serves as the national representative of more than seventy chapters.

Tuberous Sclerosis Alliance (TS Alliance)
8181 Professional Place, Suite 110
Landover, MD 20785
(301) 459-9888
(800) 225-6872
Fax: (301) 459-0394
Web site: http://www.tsalliance.org/default.asp

The TS Alliance provides support to people with tuberous sclerosis and their families, awards grants to researchers, and offers education to the public and professional communities.

United Cerebral Palsy Association (UCP)
1522 K Street NW, Suite 1112
Washington, DC 20005
(800) 872-5827
Web site: http://www.ucpa.org/

A national organization whose mission is to serve people with cerebral palsy through programs and research.

✓**U.S. Department of Education**
400 Maryland Avenue SW
Washington, DC 20202
(202) 205-9021 (Assistance to States)
(202) 205-9084 (Early Childhood Branch)
(800) USA-LEARN (872-5327)
Web site: http://www.ed.gov/

The administration's priorities include national efforts to improve reading and math, reduce class size, strengthen school construction, and promote major initiatives and partnerships for family involvement in education.

U.S. Department of Transportation (DOT)
400 Seventh Street SW
Washington, DC 20590
(202) 366-9305
Web site: http://www.dot.gov/

The DOT is charged with providing safe, efficient, accessible, and convenient transportation for all persons within the United States.

✓**World Council for Gifted and Talented Children**
Lamar University
P.O. Box 10034
Beaumont, TX 77710
Web site: http://www.worldgifted.org/

The purpose of this group is to promote worldwide communication related to gifted and talented children.

ADVOCACY AND LEGAL ASSISTANCE

Association for Retarded Citizens
2709 Avenue E East
Arlington, TX 76011
Web site: http://www.thearc.org/

This organization advocates for parents and professionals of children with mental retardation and has local chapters in each state.

Association for the Care of Children's Health (ACCH)
7910 Woodmont Avenue, Suite 300
Bethesda, MD 20814-9635
(301) 654-6549

Advocates for the improvement of child development skills.

Children's Defense Fund (CDF)
25 E Street NW
Washington, DC 20001
(202) 628-8787
Web site: http://www.cdinfo@childrensdefense.org/

The CDF's online Parent Resource Network provides access to a variety of national Web sites offering parents information on caring for their children and on getting involved in group efforts to help children in their own communities or states.

Children's Institute International
711 South New Hampshire Avenue
Los Angeles, CA 90005
Web site: http://www.childrensinstitute.org/

This private, nonprofit organization works to protect, preserve, and strengthen the family through child abuse prevention and treatment services for high-need, low-resource families, as well as through professional training, research, and advocacy.

Consortium for Citizens with Disabilities
1730 K Street NW, Suite 1212
Washington, DC 20006
(202) 785-3388
Fax: (202) 467-4179
Web site: http://www.c-c-d.org/about.htm

This is a coalition of national consumer, advocacy, provider, and professional organizations that advocates on behalf of people of all ages with physical and mental disabilities and their families.

✓ Consumer Information Bureau

445 12th Street SW
Washington, DC 20554
(888) CALL FCC (225-5322)
Web site: http://www.fcc.gov/cib/

The bureau provides consumers with disabilities information regarding resolution of their complaints and rights concerning telecommunications.

✓ Council for Exceptional Children (CEC)

Division for Early Childhood
1920 Association Drive
Reston, VA 22091
(703) 620-3660
Web site: http://www.dec-sped.org/

The CEC is a nonprofit organization advocating for individuals who work with or on behalf of special-needs children from birth through age eight and their families. It promotes policies and practices that support families and enhance the optimal development of children.

✓ Disabilities Rights Office

Federal Communications Commission (FCC)
445 12th Street SW
Washington, DC 20554
(888) CALL FCC (225-5322)
Web site: http://www.fcc.gov/cib/dro/

The FCC's Disabilities Rights Office provides information and technical assistance to consumers, business, and other entities on their rights and responsibilities to provide disability access and to protect consumers with disabilities.

✓ Disability Government

U.S. Department of Justice
P.O. Box 66118
Washington, DC 20035
(800) 514-0301
Web site: http://www.disability.gov/

This is a new site created by the Presidential Task Force on Employment of Adults with Disabilities in honor of the tenth anniversary of the signing of the Americans with Disabilities Act. It provides access to resources, services, and information available throughout the federal government.

✓ The National Association of Developmental Disabilities Councils (NADDC)
1234 Massachusetts Ave NW, Suite 103
Washington, DC 20005
(202) 347-1234
Fax: (202) 347-4023
Web site: http://www.igc.apc.org/NADDC/

NADDC advocates and works for change on behalf of people with developmental and other disabilities and their families. It promotes national policy to enhance the quality of life for all people with developmental disabilities.

National Association of Protection and Advocacy Systems (NAPAS)
900 Second Street NE, Suite 211
Washington, DC 20002
(202) 408-9514
Fax: (202) 408-9520
Web site: http://www.iser.com/NAPAS.html

NAPAS works to promote and strengthen the role and performance of its members in providing quality legally based advocacy services.

✓ National Council on Disability
1331 F Street NW, Suite 1050
Washington, DC 20004
(202) 272-2004
Fax: (202) 272-2022
Web site: http://www.ncd.gov/

The council is an independent federal agency making recommendation to the president and Congress on issues affecting 54 million Americans with disabilities. Its purpose is to promote policies, programs, practices, and procedures that guarantee equal opportunity for all individuals with disabilities, regardless of the nature of severity of the disability; and to empower individuals with disabilities to achieve economic self-sufficiency, independent living, and inclusion and integration into all aspects of society.

✓**National Information Center for Children and Youth with Disabilities**
P.O. Box 1492
Washington, DC 20013-1492
(800) 695-0285
Web site: http://www.nichcy.org/

This center provides information on disabilities and disability-related issues for families, educators, and other professionals, as well as referrals. Its focus is on children and youth from birth to age twenty-two.

National Maternal and Child Health Clearinghouse (NMCHC)
2070 Chain Bridge Road, Suite 450
Vienna, VA 22182
(703) 821-8955, ext. 254
Web site: http://www.nmchc.org/

The NMCHC produces and disseminates educational materials to the public.

Stand For Children
1834 Connecticut Avenue NW
Washington, DC 20009
(800) 663-4032
Fax: (202) 234-0217
Web site: http://www.stand.org/

Stand For Children identifies, trains, and connects local children's activists engaging in advocacy, awareness-raising, and service initiatives on an ongoing basis.

✓**U.S. Department of Health and Human Services**
Administration of Children, Youth, and Families
Child Care Bureau
330 C Street SW
Washington, DC 20447
(202) 690-6782
Web site: http://www.acf.dhhs.gov/programs/

The Child Care Bureau examines child care as an essential support to low-income families in achieving economic self-sufficiency while balancing work and family life. It has funded two waves of research partnerships with state child care agencies; university research teams; national, state, and local child care resource and referral networks; providers and parents; professional organizations; and businesses.

U.S. Department of Justice
Civil Rights Division
Office of the Americans with Disabilities Act
P.O. Box 66118
Washington, DC 20035-6118
(800) 514-0301 (Voice)
(800) 514-0383 (TDD)
Web site: http://www.usdoj.gov/

The Department of Justice has an office to provide information about the Americans with Disabilities Act (ADA) to businesses, state and local governments, and individuals. It answers questions concerning specific ADA requirements, including questions about the ADA Standards for Accessible Design, provides free ADA materials, and explains how to file a complaint.

U.S. Equal Employment Opportunity Commission (EEOC)
1801 L Street NW
Washington, DC 20507
(202) 663-4900
(202) 663-4494 (TTY)
(800) 669-4000
Web site: http://www.eeoc.gov/

The EEOC is an independent federal agency originally created by Congress in 1964 to enforce Title VII of the Civil Rights Act of 1964. It provides informational materials and assistance to individuals and entities concerning rights and responsibilities under EEOC-enforced laws. Most materials and assistance are provided to the public at no cost.

Zero to Three
National Center for Infants, Toddlers, and Families
734 15th Street NW, Suite 1000
Washington, DC 20005
(202) 638-1144
Web site: http://www.zerotothree.org/

This national nonprofit organization was founded by pediatricians, child development specialists, and researchers in 1977 to promote the healthy social, emotional, and intellectual development of babies and toddlers by supporting and strengthening families, communities, and those who work on their behalf.

FREE MEDICAL SERVICES

Alexander Graham Bell Association for the Deaf
3417 Volta Place NW
Washington, DC 20007
(202) 337-5220
Web site: http://www.agbell.org/

Provides financial aid to the parents of severely to profoundly hearing-impaired infants enrolled in preschool.

American Amputee Foundation—Give a Limb Program
P.O. Box 250218, Hillcrest Station
Little Rock, AR 72225
(501) 666-2523

Prostheses available.

Children's Hope Foundation: Childcare Necessities Program
295 Lafayette, Suite 801
New York, NY 10012
(212) 941-7432

Provides vital equipment such as strollers, cribs, diapers, and beds to children who are infected with HIV or have AIDS.

Deborah Heart and Lung Association
Department of Pediatric Cardiology
200 Trenton Road
Brown Mills, NJ 08015
(609) 735-2923

Cardiac surgery.

Disabled Children's Relief Fund
50 Harrison Avenue
Freeport, NY 11520
(516) 377-1605

Assistive devices/equipment and rehabilitative services.

Gift of Life
P.O. Box 776
Middle Island, NY 11953
(516) 924-4434

Cardiac surgery.

Hear Now
9745 East Hampden Avenue, Suite 300
Denver, CO 80231
(800) 648-4327

Provides hearing aids to doctors, who will prescribe and fit them to needy patients.

Hearing Aid Foundation
c/o National Hearing Aid Society
20361 Middlebelt Road
Livonia, MI 48152
(313) 478-2610

Hearing aids.

Miracle Ear Children's Foundation
P.O. Box 59261
Minneapolis, MN 55459
(800) 234-5422

Hearing aids. Money is sent directly to vendor.

Operation Smile
717 Boush Street
Norfolk, VA 23510
(804) 625-0375

For children with craniofacial abnormalities, burns, and orthopedic impairments.

Pharmaceutical Research and Manufacturers of America
1100 Fifteenth Street NW
Washington, DC 20005
(800) 762-4636

Free medications.

Shriners Hospitals for Crippled Children
P.O. Box 31356
Tampa, FL 33631
(800) 237-5055

For children with burns or orthopedic impairments.

St. Jude Children's Research Hospital
332 North Lauderdale
Memphis, TN 38105
(901) 495-3300

Cancer treatment for children (birth–18 years of age) who are newly diagnosed. Referring physician should call.

FEDERAL ASSISTANCE

Medicaid
Call your local Medicaid Office telephone number.

Medicaid is a government assistance program that pays for a range of medical services for persons with low income and limited resources. There are income and other eligibility requirements.

Supplemental Security Income (SSI)
Call your local Social Security Office telephone number.

SSI consists of monthly cash benefits to low-income families having a child with a disability. Not all children with disabilities will qualify. You should obtain as much detailed medical and social/emotional documentation as possible before applying. If denied, file for a hearing. With the denial letter, information will be provided about the hearing process. Legal Aid can assist the family with this process.

FRATERNAL ORGANIZATIONS

The following charitable organizations maintain local chapters throughout the nation. They often will consider assisting families in need who live in their geographic area. It is always best to contact your local branch, which can be accessed through the national office.

Elks
2750 North Lakeview Avenue
Chicago, IL 60614
(312) 477-2750

Kiwanis International
3636 Woodview Trace
Indianapolis, IL 46268
(317) 875-8755

Lions Club
300 22nd Street
Oakbrook, IL 60521
(708) 571-5466

Rotary Club
1560 Sherman Avenue
Evanston, IL 60201
(708) 866-3000

WISH ORGANIZATIONS

Wish granting organizations most often only consider children who have life-threatening conditions, but not always! It never hurts to contact them.

Children's Hopes and Dreams Foundation
280 Route 46
Dover, NJ 07801
(201) 361-7348

Children's Wish Foundation International
7840 Roswell Road, Suite 301
Atlanta, GA 30350
(800) 323-9474

Dream Factory
315 Guthrie Green
Louisville, KY 40202
(800) 456-7556

Friends of Karen
P.O. Box 190, 118 Titicus Road
Purdys, NY 10578
(914) 277-4547

Give Kids the World
210 South Bass Road
Kissimmee, FL 34746
(407) 396-1114

Make a Wish Foundation
85 Old Shore Road
Port Washington, NY 11050
(212) 505-9474

The Marty Lyons Foundation, Inc.
333 Earle Ovington Boulevard, Suite 600
Mitchel Field, NY
(516) 745-8966

Rainbows Hope, Inc./Wish Is Granted Foundation
48 Heinz Avenue
Staten Island, NY 10308
(718) 317-9078

A Special Wish Foundation
2244 South Hamilton Road, Suite 202
Columbus, OH 43232
(614) 575-9474

Starlight Foundation
1560 Broadway, Suite 402
New York, NY 10036
(212) 354-2878

Sunshine Foundation
P.O. Box 255
Loughman, FL 33858
(800) 457-1976

Wish Is Granted
43 West Main Street
Smithtown, NY 11787
(800) 357-9229

A Wish with Wings
P.O. Box 3479
Arlington, TX 76007
(817) 469-9474

FREE MEDICAL AIR TRANSPORTATION

The following organizations provide free air transportation for appointments with medical specialists. Call for details. You can also contact the National Patient Air Transport Hotline at (800) 296-1217, which will refer you to the best type of transportation for your need.

Air Care Alliance
P.O. Box 1940
Manassas, VA 22110
(800) 296-1217

Air Life Line
6133 Freeport Boulevard
Sacramento, CA 95822
(800) 446-1231

American Airlines—Miles for Kids
P.O. Box 619688, Mail Drop 1396
Dallas–Fort Worth, TX 75261
(817) 963-8118

Angel Planes
2756 North Green Valley Parkway, Suite 115
Green Valley, NV 89014
(800) 359-1711

Care Force
P.O. Box 3816
Humble, TX 77347
(713) 438-0376

Corporate Angel Network
Westchester City Airport, Building 1
Westchester, NY 10604
(914) 328-1313

Transportation for Cancer Patients and Organ Donors

Lifeline Pilots
1028 East Avenue South
Oak Park, IL 60304
(217) 373-4195

Roads to Recovery
2516 Wilkins Avenue
Baltimore, MD 21223
(410) 945-6761

Volunteer Pilots Association
P.O. Box 95, 100 Main Street
Hickory, PA 15340
(412) 356-4007

Wings for Children
20th and Smallman Street, Second Floor
Pittsburgh, PA 15222
(800) 743-5527

Wings of Mercy
A-5006 146th Avenue
Holland, MI 49423
(616) 396-1077

Chapter Eight

●◆ Selected Print and Nonprint Resources

BOOKS AND CD-ROMS

Adaptive Play for Special Needs Children: Strategies to Enhance Communication and Learning, by C. R. Musselwhite (Borgo Press, 1991).
Order from:
Exceptional Parent Magazine
555 Kinderkamack Road
Aradell, NJ 07649
(201) 634-6550

Provides ideas for adaptive play activities for special needs children to reinforce communication and learning.

ADHD Handbook for Families: A Guide to Communicating with Professionals, by Paul L. Weingartner (Child Welfare League of America, 1999).

Offers families who have a child with ADHD real-life strategies and techniques that can be useful to their everyday existence.

Asperger Syndrome, by Ami Klin, Fred R. Volkmar, and Sara S. Sparrow, eds. (Guilford Press, 2000).

Discusses Asperger Syndrome and brings together scholars and practitioners to offer current research and information significant in this new field regarding Asperger Syndrome. It provides additional information with regard to clinical practice.

Assessing Students with Special Needs, by John J. Venn (Prentice-Hall, 1999).

Provides comprehensive coverage of assessment principles and practices for understanding how to work with individuals who have mild, moderate, and severe disabilities.

Assistive Technology in Special Education: Policy and Practice, by Diane Golden (Council for Exceptional Children, Council of Administrators of Special Education, Technology and Media Division, 1998).

Provides an overview of the critical policy and practice issues facing education in the area of assistive technology (AT) and discusses the emerging policy directives and best practices for service delivery in a way that is supportive of quality AT programs in schools.

Behavioral Intervention for Young Children with Autism: A Manual for Parents and Professionals, by Catherine Maurice, Stephen C. Luce, and Gina Green, eds. (PRO-ED International Publisher, 1996).

Provides information concerning effective treatment strategies for young children with autism.

Characteristics of and Strategies for Teaching Students with Mild Disabilities, by Martin Henley, Roberta S. Ramsey, and Robert F. Algozzine (Allyn and Bacon, 1998).

Written by experts in the field who have produced other important works regarding children with disabilities, this is intended for undergraduate and graduate students majoring in either general or special education. The authors provide a comprehensive overview of educational practices influencing the identification, placement, and teaching of students with mild disabilities.

The Child with Special Needs: Encouraging Intellectual and Emotional Growth, by Stanley I. Greenspan, Robin Siomon, and Serena Wieder (Addison Wesley Longman, 1997).

Provides information to parents concerning ways of helping special needs children.

The Classroom Observer: Developing Observation Skills in Early Childhood Settings, by Ann E. Boehm and Richard A. Weinberg (Teachers College Press, 1996).

Emphasizes early childhood and focuses on those skills that will enable the observer to make appropriate, valid inferences and to arrive at decisions based on objective observational data gathering in natural learning environments and diverse educational settings.

Collaboration: A Success Strategy for Special Educators, by Sharon F. Cramer (Allyn and Bacon, 1998).

A book for educators who would like to improve their skills by collaborating with other educators.

Collaboration for Inclusive Education: Developing Successful Programs, by Chriss Walther-Thomas, Lori Korinek, Virginia L. McLaughlin, and Brenda Toler Williams (Allyn and Bacon, 2000).

Teaches professionals how to work with others to develop education programs for students with special learning needs.

The Complete IEP Guide: How to Advocate for Your Special Ed Child, by Lawrence M. Siegel; edited by Marcia Stewart (Nolo Press, 1997).

A research book for learning how to advocate for children with special needs.

Consultation, Collaboration, and Teamwork for Students with Special Needs, by Peggy Dettmer, Norma Dyck, and Linda P. Thurston (Allyn and Bacon, 1999).

Explains the roles and responsibilities of collaborative school consultants in providing for the needs of students with special needs.

Controversial Issues Confronting Special Education: Divergent Perspectives, by William Stainback and Susan Stainback (Allyn and Bacon, 1995).

Perspectives on hot issues in special education.

Creative Play Activities for Children with Disabilities, by Lisa Rappaport Morris and Linda Schulz (Redleaf Press, 1989).
Order from:
Redleaf Press
450 North Syndicate, Suite 5
St. Paul, MN 55104
(800) 423-8309

The authors suggest a variety of activities and include directions, a list of equipment needed, an explanation of the benefits of the activity, and possible adaptations for children with particular disabilities.

Educational Care: A System for Understanding and Helping Children with Learning Problems at Home and in School, by Melvin D. Levine (Educators Publishing Service, 1998).

Topics regarding curriculum and testing tools to assist teachers who serve special needs children.

Exceptional Learners: Introduction to Special Education, by Daniel P. Hallahan and James M. Kauffman (Allyn and Bacon, 1999).

Written by authors with great experience in the publication of special education texts, this is a general introduction to the characteristics of exceptional persons and their education.

Final Gifts: Understanding the Special Awareness, Needs, and Communications of the Dying, by Maggie Callanan and Patricia Kelly (Bantam Doubleday Dell Publishing Group, 1997).

Advice for family members and professionals regarding death awareness.

Financial Aid for the Disabled and Their Families, by Gail Ann Schlachter and R. David Weber (Reference Service Press, 1998).
Order from:
Reference Service Press
1100 Industrial Road, Suite 9
San Carlos, CA 94070
(415) 594-0411

A reference book that provides information concerning foundations, scholarships, and assistance for the disabled and their families.

The Gift of Dyslexia: Why Some of the Smartest People Can't Read and How They Can Learn, by Ronald D. Davis, with Eldon M. Braun (Berkley Publishing Group, 1997).

The author discusses his own experience with dyslexia and provides a plan as to how readers can help themselves overcome the disability.

The Gifted Kids' Survival Guide: For Ages 10 and Under, by Judy Galbraith, Pamela Espeland, and Albert Molnar (Free Spirit Publishing, 1998).

Designed for young children, this book explains giftedness and provides encouragement.

Guide to Writing Quality Individualized Education Programs: What's Best for Students with Disabilities, by Gordon S. Gibb and Tina Taylor Dyches (Allyn and Bacon, 1999).

A guide for professionals that provides information for enhancing IEP writing skills.

Holler If You Hear Me: The Education of a Teacher and His Students, by Gregory Michie (Teachers College Press, Teachers College, Columbia University, 1999).

Provides information concerning different teaching styles and stresses teacher/student involvement.

How Students Learn: Reforming Schools through Learner-Centered Education, by Nadine M. Lambert and Barbara L. McCombs, eds. (American Psychological Association, 1997).

Examines current research on how students learn and presents the theoretical perspectives and research findings of leading authors in educational psychology.

How to Get Services by Being Assertive, by Charlotte Des Jardins (1998). *Order from:*
Family Resource Center on Disabilities
20 East Jackson Boulevard, Room 900
Chicago, IL 60604
(313) 939-3513

A handbook on assertive communication techniques for parents and professionals.

How to Reach and Teach ADD/ADHD Children: Practical Techniques, Strategies, and Interventions for Helping Children with Attention Problems and Hyperactivity, by Sandra Rief (Center for Applied Research in Education, 1995).

Provides information for professionals concerning techniques, strategies, and interventions for reaching and teaching children with attention problems and hyperactivity.

Human Exceptionality: Society, School, and Family, by Michael L. Hardman, Clifford J. Drew, and M. Winston Egan (Allyn and Bacon, 1999).

Focuses on the challenges that individuals with exceptionalities face on a daily basis.

The Inclusive Classroom: Strategies for Effective Instruction, by Margo A. Mastropierie and Thomas E. Scruggs (Prentice-Hall, 1999).

Focuses on inclusive teaching ideas and lessons with curriculum and instructional strategy implications in content areas for children in the K–12 teaching experience.

Inclusive High Schools: Learning from Contemporary Classrooms, by Douglas Fisher, Caren Sax, and Ian Pumpian (Paul H. Brooks Publishing, 1999).

This text provides a framework for developing inclusive high schools and addresses processes and outcomes. Issues include building school-based relationships, developing support strategies, communicating responsibilities, preparing for the classroom, establishing continuity, planning lessons and adapting curricula, and redistributing school resources.

Infant Development and Risk: An Introduction, by Anne H. Widerstrom, Barbara A. Mowder, and Susan R. Sandall (Paul H. Brookes Publishing, 1997).

This book provides a comprehensive overview of typical and atypical infant development while explaining key assessment issues and intervention programs.

Interprofessional Collaboration in Schools: Practical Action in the Classroom, by Mark P. Mostert (Allyn and Bacon, 1998).

Practical information for teachers to use in the classroom. Teaching collaboration between students is stressed.

Introduction to Special Education: Teaching in an Age of Challenge, by Deborah Deutsch Smith (Prentice Hall, 1997).

Discusses insight to important issues in special education.

The K & W Guide to Colleges for Students with Learning Disabilities or Attention Deficit Disorders: A Resource Book for Students, Parents, and Professionals, by Marybeth Kravets (Random House, 1999).

A resource book that provides information concerning college-level programs and services for the learning disabled.

The Language of Toys: Teaching Communication Skills to Special Needs Children, by S. Schwartz and J. E. Heller Miller (1998).
Order from:
Exceptional Parent Magazine
555 Kinderkamack Road
Aradell, NJ 07649
(800) 535-1910

Teaches parents how to improve their child's communication skills at home with fun exercises.

Learning to Read and Write: Developmentally Appropriate Practices for Young Children, by Susan B. Neuman, Carol Copple, and Sue Bredekamp (National Association for Education, 2000).

Focuses on research-based strategies for children's learning in elementary and infant and toddler classrooms. Classroom photos and children's work accompany innovative ideas for teachers to help young children progress in their reading and writing competence.

Making a Difference: Advocacy Competencies for Special Education Professionals, by Craig R. Fiedler (Allyn and Bacon, 2000).

A source on the role and responsibilities of special education professionals as advocates for children with disabilities.

Models of Collaboration, by Mary E. Fishbaugh (Allyn and Bacon, 1997)

Collaboration models such as consulting, coaching, and teaming are discussed.

Mrs. Jeepers in Outer Space (Adventures of the Bailey School Kids Series), by Debbie Dadey and John Steven Gurney (Scholastic, 1999).

A children's book that focuses on how children can deal with fear and insecurities through the use of an interesting and easy-to-read narrative.

Peterson's Colleges: With Programs for Students with Learning Disabilities or Attention Deficit Disorders, by Charles T. Mangrum and Stephen Strichart, eds. (Peterson's, 1997).

A directory that provides information about programs and services for college students with learning disabilities.

Physical, Sensory, and Health Disabilities: An Introduction, by Frank G. Bowe (Prentice-Hall, 1999).

This text covers all major disability areas and presents material on barriers that can hinder a full and rewarding life. It focuses on the delivery of services to children and individuals with disabilities.

Restructuring for Caring and Effective Education: Piecing the Puzzle Together, by Richard A. Villa and Jacqueline S. Thousand, eds. (Paul H. Brookes Publishing, 1999).

Reexamines the purposes of schooling and the rationalities for inclusive schooling.

Savage Inequalities: Children in America's Schools, by Jonathan Kozol (Harper Trade, 1992).

Describes and provides insight into the classrooms of the minority poor.

The Self-Help Sourcebook: Finding and Forming Mutual Aid Self-Help Groups, by Barbara White (1995).
Order from:
American Self-Help Clearinghouse
Northwest Covenant Medical Center
Denville, NJ 07834
(201) 625-7101

A directory of over 700 groups that offer support and information about particular issues and concerns.

Skills for Success: A Career Education Handbook for Children and Adolescents with Visual Impairments, by Karen E. Wolffee, ed. (American Foundation for the Blind, 1999.)

Written to establish a foundation that will enable children with visual impairments to compete and cooperate with sighted children, this book provides practical learning experiences in the environments that children frequent: school, home, and community. Topics include career education, high expectations, socialization, compensatory skills, and realistic feedback.

Songs in Sign, by S. Harold Collins; illustrated by Kathy Kifer and Dahna Sola (Garlic Press, 1995).

Provides six songs in signed English with easy-to-follow illustrations.

The Special Education Yellow Pages, by Roger Pierangelo and Rochelle Crane (Prentice-Hall, 1999).

A resource guide for finding information on organizations, specific disabilities, Web sites, professional organizations, books, materials, laws and legal issues, federal agencies, university libraries, transportation issues, computer and technology resources, free materials, employment issues, and much more.

Staff Development: The Key to Effective Gifted Education Programs, by Peggy Dettmer and Mary Landrum, eds. (Kentucky Department of Education Middle School Initiative, 1998).

Guides the reader through the process of staff development—from organizing, planning, and conducting to following up. By learning skills as staff developers, education professionals can help teachers adopt more accepting and facilitative attitudes toward highly able students.

The Survival Guide for Parents of Gifted Kids: How to Understand, Live with, and Stick up for Your Gifted Child, by Sally Yahnke Walker (Free Spirit Publishing, 1991).

An easy-to-understand approach to some of the problems faced by parents of gifted children.

Tax Guide for Parents, by Family Resource Center on Disabilities (1999).
Order from:
The Connecticut Association for Children with Learning Disabilities
18 Marshall Street
South Norwalk, CT 06854
(203) 838-5010

Provides information and helpful tips as to accounting for purchases and expenses related to special-needs children.

Teacher Unions and TQE (Total Quality Education): Building Quality Labor Relations, by William A. Streshly and Todd A. DeMitchell (Corwin Press, 1994).

An overview of the educational labor movement, principles in union relations, the ins and outs of collective bargaining, and the transition of unionism.

Teaching Gifted Kids in the Regular Classroom: Strategies and Techniques Every Teacher Can Use to Meet the Academic Needs of the Gifted and Talented, by Susan Winebrenner and Pamela Espeland, eds. (Free Spirit Publishing, 2000).

A resource book for parents and teachers of gifted children who are in the regular classroom.

Toy Resource List, by Colleen Roth (Toledo Association for the Blind, 1993).
Order from:
Network on the Blind Multiple-Handicapped Child/Adult
1912 Tracy Road
Northwood, OH 43619
(419) 666-6212

Toys are listed by developmental age and are chosen for durability.

Toys "R" Us Toy Guide for Differently Abled Kids! (1999; updated regularly).
Order from:
Toys "R" Us
P.O. Box 8501
Nevada, IA 50201

Toys are categorized by skill (gross motor, fine motor, tactile, visual, language, social, etc.).

Transdisciplinary Play-Based Intervention (TPBI) Guidelines for Developing a Meaningful Curriculum for Young Children, by Toni W. Linder (Paul H. Brookes Publishing, 1993).

This guide offers individualized play-based intervention activities for young children in home- and center-based environments.

What's Best for Matthew? Interactive CD-ROM Case Study for Learning to Develop Individualized Education Programs, by M. Winston Egan (Allyn and Bacon, 2001).

Helps preservice and inservice teachers develop IEP writing skills.

A Work in Progress: Behavior Management Strategies and a Curriculum for Intensive Behavioral Treatment of Autism, by John McEachin, Ron Leaf, Marlene Boehm, and Jamison Day Harsh (Different Roads to Learning, 1999).

The authors use applied behavioral analysis (ABA) to suggest individualized programs and curricula for teaching skills to autistic children.

GUIDES AND REFERENCE MATERIALS

The Americans with Disabilities Act: A Guide for People with Disabilities, Their Families, and Advocates (1993)
Order from:
Pacer Center
4826 Chicago Avenue South
Minneapolis, MN 55417
(612) 827-2966

Drugs, Alcohol, and Other Addictions: A Directory of Treatment Centers and Prevention Programs Nationwide

Order from:
The Oryx Press
2214 North Central at Encanto
Phoenix, AZ 85004

Early Warning, Timely Response: A Guide to Safe Schools

To order, call:
(800) 279-6799
Published by the Office of Special Education and Rehabilitative Services, this guide helps school personnel, parents, community members, and others identify early indicators of problems within the school setting.

Financial Aid for the Disabled and Their Families

By Gail Ann Schlachter and R. David Weber (1995)
Order from:
Reference Service Press
1100 Industrial Road, Suite 9
San Carlos, CA 94070

How to Get Services by Being Assertive

By Charlotte Des Jardins (1993)
Order from:
Family Resource Center on Disabilities
20 East Jackson Boulevard, Room 900
Chicago, IL 60604
A handbook on assertive communication techniques for parents and professionals.

Parents Guide to the Internet

Order from:
U.S. Department of Education
Office of Educational Research and Improvement

Media and Information Services

555 New Jersey Avenue NW
Washington, DC 20208
(800) USA-LEARN (872-5327)

The full text of this publication also is available on-line at the department's home page (see Web Directories in this chapter).

The Self-Help Sourcebook: Finding and Forming Mutual Aid Self-Help Groups (1995)
Order from:
American Self-Help Clearinghouse
Northwest Covenant Medical Center
Denville, NJ 07834
(201) 625-7101

JOURNALS AND MAGAZINES

American Journal on Mental Retardation
1719 Kalorama Road NW
Washington, DC 20009

A bimonthly publication by the American Association on Mental Retardation, this journal publishes studies and discussions dealing with behavioral and biological aspects of mental retardation.

Behavioral Residential Treatment
605 Third Avenue
New York, NY 10158

Quarterly reports of behavioral treatment programs.

Career Development for Exceptional Individuals
Division on Career Development, CEC
1920 Association Drive
Reston, VA 22091

Published semi-annually with a focus in vocational, residential, and leisure activities for children and adults with disabilities.

Child Abuse and Neglect, The International Journal
Elsevier, Inc.
655 Avenue of the Americas
New York, NY 10011
(212) 633-3950

Published monthly.

Childhood Education
Association for Childhood Education International
17904 Georgia Avenue, Suite 215
Olney, MD 20832

(301) 570-2111

Published six times a year. Articles related to infancy through early adolescence.

Day Care and Early Education
Behavioral Publications
72 Fifth Avenue
New York, NY 10016

Published bimonthly, directed at day care personnel focusing on new ideas for educating preschool children.

Early Childhood Education Journal
Human Sciences Press, Inc.
233 Spring Street
New York, NY 10013

Published quarterly. A professional publication of original peer-reviewed articles, both invited and unsolicited, that reflect exemplary practices in the rapidly changing field of contemporary early childhood education.

Early Childhood Research and Practice
Web site: http://ecrp.uiuc.edu/

An Internet journal on the development, care, and education of young children.

Early Childhood Research Quarterly
Ablex Publishing Corporation
55 Old Post Road, No. 2
P.O. Box 5297
Greenwich, CT 06831
(203) 661-7602

Quarterly publication. Includes articles presenting significant research and scholarship on all topics related to the care and education of children from birth through eight years.

Education and Training of the Mentally Retarded
Division of Mental Retardation of CEC
1920 Association Drive
Reston, VA 22091

Published four times annually, this journal publishes experimental studies and articles dealing with mental retardation.

Exceptional Parent
Order from:
Council for Exceptional Children
1920 Association Drive
Reston, VA 22091

A monthly magazine for families and professionals.

Gifted Child Quarterly
National Association for Gifted Children
1155 15th Street NW, Suite 1002
Washington, DC 20005

Articles are by both parents and teachers of gifted children.

Gifted Child Today
350 Weinacker Avenue
Mobile, AL 36604

Published six times annually. Ideas and information aimed at parents and teachers of gifted, talented, and creative youngsters.

Gifted International
World Council for Gifted and Talented Children
Lamar University
College of Education
P.O. Box 10034
Beaumont, TX 77710

Published semiannually. Devoted to international communication among educators, researchers, and parents.

Infant Toddler Intervention
Singular Thomson Learning
7625 Empire Drive
Florence, KY 41042

A journal that focuses on the delivery of effective intervention services for children under three years of age.

International Journal of Rehabilitative Research Quarterly
International Society for Rehabilitation of the Disabled
432 Park Avenue South
New York, NY 10016

A quarterly publication that focuses on rehabilitation of the disabled.

Journal for the Education of the Gifted
Association for the Gifted, CEC
1920 Association Drive
Reston, VA 22091

Published quarterly. Presents theoretical, descriptive, and research articles of diverse ideas and points of view on the education of the gifted and talented.

Journal of Creative Behavior
Creative Educational Foundation, Inc.
State University College
1300 Elmwood Avenue
Buffalo, NY 14222

Contains research reports and suggestions to encourage creative behavior in children and adults. Published annually.

Journal of Early Intervention
Division of Early Childhood Education, CEC
1920 Association Drive
Reston, VA 22091

Provides information and research regarding early childhood intervention, education, and strategies.

Journal of Educational Research
Heldref Publications
1319 18th Street NW
Washington, DC 20036
(202) 296-6267

This quarterly publishes articles that describe or synthesize research of direct relevance to educational practice in elementary and secondary schools.

Journal of Special Education
Pro-Ed
8700 Shoal Creek Boulevard
Austin, TX 78757

Published quarterly.

Journal of the International Association of Special Education
IASE
Box 2950

Storm Lake, IA 50588

Published two times a year.

Journal of the National Center for Clinical Infant Programs
P.O. Box 25494
Richmond, VA 23260
(800) 899-4301

Focuses on the first three years of life and of the importance of early intervention and prevention to healthy growth and development.

Journal of Vocational Rehabilitation
Andover Medical Publishers, Inc.
80 Montvale Avenue
Stoneham, MA 02180

This publication concerns itself with vocational rehabilitation issues.

Remedial and Special Education
Pro-Ed
8700 Shoal Creek Boulevard
Austin, TX 78757

Published bimonthly.

Research in Developmental Disabilities
Maxwell House, Fairview Park
Elmsford, NY 10523

Published six times a year by ProgMan Press.

Roeper Review
Roeper City and County Schools
2190 North Woodward
Broomfield Hills, MI 48013

Published quarterly. Contains articles by teachers, researchers, and students in gifted education.

Topics in Early Childhood Special Education
Pro-Ed
8700 Shoal Creek Boulevard
Austin, TX 78757

Quarterly publication.

The Transdisciplinary Journal
Singular Publishing Group
4284 41st Street
San Diego, CA 92105

Quarterly publication. Provides members of the early intervention team with information that will enhance the clinical services they provide to infants and toddlers who are at-risk or have disabilities, and their families.

Young Children
National Association for the Education of Young Children
1834 Connecticut Avenue NW
Washington, DC 20001

Published bimonthly. Focuses on projects and research in early childhood education.

Young Exceptional Children
Division for Early Childhood, CEC
Executive Office
1444 Wazee Street, Suite 230
Denver, CO 80202
(303) 620-4579

Quarterly publication.

WEB DIRECTORIES

Whenever possible, the following Web sites have been listed according to official site name. A listing of sites specifically helpful for children's advocates can be found at the section's end.

Americans with Disabilities Act (ADA) Technical Assistance Programs Centers: http://www.ncddr.org/relativeact/adatech/index.html

This page within the National Center for the Dissemination of Disabilities Research (NCDDR) Web site lists centers that provide technical assistance, training, and resource referral on all aspects of the ADA.

Child Care Bureau: http://www.acf.dhhs.gov/programs/ccb/index.htm

Research, data, and systems information.

Children's Defense Fund: http://www.childrensdefense.org/

Provides information regarding advocacy for children.

Consumer Information Bureau: http://www.fcc.gov/cib/

The FCC's page for its Consumer Information Bureau provides useful links to sites concerning communications and consumer rights.

Department of Defense Education Activity (DODEA) Special Education Resource Directory for Special Educators: http://www.brusdso.odedodea.edu/special/home.html

This exhaustive guide to education and technology resources includes a list of professional associations and related organizations, education and federal government sites, teacher resources, recommended software, and a special education parent guide.

Disability Resources: http://www.disabilityresources.org/DRMabout.html

Organized and maintained by volunteers who work in disability-related fields.

Disabilities Rights Office: http://www.fcc.gov/cib/dro/

This government-run site provides information specific to the FCC's Disabilities Rights Office.

Early Head Start National Resource Center (EHS NRC): http://www.ehsnrc.org/

Provides training and technical assistance for the Early Head Start program. The site is operated by Zero to Three: National Center for Infants, Toddlers, and Families and West End's Center for Child and Family Studies.

Federation for Children with Special Needs: http://www.fcsn.org/

Useful for families of children with special needs, this site will keep them informed of their rights in the areas of education, health care, and many other topics of concern.

Ideal Lines: http://www.emtech.net/

Maintained by Lisa Simmons, a certified education advocate, teacher, and music therapist, this site provides links to other sites related to disabilities and is divided into categories such as education and associations, legal, disabilities and exceptionalities, medical, and assistive technology.

Inclusion and Parent Advocacy: A Resource Guide: http://www.disabilityresources.org/DRMincl.html

An on-line guide to multicultural multimedia materials about inclusion and parent advocacy.

Inside HealthCare: http://www.insidehealthcare.com/

An information service offering news, directories, search engines, business research tools, funding sources, organizations, and publications related to health care.

Internet Special Education Resources (ISER): http://www.iser.com/index.shtml

A nationwide directory of professionals who serve the learning disabilities and special education communities. Helps parents and caregivers find local special education professionals to help with learning disabilities and attention deficit disorder assessment, therapy, advocacy, and other special needs.

- **Resources for Special Education and Learning Disabilities Professionals:** http://www.iser.com/proresources.html
- **Special Education Nonprofit Resources:** http://www.iser.com/nps. html

National Advisory Panel (NAP) on the Education of Dependents with Disabilities: http://www.brus-dso.odedodea.edu/special/charter.htm

The NAP advises the DODEA on matters affecting the education of children with disabilities.

National Association for Rights Protection and Advocacy (NARPA): http://www.connix.com/~narpa/

Represents protection and advocacy systems.

National Association for the Education of Young Children (NAEYC): http://www.naeyc.org/

Provides numerous links to key sources of information for children's advocates.

National Association of Developmental Disabilities Council's Home Page: http://www.igc.apc.org/NADDC/

Provides links to information concerning public policy and resources.

Netscape

Netscape is a leading provider of open software that links people and information over the Internet.

- ◦ **Resources and Guides:** http://directory.netscape.c.on/ Special_Education/Resources_and_Guide
- ◦ **Special Education Institutes:** http://directory.netscape.c. nce/Education/Special_Education/Institute
- ◦ **Special Education Materials:** http://directory.netscape.c.nce/ Education/Special_Education/Material
- ◦ **Special Education Resources on Inclusion:** http://directory. netscape.c. nce/Education/Special_Education/Inclusion
- ◦ **Special Education Schools:** http://directory.netscape.c. rence/Education/Special_Education/School
- ◦ **Special Education Support:** http://directory.netscape.c. rence/Education/Special_Education/Support

The New York Institute for Special Education: http://www. nyise.org/

A private, nonprofit, nonsectarian educational facility that provides quality programs for children who are blind or visually disabled, emotionally and learning disabled, and preschoolers who are developmentally delayed.

Office of Special Education and Rehabilitative Services (OSERS): http://www.ed.gov/offices/OSERS/OSEP/links.html

The following OSERS-sponsored Web sites can be accessed from this site: The National Information Clearinghouse on Children Who Are Deaf-Blind (DB-Link), The National Technical Assistance Consortium for Children and Young Adults Who Are Deaf-Blind (NTAC), Center for Appropriate Dispute Resolution in Special Education (CADRE), The National Early Childhood Technical Assistance System (NEC*TAS), National Center on Educational Outcomes (NCEO), Center for Effective Collaboration and Practice, Center for Special Education Finance, National Information Center for Children and Youth with Disabilities (NICHCY), ERIC Clearinghouse on Disabilities and Gifted Education, Health Resource Center, IDEA 1997, Association of Service Providers Implementing IDEA Reforms in Education (ASPIIRE) (or log on to http://www.ideapractices.org), Families and Advocates Partnerships for Education (FAPE) (or log on to http://www.fape.org), IDEA Local Implementations by Local Administrators (ILIAD) (or log on to http://www.ideapractices.org), The Policy Maker Partnership for Implementing IDEA 97 (or log on to http:// www.ideapolicy.org/pmp.htm), Consortium on Inclusive Schooling Practices, Center of Minority Research in Special Education (COMRISE), Technical Assistance Alliance for Parent Center, Parents Engaged in Education Reform, OSEP Center on Positive Behavioral Interventions and Supports, Federal Resource Center for Special Education (FRC), and OSERS Regional Resource and Federal Centers Network.

Office of Special Education and Rehabilitative Services (OSERS), Teachers Guide: http://www.ed.gov/pubs/TeachersGuide/osers.html

The new teacher's guide to the U.S. Department of Education.

Special Education Books: http://www.respond.com/

After a search, can provide a list of suggested books along with news, information, and ideas.

Special Education Network: http://www.specialednet.com/

Provides information and resources on the education of children with special needs.

Special Education Resources on the Internet (SERI): http://www. seriweb.com/

A collection of Internet-accessible information resources of interest to those involved in fields related to special education.

Starting Points for Advocacy of Special Education and Children's Services

Each of the following sites contains a vast array of information relevant to professionals, parents, policymakers, and the general public. Search them for publications, news, federal regulations, and links to related sites.

—Child Care Bureau: http://www.acf.dhhs.gov/programs/ccb/
—ERIC Clearinghouse on Elementary and Early Childhood Education: http://ericeece.org/
—Head Start Bureau: http://www.acf.dhhs.gov/programs/hsb/
—National Child Care Information Center: http://www.nccic.org/
—U.S. Department of Education: http://www.ed.gov/
—Welfare Information Network: http://www.welfareinfo.org/

On-line Legislative Resources

The following Web sites provide detailed information about legislative proposals, congressional committee membership, and congressional activity. You can also link to your representatives' home pages and send them e-mail messages.

—Daily Digest of the House of Representatives and the Senate:
  http://www.access.gpo.gov/su_docs/aces/digest001.shtml
—House of Representatives: http://www.house.gov/
—Senate: http://www.senate.gov/
—Thomas Legislative Information on the Internet:
  http://thomas.loc.gov/
—White House: http://www.whitehouse.gov/

Sites for Community Outreach

The organizations listed here offer children's advocates useful information, on-line tools, and networking opportunities to stimulate community involvement.

—America Reads Challenge Resource Kit: pubaff@naeyc.org/
—Children's Defense Fund: http://www.childrensdefense.org/
—Families and Work Institute: http://www.familiesandworkinst.org/
—I Am Your Child: http://www.iamyourchild.org/
—Stand for Children: pubaff@naeyc.org/

TOYS

Abledata
(800) 346-2742

This is the National Rehabilitation Center's computer database of products. They will do a search for any product.

A.D.D. WareHouse
300 NW 70th Avenue, Suite 102
Plantation, FL 33317
(800) 233-9273

Specializes in products for attention deficit disorder/hyperactivity and related problems. Includes books and videos.

Childcraft Education Corporation
20 Kilmer Road
Edison, NJ 08817
(800) 631-5652

Educational materials for early childhood professionals, including storage cabinets, shelving and unit blocks, arts and crafts, and literature.

Childswork/Childsplay
Genesis Direct
P.O. Box 1600
Secaucus, NJ 07096
(800) 962-1141
Fax: (201) 583-3644

Play equipment, board games, and literature.

Constructive Playthings
1227 East 119th Street
Grandview, MO 64030
(800) 832-0224

Toys designed for early childhood education and first learning.

Flaghouse
150 North MacQuesten Parkway
Mount Vernon, NY 10550
(800) 793-7900

Toys and developmental activities for children with special needs.

Funtastic Learning
206 Woodland Road
Hampton, NH 03824
(800) 722-7375

Toys, games, and tools for children with skill-development needs.

Jesana Limited
P.O. Box 17
Irvington, NY 10533
(800) 443-4728

Catalog includes adapted toys and augmentative communication equipment.

Kapable Kids
P.O. Box 250
Bohemia, NY 11716
(800) 356-1564

Catalog is coded to indicate a toy's educational benefit.

Lakeshore Learning Materials
2695 East Dominguez Street
Carson, CA 90749
(800) 421-5354

Educational toys, language materials, and multicultural materials.

National Lekotek Center
2100 Ridge Avenue
Evanston, IL 60201
(847) 328-0001
(800) 366-PLAY (7529; Helpline)
Web site: www.lekotek.org/

This nonprofit organization with a national network of fifty affiliates promotes access to play for children with special needs and provides supportive services for their families.

Network on the Blind Multiple-Handicapped
1912 Tracy Road
Northwood, OH 43619
(419) 666-6212

Toys are listed by developmental age and chosen for durability.

Sportime Abilitations
One Sportime Way
Atlanta, GA 30340
(800) 444-5700

Equipment for development of physical and mental ability through movement.

TFH Limited
4537 Gibsonia Road
Gibsonia, PA 15044
(412) 444-6400

Distributes outdoor play equipment, toys that help with dexterity and speech, toys that are sensitive to sound, and more.

Therapeutic Toys
P.O. Box 418
Moodus, CT 06469
(800) 638-0676

Toys and playground equipment for physically challenged children.

Therapro
225 Arlington Street
Framingham, MA 01702
(800) 257-5376

Developmental devices, products, and toys that address the needs of children with special needs.

Toys for Special Children
385 Warburton Avenue
Hastings-on-Hudson, NY 10706
(800) 832-8697

Toys, games, and tools designed to improve the skills of special needs children.

Toys "R" Us Toy Guide for Differently Abled Kids!
Toys "R" Us
P.O. Box 8501
Nevada, IA 50201

Toys are categorized by skill (gross motor, fine motor, tactile, visual, language, social, etc.).

VIDEOS

A Is for Autism (1992)
This video examines people who lack a small piece of their frontal cortex and suffer from a mild form of autism. 30 minutes. Produced by the BBC.

Augmentative and Alternative Communication (1998)
This video program provides an overview of augmentative and alternative communication (AAC) and the considerations that should be made in choosing an AAC system for individuals. 22 minutes. Produced and distributed by Assistive Technology Programs, Center for Development and Disability, University of New Mexico, (505) 272-3000.

"But He Knows His Colors": Characteristics of Autism in Children Birth to Three

In this video four children with a diagnosis of autism demonstrate some of the characteristic behaviors. It helps in teaching families, educators, early interventionists, occupational therapists, speech and language pathologists, and physicians about the spectrum of behavioral characteristics seen in children with autism who are under the age of three. It speaks to the importance of early diagnosis and intervention for children and their families. 28 minutes. Produced by the New Mexico Autism Program. Order from Child Development Media, Inc., (800) 405-8942.

Child Care and Children with Special Needs (2001)

This is a training tool for program directors who wish to meet the needs of children with disabilities. Two-video set. Produced by Video Active Productions. To order, log on to http://www.naeyc.org/resources/catalog/.

Classroom Interventions for ADHD (1999)

This video program is designed specifically to help teachers with students who have ADHD and to help them provide a better learning environment for the entire class. 35 minutes. Produced and distributed by National Professional Resources, Inc., (800) 453-7461.

Curriculum (1994)

In this video you will observe toddlers, preschoolers, and kindergarten-aged children in three classrooms. Their teachers each provide a learning environment with a wide variety of hands-on activities and open-ended materials. 35 minutes. Produced by Magna Systems, Inc. Order from Child Development Media, Inc., (800) 405-8942.

A Day at a Time (1992)

Filmed over a period of four years, this unforgettable story will inspire everyone concerned with the challenges of family life and the place of disabled children in our society. 58 minutes. Produced by William Garcia and Charles Schultz. Order from Child Development Media, Inc., (800) 405-8942.

Developing the Young Bilingual Learner (2000)

Today many children enter early childhood programs with home languages other than English. This video explores the importance of supporting children's home language while helping them learn English, and it gives strategies for helping children become bilingual learners. 21 minutes. Produced for NAEYC by Resources and Instruction in Staff Excellence in Cincinnati, Ohio. To order, log on to http://www.naeyc.org/resources/catalog/.

Effective Education: Adapting to Include All Students (1998)
Shows how to adapt regular education classrooms to include students with several disabilities. 19 minutes. Produced by the South Dakota Department of Education and Cultural Affairs, and the Indiana Deafblind Project, the Blumberg Center.

The Exceptional Child I: Building Understanding (1999)
Defines the educationally exceptional child by using scenes of children and interviews to help viewers develop an understanding of a wide span of exceptionalities. 30 minutes. Produced and distributed by Magna Systems, Inc., (800) 405-8942.

The Exceptional Child II: Focusing on Nurturing and Learning (1999)
Explores how families feel and change in response to having children with exceptional needs. 30 minutes. Produced and distributed by Magna Systems, Inc., (800) 405-8942.

A Family's Guide to the Individualized Family Service Plan (1999)
Tells families what the IFSP process is all about. It shows parents how an IFSP is developed and implemented. 17 minutes. Produced by Juliann J. Woods Cripe. Distributed by Child Development Media, Inc., (800) 405-8942.

The IEP: A Tool for Realizing Possibilities (1998)
Produced by parents for parents, this video gives an overview of the individual educational plan (IEP) process from referral for assessment to the IEP meeting. Included are interviews with parents, teachers, paraprofessionals, principals, and peers. 20 minutes. To order, contact Howard George, georgeh@mail.doe.state.fl.us.

Learning and Communication: Functional Learning Programs for Young Children (1998)
Shows brief, longitudinal studies of three children and their parents involved together in functional learning activities. 18 minutes. Produced by Katrin Stroh and Thelma Robinson, Highgate, London, England.

A New I.D.E.A. for Special Education (1998)
Seeks to help educators and parents better understand the 1997 changes to the Individuals with Disabilities in Education Act. 45 minutes. Produced and distributed by Edvantage Media, Inc., (800) 375-5100.

Shining Bright: Head Start Inclusion (1998)

Presents the experiences of a Head Start and local education agency's collaborative effort to include children with severe disabilities in a Head Start program. 23 minutes. Produced and distributed by the Kansas University Affiliated Program, (785) 864-4950.

Standards and Inclusion: Can We Have Both? (1999)

Addresses the issue of inclusion for educators in both pre-service and in-service training. 40 minutes. Produced by Dorothy Kerzner Lipsky and Alan Gartner for the National Center on Educational Restructuring and Inclusion.

Success with Technology: Practices and Programs for Students with Special Needs (1999)

Vignettes that demonstrate successful applications of technology in educational programs that include students with disabilities are the focus of this video. 50 minutes. Produced and distributed by MACRO International, Inc., (800) 227-0216.

Three R's for Special Education: Rights, Resources, and Results.
A Guide for Parents, a Tool for Educators (1999)

A practical step-by-step guide that enables parents to be effective managers on behalf of their special-needs child. It shows parents how to work with the system, what resources are available, and how to plan for the disabled person's future. 48 minutes. Produced and distributed by Edvantage Media, Inc., (800) 375-5100.

Transition: A Time for Growth (1998)

This short video was developed from numerous interviews with families in transition. 12 minutes. Produced and distributed by Bridging Early Services Transition Project. Close captioned.

EDUCATIONAL SOFTWARE VENDORS

American Education Corporation

7506 North Broadway Extension
Oklahoma City, OK 73116
(800) 342-7587
Web site: www.amered.com/

Advanced Learning System—Reading, writing, language arts, math, science, and social studies software with on-line capabilities featuring more than 4,000 lessons for grade levels K–12.

Attainment Company, Inc.
P.O. Box 930160
Verona, WI 53593
(800) 327-4269
Web site: http://www.attainmentcompany.com/

Academic and Life Skills Software, First Money, Time Scales.

Broderbund Software, Inc.
500 Redwood Boulevard
P.O. Box 6125
Novato, CA 94948
(800) 521-6263
Web site: http://www.broderbund.com/

Living Books Series CD-ROMs—twelve titles, including *Just Grandma and Me, Arthur's Birthday,* and *The Cat in the Hat.*

Cognitive Concepts, Inc.
(888) 328-8199
Web site: http://www.cogcon.com/

Earobics Step 1 for ages 4–7, Earobics Step 2 for ages 7–11.

Computer Curriculum Corporation
1287 Lawrence Station Road
Sunnyvale, CA 94088
(800) 227-8324
Web site: http://www.ccclearn.com/

CCC Successmaker—Multidiscipline software with an Internet subscription service that provides on-line activities in math, reading, language arts, science, and social studies.

Davidson and Associates, Inc.
19840 Pioneer Avenue
Torrance, CA 90503
(310) 793-0600

Web site: http://www.davd.com/

Games and entertainment software designed for children.

Don Johnston, Inc.
1000 North Rand Road, Building 115
P.O. Box 639

Wauconda, IL 60084
Web site: http://www.donjohnston.com

Co:Writer and Write:Outland (revised version contains Franklin speller), Simon Spells, Simon Sound It Out, Story Time Tales and Circle Time Tales Deluxe, Ensy and Friends, Blocks in Motion, Press-to-Play Series, UkanDu Little Books (primary), Start to Finish Books (middle/high school).

Edmark Corporation
P.O. Box 3218
Redmond, WA 98073
(800) 362-2890
Web site: http://www.edmark.com/

Millie's Math House, Bailey's Book House, Stanley Sticker Stories, Sammy's Science House, Trudy's Time and Place, Let's Go Read, Mighty Math Series, Imagination Express.

Heartsoft
P.O. Box 691381
Tulsa, OK 74169
(800) 285-3475

Web site: http://www.heartsoft.com/
Software designed to teach basic skills, thinking, and learning.

Inspiration Software, Inc.
7412 SW Beaverton Hillsdale Highway, Suite 102
Portland, OR 97225
(800) 877-4292
Web site: http://www.inspiration.com/

Visual thinking and learning software.

Intelligent Peripherals
20380 Town Center Lane, Suite 270
Cupertino, CA 95014
(408) 252-9400
Web site: http://www.alphasmart.com/

Turbo Charger, Get Utility, Writing Activity CD-ROM, Keywords to be used with AlphaSmart 2000.

Intellitools
5221 Central Avenue, Suite 205
Richmond, CA 94804

(800) 899-6687

Web site: http://www.intellitools.com/

IntelliPics, IntelliTalk, Overlay Maker, Click It.

Knowledge Adventure

19840 Pioneer Avenue
Torrance, CA 90503
(800) 545-7677
Web site: http://www.KnowledgeAdventure.com/

Classworks Gold—Curriculum management software for math and language arts in K–8 with more than 8,000 activities. Hyper Studio, Jump Start series.

Laureate Learning Systems

110 East Spring Street
Winsooski, VT 05404
(800) 562-6801
Web site: http://www.LLSys.com/

First Words; Talking Nouns I, II; Talking Verbs I, II; Tiger's Tale; Creature Chorus; Creature Magic.

The Learning Company (TLC)

One Anthenaeum Street
Cambridge, MA 09214
(800) 685-6322
Web site: http://www.learningcompanyschool.com/school/

Instructional software titles featuring Broderbund, Creative Wonders, Mindscape, The Learning Company, MECC, and Compton's plus Resource Center and Free demos.

The Lightspan Partnership, Inc.

10140 Campus Point Drive
San Diego, CA 92121
(888) 425-5543
Web site: http://www.lightspan.com/

Lightspan Achieve Now—Interactive software for reading, math, and language arts for grades K–8. Includes school and home learning activities, teacher materials, interactive software, student assessment, professional development, and Internet resources.

Linda Burkhart

6201 Candle Court
Eldersburg, MD 21780
(410) 795-4561
Web site: http://www.lburkhart.com/

Early Play Activities (contains activities authored in IntelliPix), switches, devices, and books regarding software use.

Macmillan/McGraw-Hill

10 Union Square East
New York, NY 10003-3384
(212) 353-5676
Web site: http://www.mmhschool.com/

An array of software designed to teach skills and provide teaching ideas and curriculum.

Marblesoft

12301 Central Avenue NE, Suite 205
Blaine, MN 55434
(612) 755-1402
Web site: http://www.marblesoft.com/

Early Learning (I, II, III), Functional Life Skills, Money Skills, Overlays for IntelliKeys.

Mayer-Johnson Company

P.O. Box 1579
Solana Beach, CA 92075
(619) 550-0449
Web site: http://www.mayerjohnson.com/

Boardmaker, Communication Board-Builder, HyperSign-Interactive ASL Dictionary, Picture Communications Symbols (PCS), Writing with Symbols 2000.

McGraw-Hill Learning Technologies

8787 Orion Place
Columbus, OH 43240
(800) 598-4077
Web site: http://www.passkeylearning.com/

Passkey, a Prescriptive Learning System—A networkable CD-ROM program for basic skills and test preparation in math, reading, writing, and science.

National Computer Systems, Inc.
3450 East Sunrise Drive, Suite 140
Tucson, AZ 85718
(800) 937-6682
Web site: http://www.novanet.com/

The Novanet System—An on-line standards-based curriculum for children ages 3–12+ featuring more than 600 new lessons, multimedia resources, and a management system.

Psychological Corporation
555 Academic Court
San Antonio, TX 78204
(800) 232-1223
Web site: http://www.hbtpc.com/

CELF-3, clinical assistant-scoring software for the CELF-3 test.

R. J. Cooper and Associates
24843 Del Prado, Suite 283
Dana Point, CA 92629
(800) 752-6673
Web site: http://www.rjcooper.com/

Early and Advanced Switch Games, Point to Pictures, Turn-Taking.

Scholastic, Inc.
730 Broadway
New York, NY 10003
(212) 353-8219
Web site: http://www.scholastic.com/

Wiggleworks Plus (K–2), Smart Place (3–6) CD-ROMs.

Simtech Publications
134 East Street
Litchfield, CT 06759
Web site: http://www.hsj.com/

Single-switch software called Switch Kids, New Frog, and Flyk; Scan and Match series (for preschoolers and teens).

Soft Touch Software
4300 Stine Road, Suite 401
Bakersfield, CA 93309
(877) 763-8868

Web site: http://www.funsoftware.com/

Teach Me to Talk, Songs I Sing at Preschool, Old MacDonald's Farm Delux, Monkeys Jumping on the Bed, Switch Basics Software, IntelliKeys Overlays.

Sunburst
101 Castleton Street
Pleasantville, NY 10570
(800) 321-7511
Web site: http://www.sunburst.com/

Write On! Plus (middle/high school series).

Tom Snyder Productions
80 Coolidge Hill Road
Watertown, MA 02172
(617) 926-6000
Web site: http://www.tomsnyder.com/index.shtml

Educational software designed to enhance the teaching process and improve performance and understanding.

UCLA Microcomputer Project
1000 Veteran Avenue, Room 23-10
Los Angeles, CA 90095
(310) 825-4821

Wheels on the Bus (for Mac and old Apple computers only).

ADAPTIVE DEVICE VENDORS

Ability Research
P.O. Box 1791
Minnetonka, MN 55345
(612) 939-0121

Products and devices that make computer access easier for individuals with special needs, including switches such as Dynamic Delux Talk Back and Big Red.

AbleNet, Inc.
1081 10th Avenue SE
Minneapolis, MN 55414

(800) 322-0956

Web site: http://www.ablenetinc.com/

BIGmack Single Message One Step Communicator, Step-by-Step Communicator 75, Speak Easy Communication Device, Big Red and Jellybean Switches.

Adaptive Communication Systems, Inc.

P.O. Box 12440

Pittsburg, PA 15231

(800) 247-3433

The Great Talking Box, alternative keyboards such as the Fixed-Split Keyboard, AdapTek, and Mouse Emulator.

Adaptive Consulting Services

253 Merritt Square Mall, Suite 642

Merritt Island, FL 32952

(407) 639-7116

Communication devices such as DynaVox and DynaMyte, and Dectalk voice synthesis.

Adaptive Devices Group

1278 North Farris Avenue

Fresno, CA 93728

(800) 766-4234

Vocalize, Double Touch Switch.

Attainment Company, Inc.

P.O. Box 930160

Verona, WI 53593

(800) 327-4269

Web site: http://www.attainmentcompany.com/

15 Talker, 5 Talker, Memory Pad, Talking Picture Frame.

Crestwood Company

6625 North Sidney Place

Milwaukee, WI 53209

(414) 352-5678

Web site: http://www.communicationaids.com/

Adapted toys: Fireman, Cutie Penguin, Leo the Lion, Baby Brontosaurus, and more (work with switches like the Big Red and Jelly Bean from

AbleNet). Communication devices: Dynamic Delux Talk Back 24, Mini Talk Back I and II, Talk Back III.

Dragon Systems, Inc.
320 Nevada Street
Newton, MA 02160
(617) 965-2374
Web site: http://www.dragonsys.com/

Dragon Naturally Speaking for Teens (for ages 11 and up).

ENABLING DEVICE VENDORS

Edmark Corporation
P.O. Box 3218
Redmond, WA 98073
(800) 362-2890
Web site: http://www.edmark.com/

Touch Window (touchscreen).

Flaghouse Special Populations
601 Flaghouse Drive
Hasbrouck Heights, NJ 07604
(800) 793-7900
Web site: http://www.flaghouse.com/

Super Sensitive switch.

Intelligent Peripherals
20380 Town Center Lane, Suite 270
Cupertino, CA 95014
(408) 252-9400
Web site: http://www.alphasmart.com/

AlphaSmart 2000.

Intellitools
5221 Central Avenue, Suite 205
Richmond, CA 94804
(800) 899-6687
Web site: http://www.intellitools.com/

IntelliKeys.

Mayer-Johnson Company
P.O. Box 1579
Solana Beach, CA 92075
(619) 550-0084
Web site: http://www.mayerjohnson.com/

Tech/Speak, Tech/TALK, Tech/Four, Magic Touch (touchscreen).

R. J. Cooper and Associates
24843 Del Prado, Suite 283
Dana Point, CA 92629
(949) 661-6904
(800) 752-6673
Web site: http://www.rjcooper.com/

Magic Touch screens, Switch-Adapted Mouse devices/interfaces.

Toys for Special Children
385 Warburton Avenue
Hastings-on-Hudson, NY 10706
(914) 478-0960
Web site: http://www.enablingdevices.com/

Cheap Talk, Cheap Talk 4 Inline, Cheap Talk 8, Talking Switch Plate, Twin Talk, Step Talk Switch Plate, Hip-Step Talker, Specially-Adapted Toys, Sensory Devices.

SELECTED INTERNET RESOURCES FOR ASSISTIVE TECHNOLOGY

Abledata
http://www.abledata.com/

Access Unlimited (numerous links to other disability sites)
http://www.accessunlimited.com/

Apple Computer's Disability Home Page
http://www.apple.com/education/k12/disability/

Archimedes Project (Design Issues for Tomorrow's Technology)
http://archimedes.stanford.edu//arch.html

DDInsite (Developmental Disabilities/Assistive Technology)
http://ddinsite.gatech.edu/
disABILITY Resource on the Internet
http://www.dinf.org/disability_resources/

DO-IT
http://www.washington.edu/doit/

DREAMMS for Kids, Inc.
http://www.dreamms.org/

EASI, Access to Information for Persons with Disabilities
http://www.rit.edu/~easi/

Information Technology and Disabilities (a refereed journal)
http://www.rit.edu/~easi/itd.html

Job Accommodation Network (JAN)
http://janweb.icdi.wvu.edu/

Microsoft's Accessibility and Disability Home Page
http://www.microsoft.com/enable/

National Rehabilitation Information Center (NARIC)
http://www.naric.com/naric/

NCSA Mosaic Disability Access Page
http://bucky.aa.uic.edu/

Project Link
http://cosmos.buffalo.edu/t2rerc/

RESNA Technical Assistance Project
http://www.resna.org/

SuperKids Educational Software Review
http://www.superkids.com/

Trace Research and Development Center
http://www.trace.wisc.edu/

Way Cool Software Reviews by Students

http://www.ucc.uconn.edu/~wwwpcse/wcool.html

WebABLE

http://www.webable.com/

❧ Glossary

The following terms and concepts have been defined as they relate to the topic of special education.

ABC model—A framework for analyzing behavior that takes into account both the events that precede the behavior and the events that are subsequent to it; A = antecedent, B = behavior, C = consequence.

Ability grouping—Placement of students with comparable achievement and skill levels in the same classes or courses, an arrangement often used in the education of students who are gifted.

Academic—Having to do with subjects such as reading, writing, math, social studies, and science.

Academic achievement—The grade level at which a student functions in specific academic areas such as reading and mathematics, typically determined through standardized achievement tests.

Acceleration—More-rapid-than-usual passage by a student through a curriculum or grades in school.

Accommodation—Learning to do things differently from other students because of a handicap, impairment, or disability; the tendency to change one's way of thinking to fit a new objective or stimulus.

Achievement—The quality and quantity of a student's work.

Acquired disability—A disability occurring after birth.

Acquired handicap—A disabling condition having onset after birth.

Adaptive behavior—Individual behavior that meets the standards of personal independence and social responsibility expected for age and culture group; an essential component in the diagnosis of mental retardation.

Adaptive instruction—Instructional practice by which materials are modified to accommodate the unique characteristics of the learner.

Advance organizers—Written materials or statements made by a teacher to focus students' attention on the upcoming lesson by previewing the material to be covered and providing a rationale for the importance of the information to be presented.

Adventitious hearing loss—A hearing loss that was acquired after the development of speech.

Adversarial bargaining—A situation that is created when both parties continually attempt to gain power over each other.

Advocacy—An advanced stage of collective bargaining in which the two sides respect and accept the rights and roles of the other and do not challenge or threaten each other's leadership.

Advocate—An individual, parent, or professional who promotes the interests of persons with disabilities.

Age-appropriate and functional curricula—Real-life materials, activities, and teaching methods.

Age of onset—The age at which a handicap begins.

Aggression—Hostile and attacking behavior—which can include verbal communication—directed toward self, others, or the physical environment.

AIDS—Acquired immune deficiency syndrome.

American Association on Mental Deficiency (AAMD)—An earlier name for the American Association on Mental Retardation.

American Association on Mental Retardation (AAMR)—The oldest and largest multidisciplinary mental retardation organization. It investigates and promotes the best practices for people with mental retardation.

American Federation of Labor–Congress of Industrial Organizations (AFL-CIO)—The nation's largest private sector union.

American Federation of Teachers (AFT)—An affiliate of the AFL-CIO. It was formed in 1916 out of the belief that the organizing of teachers should follow the model of a labor union rather than that of a professional association. It promotes collective bargaining for teachers and other educational employees; conducts research on teacher stress, special education, and other education-related issues; and lobbies for the passage of legislation of importance to education.

American Sign Language (ASL)—A fully developed natural language, one of the world's many signed languages; the sign language or manual communication system preferred by many adults in the United States who are deaf.

American Speech-Language-Hearing Association (ASHA)—A professional organization concerned with communication disorders.

Americans with Disabilities Act (ADA)—Federal disability antidiscrimination legislation originally enacted in 1990.

Analytical listening—Hearing, analyzing, and possibly interpreting another person's communication or verbal message.

Anencephaly—A condition in which the brain fails to develop completely or is absent.

Annual appeal—A written request for a court to review or change the decision of a hearing officer.

Annual goal—A statement of an IEP as directed in IDEA of what an exceptional student needs to learn and should be able to learn in his special program over the time period of a year.

Anoxia—Inadequate supply of oxygen to the body and brain, usually at birth.

Anxiety—A state of painful uneasiness, emotional tension, or emotional confusion.

Aphasia—Impaired ability to use language or articulate ideas due to brain injury or stroke.

Appropriate education—A standard, required by IDEA, which guarantees that students with disabilities receive an educational program individually tailored to their abilities and needs.

Aptitude—Capacity for learning.

Array of services—A wide selection of services that are available so that an appropriate education can be provided to each student with special needs.

Articulation—The process of forming speech sounds.

Assessment—A way of collecting information about a student's special learning needs, strengths, and interests. An assessment may include giving individual tests, observing the student, looking at records, and talking with the student and/or parent.

Assimilation—The incorporation of a new object or stimulus into an existing way of thinking.

Assistive technology (AT)—Technological equipment designed to help individuals function in their environment.

Association for Children and Adults with Learning Disabilities (ACALD)—*See* Learning Disability Association of America.

Associative thinking—The ability to see relationships among differing concepts or knowledge bases.

At risk—Children whose history (family, developmental, medical), physical characteristics, life circumstances, or environment suggest that without interventions they will be identified as having disabilities later in life; a category of preschoolers under the age of three who are suspected of having a handicap and are eligible for special services without needing a specific label.

Ataxia—A form of cerebral palsy characterized by poor muscle coordination that negatively influences balance and coordination.

Attentive listening—Focusing on one specific form of heard communication while ignoring others heard simultaneously.

Attention deficit disorder (ADD)—A condition characterized by hyperactivity, inability to control one's own behavior, and constant movement.

Attention deficits—Characteristics often associated with learning disabilities that impair learning; students do not pay attention to the learning task or to the correct features of the task.

Attentional capacity—A limited pool of energy available to receive and process information.

Augmentive communication device—Equipment, such as a microcomputer with synthesized speech, that helps individuals communicate with others.

Autism—A severe disorder of thinking, communication, interpersonal relationships, and behavior; a disturbance of behavior noted in early childhood that may be characterized by self-stimulation, self-injurious behavior, or the absence of speech.

Autistic—A word describing a handicap or exceptionality where the student seems to act, talk, think, or behave differently from other students in that he or she does not want to physically be close to others.

Autistic behavior—A term used in reference to children and youth with autism; a subgroup of pervasive developmental disorder.

Aversive treatment—A noxious and sometimes painful consequence that would usually be avoided, for example electric shock, used for behavior modification.

Behavior modification—Systematic use of the principles of learning, including rewards and punishment, to promote desired behaviors and discourage undesired behaviors in an individual.

Behavior rating instruments—Checklists consisting of a list of behavioral descriptors to which an observer responds by indicating a choice along a positive-negative continuum.

Behavioral approach—A theory that views human behavior as learned.

Behavioral disorders—A condition of disruptive or inappropriate behaviors that interferes with a student's learning, relationships with others, or personal satisfaction to such a degree that intervention is required.

Behavioral goals and objectives—Expected and desired learning outcomes for students; stated in measurable terms so the teaching and learning process can be evaluated.

Behavioral management—Systematic use of behavioral techniques, such as behavior modification, to control or direct responses.

Biochemical disorders—Any number of disorders (such as learning disabilities) that are caused by biological or physiological imbalances or dysfunctions.

Blindisms—Inappropriate social behaviors possibly due to understimulation of infants with low vision.

Braille—A system of reading and writing that uses dot codes that are embossed on paper, developed by Louis Braille around 1829.

Brain damage—An identifiable insult to the structure of the brain.

Brainstem-evoked response—A technique involving electroencephalograph measurement of changes in brainwave activity in response to sound.

Career education—A curriculum designed to teach individuals the skills and knowledge necessary in the world of work.

Cascade of services—A model associating particular special education services and placements with severity of handicap.

Categorical—A system of labeling using specific classifications such as "learning disabled" or "mentally retarded."

Categorical programs—Classes available only to those students identified as having a specific disability, such as learning disabilities, mental retardation, visual impairments, and hearing impairments.

Center schools—Segregated school settings that typically serve students with a particular type of handicapping condition (for example, visual impairments, hearing impairments); some of these schools are residential.

Central nervous system dysfunction—An improper functioning of a component of the brain, spinal cord, or nervous system.

Cerebral palsy—A nonprogressive disorder due to brain damage that results in lack of control of voluntary muscles, paralysis, weakness, or lack of coordination of certain large and small muscles. Can be very mild or extremely debilitating. Often causes speech problems.

Chaining—A strategy to teach the steps of skills that have been task analyzed; in the chain either the first step can be taught first (*forward chaining*) or the last taught first (*backward chaining*).

Child Find—An organized effort funded by the federal government to enable each state to find and identify children with disabilities.

Child study team (CST)—A group of people working within the school and providing help to the teacher. This team tries to help the teacher meet the learning needs of students within the classroom.

Chronologically ill—Long-term illness.

Clinical teaching—An informal strategy involving systematic presentation of curriculum and response requests to children undergoing evaluation.

Cluster programs—A plan where gifted students spend a part of their day in the regular classroom on enriched or accelerated activities.

Cognitive behavior modification (CBM)—Instructional strategies that use internal control methods (such as self-talk) in structured ways to help students learn how to learn; the approach was initially developed by Donald Meichenbaum.

Cognitive development—Learning skills associated with memory, concepts (e.g., color, shape, size), recognition, and attention.

Collaboration—Group effort of special education teachers, regular education teachers, other service providers, and families working together to provide the best possible services and education.

Communication symbols—Spoken words or utterances, letters of the alphabet, pictures, or gestures used to relay a message; these usually refer to a past, present, or future event, person, object, action, or emotion.

Community-based instruction (CBI)—A strategy of teaching functional skill in the environments in which they occur; for example, shopping skills taught in the local market rather than in the classroom.

Compliance training—A method of assessing children and youth with autism by giving simple commands requiring motor and other nonverbal responses.

Computer-assisted instruction (CAI)—Instructional programs focusing on a particular topic that supplement or replace traditional teacher-directed instructional methods and are delivered at least in part by using a computer.

Computer-enhanced instruction—Software programs that supplement traditional instruction, used primarily for drill and practice.

Conceptualize—Generate questions and formulate abstract ideas.

Concrete operational thinking—The first stage of operational thought and the third major stage in cognitive development; extends from ages seven to twelve. Characterized by ability to form mental representations, understanding of relational terms, class inclusion, and serialization.

Conduct disorder—A psychiatric classification found in the *DSM-III-R* that some school districts believe is excluded from the federal definition of seriously emotionally disturbed; a type of behavioral disorder in which persistent, negative, hostile, antisocial behavior impairs daily life functioning.

Confidential school records—Private files of students, which are often not kept at the child's school; they include test scores, observations, family history, and evaluations of social, academic, and other skills.

Conflict resolution curriculum—An educational violence prevention strategy that helps develop empathy, impulse control, and skills in communication, problem solving, and anger management.

Congenital defects—Abnormalities in the child originating before birth.

Congenital onset—The presence of a condition at birth.

Consent—Parents demonstrate that they agree to let the school take an action that affects their child's education. This is usually in the form of a parent signing his or her name to a form or letter describing the action the school wishes to take.

Consulting teacher—A specially trained teacher who serves as a resource person to advise and provide instructional support to teachers who have students with disabilities in regular classrooms.

Continuum of services—Full range of educational services arranged in a stair-step fashion, where one level of service leads directly to the next one. *See also* Cascade of services *and* Array of services.

Convergent thinking—The process of reaching conclusions by using known facts; using thinking skills associated with academic learning such as memory, classification, and reasoning.

Cooperative learning—An educational method that emphasizes group cooperation and success through activities rather than individual competition.

Council for Exceptional Children (CEC)—The largest professional organization of special educators concerned with all exceptionality areas, founded by Elizabeth Farrell in 1922.

Creativity—A form of intelligence categorized by advanced divergent thought, the production of many original ideas, and the ability to develop flexible and detailed responses and ideas.

Criterion-referenced test—A measure to ascertain an individual performance compared to a set of criterion. The person is evaluated on his or her own performance and not in comparison to others.

Critical thinking—Evaluative thinking; problem-solving abilities.

Cross-categorical—Classes available to students with a variety of disabilities, usually according to level of severity.

Curriculum—A systematic grouping of content, activities, and instructional materials.

Curriculum-based assessment (CBA)—A method of evaluating children's learning and the instructional procedures by collecting data on students' daily progress on each instructional task.

Cystic fibrosis—A disorder of chronic lung infections and malabsorption of food.

Deaf—A profound hearing disability; a person who is deaf cannot understand sounds in the environment, such as speech and language of others, with or without the use of a hearing aid; hearing cannot be used as the primary way to gain information.

Deducing—A thinking skill where a person comes to a conclusion from known facts or general principles; a type of convergent thinking.

Deinstitutionalization—Decreasing the number of individuals with disabilities living in large congregate facilities.

Delayed development—Development along the normal sequence of developmental milestones but at a slower than normal rate.

Delinquency—Illegal behavior, which may or may not be the result of a behavioral disorder, committed by juveniles.

Developing Understanding of Self and Others (DUSO)—A commercially available instructional program designed to increase language, cognitive, and social skills for students in the primary grades.

Development—Changes in functioning through the acquisition of knowledge, skills, and behavior.

Developmental delay—A lag in child development in any one or more of the five domains, which are cognitive, communication, physical, adaptive, and social or emotional.

Developmental disability—A condition that originates in childhood and results in a significant handicap for the individual, such as mental retardation, cerebral palsy, epilepsy, and conditions associated with neurological damage.

Developmental domains—An educational philosophy and approach for organizing educational objectives and classifying children's problems according to four domains: cognitive, motor, social, and communication.

Diagnosis—Process of identifying an individual as having a disability by using a series of standardized tests and observational procedures. *See also* Assessment.

Dignity of risk—Enhancing the human dignity of individuals by enabling them to experience the risk taking of ordinary life that is necessary for normal growth and development.

Direct instruction—A method of teaching academic subjects; involves systematic instruction of the skill to be learned and the collection of data evaluating the effectiveness of the teaching procedure selected.

Direction observation—A direct method of assessing problem behaviors in which the teacher systematically records, by time and condition, the frequency with which identified problem behaviors occur.

Disability—A problem or condition that makes it difficult for a student to learn in the same way as most other students. This may be short term or long term.

Disabled—Refers to an objective, measurable organic dysfunction or impairment.

Discipline—Teaching students self-control; fostering self-management of behavior; teaching students to follow the rules of proper conduct.

Discrepancy—A difference or variance; in learning disabilities, the difference between actual achievement and that expected by intellectual functioning.

Discrepancy formulas—Formulas developed by state educational agencies or local school districts to determine the difference between a students' actual achievement and expected achievement based on scores from tests of achievement and intelligence.

Discrepancy scores—The scores resulting from the application of a discrepancy formula; used in some states to determine eligibility for programs designed for students with learning disabilities.

Distance education—The use of telecommunications to deliver live instruction by content experts to remote locations.

Distractibility—A measure of an individual's inability to screen out extraneous stimuli.

Divergent thinking—Using creative thinking skills such as fluency, flexibility, originality, and elaboration; usually, conclusions are reached by reorganizing information and developing a variety of responses.

Down's syndrome (also called Down syndrome)—A chromosomal disorder that causes identifiable physical characteristics and usually causes delays in physical and intellectual development and puts individuals at high risk for communicative disorders and mental retardation.

Dual exceptionalities—Two or more noted deviations from the norm in behavioral or learning levels.

Due process—A set of rights having to do with how decisions are made; the act of following legal steps to ensure that employees are treated fairly and according to the law; a constitutional guarantee ensuring that fair laws and fair process will be used before the government can deprive a person of life, liberty, or property.

Due process hearing—A formal meeting held to settle disagreements between parents and schools in a way that is fair to the student, parents, and the school; when the parents and the special services committee cannot reach an agreement on the types of services and the educational program for a student, a third party settles the dispute. This meeting is run by an impartial hearing officer.

Duration—In relation to an IEP, this signifies the length of time an exceptional student will need a special program or service during the school year or extended school year.

Dyscalculia—Impaired ability to calculate or perform mathematical functions.

Dyslexia—Impaired ability to read, often caused by brain damage.

Early childhood programs—Preschool, daycare, and early infant school programs that involve students with disabilities and their families, designed to improve the speech, language, social, and cognitive skills of the students attending.

Early childhood special education (ECSE)—Provides meaningful and appropriate childhood experiences for children aged birth to five who because of some handicapping condition are not likely to benefit from regular early childhood and preschool experiences. These children may be at risk of becoming delayed or developmentally handicapped.

Early intervention—The provision of preventative or habilitative services to children at a very early age.

Echolalia—A stage in language development characterized by repeating (echoing) words or sentences initially spoken by other people.

Ecological assessment—Taking into consideration all dimensions of the individual's environment, including the individual him- or herself.

Educable mentally retarded (EMR)—A term formally used for people with mild mental retardation.

Educational diagnosticians—Professionals trained to test and evaluate individual children and youth to determine whether they are eligible for special education, and, if so, what special services they require.

Educational placement—The location or type of classroom program (for example, resource room) arranged for a child's education; the setting in which a student receives educational services.

Eligibility staffing—A meeting at which a group of school staff members recommend a student's eligibility for special education programs and services. This decision is made on assessment and other information, and parents may be asked to attend.

Emotional disturbance—A term used interchangeably with *behavioral disorder*.

Emotional maturity—The ability to act, think, and feel in ways similar to other students one's age.

Environmental risk factors—A category of at-risk children who are born biologically and genetically normal but whose environment includes poverty, abuse, and neglect or whose parents have mental health problems or are addicted to substances at a young age.

Enrichment—A common approach to teaching gifted students, whereby topics or skills are added to the traditional curriculum or a particular topic is studied more in depth.

Epilepsy—A physical disorder marked by repeated disturbances to the central nervous system, often manifested in recurrent seizures.

Evaluation—A manner of collecting information about special learning needs, strengths, and interests. It is used to help decide if there is a need for special services and programs. It may include giving individual tests, observing the child, reviewing records, and interviewing parents and peers. Assessment or judgment of special characteristics includes areas such as intelligence, physical abilities, sensory abilities, learning preferences, and achievement.

Exceptionality—Refers to children and youth who differ sufficiently from the norm to warrant special consideration in housing, schooling, and/or transportation. Includes gifted as well as those with mental, behavioral, sensorial, and physical disabilities.

Exclusion—The denial of educational opportunities to a student; an appropriate term to use when the educational plan is detrimentally inappropriate to the child's needs.

Externalizing behaviors—Behaviors, especially aggressive behaviors, directed toward others.

Fetal alcohol syndrome (FAS)—A condition where a baby is born with mental impairments, behavioral problems, and perhaps some physical disabilities caused by the mother drinking alcohol during the pregnancy.

Flexibility—A characteristic of creative thinking; the variety of ideas produced by an individual.

Fluency—Smoothness and rapidity in skills; this term is associated with quickness in thinking; in speech, in the rate, flow, and pattern of oral speech; in reading, the rate of correct oral reading; also used synonymously with *proficiency* or *mastery* in a variety of academic subjects.

Follow-up—To provide later monitoring, evaluation, diagnosis, or treatment after the initial diagnosis or treatment of a condition.

Follow-up study—A longitudinal research study that usually analyzes the adult outcomes of people who were subjects in a research study when they were children.

Formal operational thinking—The final stage of cognitive development, which extends from age twelve on.

Free, appropriate public education (FAPE)—The term used in the Education of the Handicapped Act and the Individuals with Disabilities Act (IDEA) to describe the right of every student to a special education that will meet his or her individual special learning needs, including supportive services and highly individualized educational programs.

Full continuum of services—With reference to special education, the availability of instructional arrangements appropriate for a full range of disabilities from least severe to most severe.

Full integration—Physical and social participation in a regular program on a full-time basis.

Full-service school—An environment providing programs and services to include all integrated support systems necessary for the education, health, and well-being of a child.

Functional exclusion—The inappropriate placement of a child in an educational program.

Functional skill—A skill or task that will be used in the individual's normal environment.

Future Problem Solving Program—A national competition and instructional program developed by Paul Torrance and his colleagues to teach creative problem solving; students attempt to find positive solutions to real issues such as the nuclear arms race and water conservation.

Generalize—The process of transferring knowledge or skills learned in one situation to untaught situations; the ability to expand upon knowledge by applying it to novel situations; the transfer of learning from particular instances to other environments, people, times, and events.

Genetic factors—Factors affecting an individual's characteristics that are of a hereditary nature.

Gifted—A term describing individuals with high levels of intelligence, outstanding abilities, and capabilities for high performance.

Goals 2000: Education America Act of 1994—Legislation that provides resources to states and communities to develop and implement education reforms that will help students reach academic and occupational standards.

Group homes—Apartments or homes in which a small number of individuals with mental retardation live together as part of their community and receive assistance from service providers.

Habilitation—An individualized program of education, training, and supportive services designed to enhance the abilities of an individual with mental retardation.

Handicap—Environmental or functional demands placed upon a person with a disability as he or she interacts in a given situation; an individual's reaction to his or her disability.

Head Start—Nationally, federally funded early intervention programs designed primarily to help young children who live in poverty; these programs typically assist at-risk preschoolers by providing an accepting and responsive environment that encourages thinking and communicative skills.

Health impairments—Physical health problems limiting strength.

Health-related problems—Problems generated by physical child abuse, AIDS, and other health problems of children and other individuals.

Hearing impaired—A general term that describes both *hard-of-hearing* and *deaf.*

Hemiplegia—Paralysis of one lateral half of the body or part of it resulting from injury to the motor centers of the brain.

High achiever—A student who expects success and views it as incentive to work harder.

High intelligence—A combination of traits such as the ability to understand complex relationships, to think abstractly, and to solve problems; usually demonstrated by achieving scores on intelligence tests that fall two standard deviations above the mean, or approximately 130 and above.

Home or hospital teacher—A special teacher who teaches in the child's home or hospital when the child must be absent from school due to health problems.

Homogeneous grouping—Placing students together in a class according to their type of disability.

Human immunodeficiency virus (HIV)—A virus that affects the immune system and impairs the individual's ability to fight infections; often develops into AIDS.

Hyperactive—Persistent, excessive movement; overactivity with or without a clearly defined purpose; the individual is unable to sit or concentrate for long periods of time.

Identification—To seek out and identify children with disabilities within special educational categories.

Illinois Test of Psycholinguistic Abilities (ITPA)—A test to identify students as learning disabled, intended to determine strengths and weaknesses of individual students; also thought to identify students' learning styles and preferences to assist in instructional planning.

Inactive learners—Students who do not become involved in learning situations, approach the learning task purposefully, ask questions, seek help, or initiate learning.

Incidental learning—Knowledge gained as a result of other activities and experiences not specifically designed to teach the knowledge learned; learning that takes place spontaneously or nondeliberately; not focused on a specific task.

Inclusion—In a school setting, inclusion involves educating all children in regular classrooms all of the time, regardless of the degree or severity of individual student disabilities. Effective inclusion programs take place in conjunction with a planned system of training and supports. Such programs usually involve the collaboration of a multidisciplinary team that includes regular and special educators (or other personnel) as well as family members and peers.

Independent study—A common approach to the education of the gifted that allows a student to pursue and study a topic in depth on an individual basis.

Individual transition plan (ITP)—A written plan that identifies the skills and supportive services that an individual needs to function in the community after schooling is completed.

Individual written rehabilitation plan (IWRP)—A written plan used to provide vocational rehabilitation for adults with disabilities.

Individualized education program (IEP)—An IEP, which is required by the Individuals with Disabilities Education Act, is a plan for an education program specific to an individual. This plan is developed collaboratively by the school and the parents. The regulations require meetings between school personnel, parents, and other individuals as well as written documents.

Individualized family service plan (IFSP)—The IFSP, which is also required by IDEA, is a written plan for infants and toddlers from birth to three years old who receive early intervention services. The regulations require that children receive early intervention services in "natural" environments (settings that are natural and normal for the child's age peers who do not have disabilities) to the maximum extent possible. Like the IEP, the IFSP must be written with the family's involvement and approval.

Individualized habilitation plan (IHP)—A written plan used to provide educational and social services to individuals living in an intermediate care facility.

Individualized instruction—Instruction planned to meet the individual needs of students; they are presented with instructional tasks reflecting their own pace of learning, pinpointing exactly what the student does and does not know and providing instruction based on that information.

Individuals with Disabilities Education Act (IDEA)—Formally referred to as the Education for All Handicapped Children Act (EHA); originally passed as P.L. 94-142 in 1975; amended in 1986 by P.L. 99-457 to also provide instruction and services to infants and toddlers; amended and reauthorized again in 1990 under P.L. 101-476, which strengthened transitional programs for adolescents and young adults with handicaps; ensures a free appropriate public education in the least restrictive environment for all children and youth with disabilities.

Inference—Decision or opinion based on assumptions; a conclusion drawn by using reason.

Information processing theory—The suggestion that learning disabilities are caused by an inability to organize thinking and to approach learning tasks systematically.

Instructional goals—A statement about learning that includes a result to be achieved after specific instruction.

Instructional objectives—Statements about learning that relate to an overall goal; includes a description of the student's behavior, the conditions under which the behavior is to occur, and the criteria for acceptable performance.

Integrated classes—Regular education classes where students with special needs learn alongside students without disabilities.

Integration—Often used synonymously with *mainstreaming* to encompass efforts to move students from segregated classes into the mainstream. However, it is sometimes used to represent the ultimate objective of inclusion.

Intellectual functioning—The actual performance of tasks believed to represent intelligence, such as observing, problem solving, and communicating.

Intelligence—A person's ability to think, learn, or understand, often measured by standardized tests.

Intelligence quotient (IQ)—The numerical figure, with a score of 100 being average, obtained from a standardized test; often used to express mental development of ability.

Interactional approach—Stresses communication with a highly interactive environment that encourages the acquisition of language.

Interactive video—A computer-controlled educational device students use to view and hear instructional presentations and make choices regarding the pace and order of the presentations.

Interdisciplinary instruction—An educational approach that involves studying a topic and its issues in the context of several different disciplines; sometimes used in the education of the gifted.

Internalizing behaviors—Behavior that is withdrawn into the individual.

Interviews—A method of gathering information from an individual by asking a set of questions.

Itinerant specialists—Specialists from various disciplines—special education, speech, occupational therapy, physical therapy—who work at different schools across the week; some travel great distances as they go from school to school.

Job coach—An individual who works alongside people with disabilities, helping them to learn all parts of a job.

Joint Committee on Learning Disabilities (JCLD)—A committee representing a number of professional, parent, and consumer organizations concerned with learning disabilities. These organizations include the International Reading Association, Orton Dyslexia Society, American Speech-Language-Hearing Association, Council for Learning Disabilities, Division for Learning Disabilities (a division of the Council for Exceptional Children), Learning Disability Association of America (formerly ACLD), Council for Children with Communication Disorders (a division of the Council for Exceptional Children), and the National Association of School Psychologists.

Labeling—Assigning an individual as belonging to a group; associating an individual with a specific handicapping condition.

Language—The formalized method of communication used by people; includes the signs and symbols by which ideas are represented and the rules that govern them so the intended message has meaning.

Language delay—When children do not develop skills as quickly as their age peers; some children with language delays are language disordered and require the special assistance of a specialist so they can ultimately use language proficiently.

Language disorder—Difficulty or inability to master the various language systems and their rules of application, morphology, phonology, syntax, and pragmatics, which then interferes with communication.

Learning disabilities—A handicapping condition whereby the individual possesses average intelligence but is substantially delayed in academic achievement.

Learning Disability Association of America (LDAA)—An advocacy organization of parents of children with learning disabilities that provides information to the public, schools, and community programs, formerly called Association for Children with Learning Disabilities (ACLD) and Association for Children and Adults with Learning Disabilities (ACALD).

Learning strategies—Instructional methods to help students read, comprehend, and study better by helping them organize and collect information strategically.

Learning styles—The systematic strategies individuals use to gain new skills and information.

Least restrictive environment (LRE)—LRE is an essential principle of IDEA, which states that "to the maximum extent appropriate, children with disabilities, including children in public or private institutions or other care facilities, are educated with children who are nondisabled." The law requires that the least restrictive environment be determined on an individual basis and be based on the child's IEP. The LRE is the legal basis for inclusive programs.

Life skills—Daily living skills used to shop and cook, and to organize, clean, and manage a home.

Likert scale—A system used in questionnaires or surveys to provide a forced-choice answer along a scale of some dimension (such as "strongly agree" to "strongly disagree," or "like" to "dislike"); the numbering system used typically ranges from 1 to 5 or from 1 to 7.

Local education agency (LEA)—Typically a local school district, but may be a cooperative district or set of districts that are funded as a single unit.

Low achiever—A student who expects failure and sees no value in expending effort to learn.

Low-incidence disability—A disability that occurs infrequently; the number of new cases is very low.

Magnet school—A center school that serves children who do not live in the immediate neighborhood; some magnet schools are designed to serve children whose parents work in a nearby area; other magnet schools emphasize a particular theme (such as theater arts, math, and science).

Mainstreaming—An older term that may imply a more gradual, partial, or part-time process (e.g., a student who is mainstreamed may attend separate classes within a regular school or may participate in regular gym and lunch programs only). In mainstreamed programs, students are often expected to fit in the regular class in which they want to participate, whereas in an inclusive program the classes are designed to fit all students.

Mean—The sum of all scores divided by the number of scores; the average.

Medically fragile—An individual who requires medical assisted technology for life support and is more acutely involved than those who are described as chronologically ill.

Mental age—An age estimate of an individual's mental ability; expressed as the average chronological age of children who can ordinarily answer the questions in the test correctly; derived from a comparison of the individual's IQ score and chronological age.

Mental retardation—A handicapping condition that affects cognitive functioning and adaptive behavior.

Mentorships—An approach to education of the gifted where a student is paired with an adult in order to learn to apply knowledge in real life situations.

Metacognition—A cognitive behavior modification strategy in which students use self-management techniques to help them remember what they are taught by taking themselves through systematic problem-solving steps.

Mild mental retardation—The level of mental retardation that usually includes individuals with IQs from approximately 50–55 to 70–75.

Minimal brain dysfunction—A condition associated with learning disabilities; a result of functional problems of the central nervous system or brain damage that can impair individuals' ability to learn or succeed at academic tasks.

Mobility—The ability to travel safely and efficiently from one place to another.

Modeling—An instructional tactic where one person demonstrates how to do a task or solve a problem while another person observes and copies those steps. The expert or teacher will demonstrate the particular skill that's being taught to address a situation (i.e., failure, teasing, accusing, and peer-pressure).

Moderate mental retardation—The level of mental retardation that usually includes individuals with IQs from approximately 35–40 to 50–55.

Morphology—Rules that govern the structure and form of words; the basic meaning of words.

Motivation—The presence of internal incentives to learn or perform, influenced by previous success or failure.

Motor development—An area in which young children are assessed that includes gross motor (large movements such as walking, jumping, rolling over) and fine motor (smaller movements such as grasping, touching, reaching).

Multicultural—Reflecting more than one culture.

Multidisciplinary team—A group of professionals responsible for evaluating a child and making decisions about the child's educational program. The team must include at least one teacher or other specialist with knowledge in the area of suspected disability.

Multihandicapped—Having more than one handicapping condition; the combination causes severe educational problems. Also called *multiply handicapped.*

Muscular dystrophy—A progressive and pervasive weakness of all muscle groups characterized by a degeneration of muscle cells and their replacement with fatty and fibrous tissue.

National Education Association (NEA)—One of the largest organizations of professional educators.

Natural setting—The environment in which individuals of comparable age typically live, work, and play.

Neurological system—Having to do with the central nervous system; the brain, spinal cord, and systems of neural pathways.

Noncategorical—An approach to special education that does not classify or differentiate among disabilities or exceptionalities in providing services.

Noncategorical classes—Classes that are available to students with a variety of handicaps, usually according to the levels of severity (mild, moderate, severe, profound) of individuals' handicaps.

Nondiscriminatory testing—Assessment that properly takes into account a child's cultural and linguistic diversity.

Nonverbal behavior—Physical or gestural communication or actions, like raising your hand for teacher attention, or smiling; body language; communications that do not use oral language.

Norm-reference tests—Instruments used to ascertain an individual's performance compared to others' performance on the same instrument.

Normal curve—A bell-shaped curve plotting the normal distribution of human traits, such as intelligence, in a population.

Normalization—Making available to people with mental disabilities patterns of life and conditions of everyday living that are as close as possible to or indeed the same as the regular circumstances and ways of life of society.

Objective permanence—The knowledge that objects exist even if they are hidden from view.

Observation systems—Systematic ways to observe and record the functioning of an individual's behavior; usually made for assessment purposes.

Occupational therapist (OT)—A professional who directs activities designed to improve muscular control as well as develop self-help skills; a medical professional who provides treatment from a physician's prescription that enhances daily living and personal care activity skills through the development of fine and gross-motor activities relating to the upper extremities.

Ophthalmologist—A medical doctor specializing in disease processes of the eye.

Oral approach or method—One method of instruction advocated for students who are deaf where they learn to communicate (both receiving and sending information) orally without using sign language.

Orthopedic impairment—A physical impairment that adversely affects academic performance, including impairments caused by congenital anomaly, disease, and trauma.

Osteogenesis imperfecta—A musculoskeletal disorder characterized by brittle bones, especially early in life.

Other health impaired—Having impaired strength, vitality, or alertness as a result of chronic or acute health problems that may require modification in the educational setting; a category in IDEA of children who have limited strength due to health problems.

Outreach programs—Specialized programs offered in local communities by residential schools or centralized agencies serving students with special needs.

Overlearning—More or longer practice than necessary for the immediate recall of a task.

Paraplegia—Paralysis of both legs.

Partial seizure—A seizure beginning in a localized area and affecting only a small part of the brain.

Peabody Language Development Kits (PLDK)—A commercially available series of instructional programs that include prepared lessons aimed at improving language and cognitive skills.

Peabody Picture Collection (PPC)—A set of picture cards that can be used to improve individuals' vocabulary and expressive language skills in teacher-prepared activities.

Peace education curriculum—An educational violence prevention strategy that looks at violence prevention interpersonally and within and among societies as a whole.

Peer coaching—A staff development process that allows fellow teachers to observe each other conducting their classes for the purpose of providing constructive, nonthreatening feedback.

Peer mediation programs—Programs that train students and teachers to identify and mediate conflicts that occur in the school.

Perceptual—Refers to selecting, organizing, and interpreting environmental stimuli.

Perceptual motor process—A basic process involved in learning (along with memory and attention); a deficit may affect the way information is perceived.

Perceptual motor training activities—The training of motor, visual, or auditory skills in an effort to improve academic performance.

Perceptual skills—Ability to decode stimuli and act accordingly.

Performance feedback—Reviewing the situation and identifying the positive and negative consequences of behaviors.

Pervasive developmental disorder (PDD)—A term used in reference to children and youth who are affected in many basic areas of psychological development at the same time and to a severe degree. This classification has only one subgroup: autistic disorder; almost always diagnosed in infancy or early childhood.

Pervasive developmental disorder, not otherwise specified—Same as pervasive developmental disorder but does not fit the autistic disorder criteria.

Phenylketonuria (PKU)—A metabolic disorder present at birth in which certain proteins are not absorbed by the body, causing damage to the central nervous system and leading to mental retardation; can be prevented by a special diet.

Physical disabilities—Problems with the body that interfere with functioning.

Physical integration—The actual physical placement of a handicapped student into an environment with nonhandicapped students.

Physical therapist (PT)—A professional trained to treat physical disabilities through nonmedical means such as exercise, massage, heat, and water therapy.

Physically challenged—A term sometimes used to describe persons with physical disabilities.

P.L. 94-142—*See* Individuals with Disabilities Education Act.

Postlingual—Refers to the period after the acquisition of speech.

Postnatal—After birth.

Prelingual—Refers to the period before the acquisition of speech; specifically, before the echolalic stage of speech development.

Prelingually deaf—Individuals who lost their ability to hear before they developed language.

Prenatal—Before birth.

Preoperational thinking—The second stage of cognitive development, which extends from eighteen months or two years to age six or seven. At this stage the child goes from egocentric and static thinking to concept formation and ability to classify objects into groups.

President's Committee on Mental Retardation (PCMR)—A committee of citizens appointed by the president of the United States to annually report to the president on issues related to mental retardation.

Presumed central nervous dysfunction—A medical term referring to the cause of some learning disabilities; thought by some special educators to be misleading because it gives the impression that nothing can be done about the condition. Indicates some brain or neurological damage that impedes individual's motor and/or learning abilities.

Problem solving—The process of searching out, analyzing, and evaluating facts using various reasoning and thinking skills in order to develop appropriate and effective solutions.

Procedural safeguards/due process—Procedural safeguards are provided in IDEA to ensure fair procedures in the identification, evaluation, and placement of children with disabilities. For example, the law requires that parents receive written notice if a change is proposed in the child's placement. If conflicts arise between parents and schools, either party may request a due process hearing with the right to be represented by others, to have a written record, and to enter an appeal. In order to advocate for their own children, parents must be familiar with these procedural safeguards.

Profound mental retardation—The level of mental retardation that usually includes individuals with IQs below approximately 20 to 25.

Program assessment—The process of gathering data from multiple sources to determine how well an organization is accomplishing its goals.

Program planning—An educational assessment that takes place after determining eligibility to determine the student's specific strengths and weaknesses and conditions under which learning will be most successful.

Protected resources—Those instructional resources that are tagged explicitly to serve low achieving students; that is, they cannot be allocated by the teacher to other students.

Psychoeducational approach—An educational outgrowth of psychodynamic theory and prescriptive approaches; this approach is child-centered and believes that the problem resides in an internal, unconscious state.

Public policy—Guidelines legitimized by government that are implemented by laws and regulations and that reflect current or future perceived needs of society or a segment of society.

Pullout programs for gifted students—The most common educational placement for gifted students; gifted students spend part of the school day in a special class.

Quadriplegia—Paralysis of all four limbs.

Reason abstractly—Ability to think about ideas and concepts; ability to draw inferences or conclusions from known or assumed facts.

Regular class—A typical classroom designed to serve students with disabilities as well as "regular" students.

Regular education initiative (REI)—A position held by some special educators that students with disabilities should be served exclusively in regular education classrooms and should not be "pulled out" to attend special classes; an attempt to reform regular and special education so they are a combined system that maximizes mainstreaming.

Related services—Services that may or may not be part of the classroom curriculum but support classroom instruction, such as transportation, physical therapy, occupational therapy, and speech and language therapy.

Reliable—Refers to the consistency and dependability of the results of information-gathering processes; consistency may be over time, from one observer to another, from one form of a test to another, or within the same observer for different times and different children.

Residential instruction—A facility in which the exceptional person receives 24-hour care.

Resocialization—The process of reestablishing values and standards held in common among the teaching staff. The phenomenon is a result of sustained staff interaction and is essential for meaningful culture changes of the sort necessary for a shift to total quality management.

Resource program—Refers to when students attend a regular class for the majority of the day and go to a special education class several hours per day or for blocks of time each week.

Resource teacher model—Students with physical disabilities who attend regular classes are provided services through a pullout program in a resource room in which a special education teacher is available.

Restructuring—Reform proposals that dramatically change the structure of school districts or the manner in which they operate.

Ritalin—A drug sometimes prescribed to help students with ADD focus their attention on assigned tasks and reduce their hyperactivity.

Role-playing—Acting out a situation in an action-oriented manner.

Schizophrenia—A type of psychosis; a severe emotional disorder in which the individual becomes irrational, and often delusional and socially withdrawn.

School nurse—A health care professional available at schools to respond to medical crises, distribute medication, and provide consultation and education.

School psychologists—Professionals trained to test and evaluate individual children to determine whether they are eligible for special education, and, if so, what special services they require.

Screening—An assessment procedure used to detect students who may be at high risk for developing serious learning or behavior problems.

Section 504 of the Vocational Rehabilitation Act—A federal law that forbids discrimination in federally funded programs against people with handicaps.

Selective attention—Ability to attend to the critical features of a task.

Selective listening—Focusing on only one sound in an environment, such as a lecture.

Self-advocacy—A social and political movement started by and for people with disabilities to speak for themselves on important issues such as housing, employment, legal rights, and personal relationships.

Self-concept analysis—A means of gaining insight into how one views self-performance or worth.

Self-contained special education classes—Special classes attended by students for most of the school day; at other times, they are mainstreamed into regular education activities. Special classes that provide intensive, specialized instruction; some of these classes are categorical, for students who have the same handicapping condition (e.g., all having hearing impairments), and some are cross-categorical, where class members have different disabling conditions (e.g., several with mental retardation, several with learning disabilities, etc.).

Self-management techniques—Strategies that assist students in identifying and solving problems independently.

Self-stimulation—Self-initiated behavior that generates a desirable sensation.

Sensorimotor—The first stage of cognitive development, occurring between birth and eighteen months or two years of age.

Sensorineural hearing loss—A hearing loss caused by a malfunction of the inner ear or the eighth cranial nerve.

Sensory development—An assessment area for young children that generally includes assessing the child's ability to see and hear.

Seriously emotionally disturbed—A condition with one or more of the following characteristics that exists over a long period of time and that substantially interferes with normal functioning: (1) an inability to learn that cannot be explained by intellectual, sensory, or other factors, (2) an inability to build or maintain satisfactory interpersonal relationships, (3) inappropriate behavior, a general pervasive mood of unhappiness, or depression, or (4) a tendency to develop physical symptoms or fears associated with problems. The term is referred to in IDEA to categorize students with behavioral disorders and emotional disturbance.

Service manager—The person who oversees the implementation and evaluation of an individualized family service plan.

Severe mental retardation—The level of mental retardation that usually includes individuals with IQs from approximately 20–25 to 30–35.

Sheltered workshops—Special segregated workshops attended by some adults with disabilities.

Sickle-cell anemia—A hereditary blood disease characterized by anemia resulting from insufficiency of red blood cells, impairment of liver function, swelling of limbs and joints, severe pain, loss of appetite, and general weakness.

Social interactions—Skills and behaviors occurring between or among people involving social, rather than academic, relationships.

Socioeconomic status (SES)—The status an individual or family unit holds in society, usually determined by one's job, level of education, and the amount of money available to spend.

Sociometric procedures—A means of assessing social preferences of individuals within a group setting.

SOMPA (System of Multicultural Pluralistic Assessment)—An assessment that is sensitive to the influence of cultural factors on performance.

Spasticity—A form of cerebral palsy characterized by involuntary muscle contractions and inaccurate and difficult voluntary motion.

Special education—Individualized education for children with special needs.

Special services committee—A multidisciplinary team, including school administrators, regular and special education teachers, diagnosticians, related service personnel, and the child's parents, who follow the process of identification, planning, writing the IEP, and evaluating the child's progress in special education.

Speech—The vocal production of language, considered the fastest and most efficient means of communicating.

Speech therapist—Responsible for the diagnosis, prescription, and treatment of a full range of communication problems, including speech and language disorders.

Standard of deviation—A statistical measure that expresses the variability of a set of scores.

Standard score—Numbers converted from raw scores with constant means and standard deviations.

State education agency (SEA)—Typically a state's department of education or division of special education.

Statute—Law passed by a legislature or Congress and signed by a governor or the president.

Strabismus—A lack of coordination of ocular muscles resulting in "cross-eyed" appearance.

Subgroups—The groups of individuals who cluster by various characteristics and are already identified as members of a larger group.

Substance abuse—The deliberate and nontherapeutic use of chemicals such as alcohol, tobacco, drugs, gasoline, cleaning fluids, and glue in ways that contribute to health risks, disruption of psychological functioning, or adverse social consequences.

Supportive services—Auxiliary services—such as adaptive physical education, speech and language, audiology, and physical or occupational therapy—required by many students with handicaps.

Systematic instruction—A data-driven method of instruction in which an instructional program is designed from data gathered from formal and informal assessment procedures, instruction is constantly evaluated, and student performance is measured to gauge the effectiveness of the program.

Task analysis—The act of breaking a task or skill into its component parts for instructional purposes.

Technology Related Assistance for Individuals with Disabilities Act of 1988—A federal act that provides funding and allows for technical assistance to persons with disabilities as they select and use assistive technology.

Telephone Devices for the Deaf (TDDs)—A teletypewriter connected to the phone system that allows people who are deaf to communicate telephonically.

Test standardization—Scores of a large number of individuals are collected and analyzed so that the score of a single individual can be compared to the norm.

Test validity—The extent to which a test actually assesses what it claims to assess.

The Association for Persons with Severe Handicaps (TASH)—A professional organization that promotes educational, policy, vocational, and habilitative research and discussion of people with severe disabilities.

Topological brain mapping—A method of analyzing the structure of the brain; used in research into biological causes of learning disabilities.

Total communication approach or method—The philosophical position regarding the development of communication skills that advocates the use of whatever enables the child who is deaf to communicate with others; also refers to the combined use of speech, signing, gestures, speechreading, fingerspelling, and even reading and writing in an attempt to extend the communication capabilities of the child who is deaf.

Trainable mentally retarded (TMR)—A term formerly used for people with moderate mental retardation.

Transfer training—How to use the skills taught in real life situations.

Transition—A period when a person is making a change; in special education, it refers to the period between one setting and another, such as from preschool to school, from elementary to middle school, and from school to work; the process of moving from adolescence to adulthood, within the context of social, cultural, economic, and legal considerations.

Traumatic brain injury—A category of disability included in IDEA in 1990; an injury to the brain that impairs learning, behavior, or motor functioning.

Triplegia—Paralysis of three limbs.

Trisomy 21—The most common cause of Down's syndrome; this genetic anomaly occurs when a third chromosome attaches to the chromosome 21 pair.

Valid—Refers to the ability of an evaluation to yield results that will serve the purposes they are intended to serve; the "truth" component of an evaluation procedure; the extent to which a test measures what the authors state it will measure.

Visual impairments—An overall term that includes all levels of visual loss.

Written symbols—Graphic means, such as the written alphabet, used to relay messages.

➤ Index

AADB. *See* American Association of the Deaf-Blind

AAF. *See* American Amputee Foundation

AAMR. *See* American Association on Mental Retardation

AAPD. *See* American Association of People with Disabilities

Academic achievement tests, 15

ACB. *See* American Council of the Blind

ACCH. *See* Association for the Care of Children's Health

ADA. *See* American Disability Association

ADA. *See* Americans with Disabilities Act

Adaptive behavior, assessment of, 16

Adaptive input devices, 22–23

Addams, Jane, 6

Administration of Children, Youth, and Families, 136

Adult Literacy and Lifelong Learning, 54

Advocacy
and films, 100–102
four types of, 98–99
and parents, 99–100
and politics, 103
and popular culture, 100–103
and the school, 97–98

Advocacy groups, 106
development of, 98–99

AFB. *See* American Foundation for the Blind

Affective domain
and integrated curriculum, 65–66

Afrocentric curriculum, 67

AFT. *See* American Federation of Teachers

Age–grade level system, 1

Aggression reduction/anger management curriculum, 67

AHA. *See* American Heart Association

AIDS, 50

Air Care Alliance, 143

Air Life Line, 143

ALA. *See* American Lung Association

Alcohol use
and at-risk children, 27

Alexander Graham Bell Association for the Deaf (AG Bell), 113, 138

Allegheny University program, 111

American Airlines—Miles for Kids, 143

American Amputee Foundation (AAF), 113
Give a Limb Program, 138

American Association of People with Disabilities (AAPD), 114

American Association of the Deaf-Blind (AADB), 114

American Association on Mental Retardation (AAMR), 114

American Council of the Blind (ACB), 114–115

American Council on Education, 115

American Disability Association (ADA), 115

American Epilepsy Society, 115

American Federation of Teachers (AFT), 105–106, 116
and regular and special education teachers, 108–109
American Foundation for the Blind (AFB), 116
American Heart Association (AHA), 116
American Lung Association (ALA), 116–117
American Paralysis Association and the Christopher Reeve Paralysis Foundation, 117
American Red Cross, 117
American Society for Deaf Children (ASDC), 117
American Society Health Association, 119–120
American Speech-Language-Hearing Foundation, 118
American Spinal Injury Association (ASIA), 118
Americans with Disabilities Act (ADA), 14, 51, 89, 92, 111, 137
Andersen, Hans Christian, 5
Angel Planes, 143
The Annie E. Casey Foundation, 118
Antisocial behavior, 32
Applied learning stations, 83
The Arc of the United States, 118
Arithmetical machine, 2
Armstrong vs. Kline, Pennsylvania, 47
ASDC. See American Society for Deaf Children
ASIA. See American Spinal Injury Association
ASPIRE. See Association of Service Providers Implementing IDEA Reforms in Education
Assessment, 8–11
and dual exceptionalities for the gifted, 13
individual student, 87
and individualized education plan, 13–14
types of, 14–16
See also Curriculum-based assessment; Tests
Assessment techniques, 12–13
Assignment menus and contracted grades, 84
Assistive technology, 23. See also Special education technology; Technology
Assistive Technology Act, 57, 93
Association for Children with Learning Disabilities, 99–100
Association for Retarded Citizens, 133
Association for the Care of Children's Health (ACCH), 133
Association of Service Providers Implementing IDEA Reforms in Education (ASPIRE), 109
At-risk children, 16
and brain research, 26–30
At-risk infants and toddlers programs for, 93–94
At-risk youth, programs for, 103
Attainment Company, 81
Attendance, school. See School attendance
Attention deficit disorder, 56
Attention deficit hyperactivity disorder, 56
Autism, 28
Autism Society of America, 119
Avenues, a National Support Group for Arthrogryposis Multiplex Congenita, 119
Awareness and advocacy, 99
Balance Materials/Curriculum, 79
Bancroft, Anne, 102
Bank Street Program, 109
Basic School Skills Inventory (diagnostic version), 15
BEES Clearinghouse/Information Center, 81

Beethoven, Ludwig van, 6
Behavior
    and integrated curriculum, 65
Behavior Evaluation Scale, 15
Behavior Problem Checklist (Quay
    and Peterson), 15
Behavior specialist
    and curriculum development, 61
Behavioral assessment, 9–10, 15–16
    and curriculum, discipline as
        part of, 77, 78
Behavioral intervention
    and curriculum, discipline as
        part of, 77, 78
Bell, Alexander Graham, 4, 6
Bender Visual Motor Gestalt Test, 16
Bereiter, Carl, 109–110
Bett's Autonomous Learning Model,
    75
Binet, Alfred, 4
Binet test of intelligence, 43
Binet-Simon Intelligence Test, 4
Blind Children's Fund, 119
Bloom's Taxonomy of Educational
    Objectives, 75
Bodily/kinesthetic intelligence, 69,
    70, 71
Bonet, Juan Pablo, 2
Braille, 3, 23
Braille, Louis, 3, 6
The Braille Forum, 115
Brain development, 25–26
Brain research, 25–31
    and at-risk children, 26–30
    and critical learning periods,
        30–31
Brain-based education, 30
Brigance Diagnostic Inventory of
    Early Development, 15
Brolin, Donn, 81
*Brookhart vs. Illinois State Board of
    Education,* 48
Brown vs. the Board of Education,
    44, 46
Buckley amendment, 46

Bureau of Education for the
    Handicapped, 45
Bureau of Elementary and
    Secondary Education, 45
Bureau of Higher Education, 45
Bureau of Vocational Education, 45
Burke's Behavior Rating Scale, 15
*Burlington School Committee vs.
    Department of Education,* 48
*Burlington vs. Department of
    Education for the
    Commonwealth of
    Massachusetts,* 49
Burnings
    and disabilities, persons with, 2

CAI. *See* Computer-assisted
    instruction
"Calabacillas" (Velazquez), 3
Care Force, 143
Career awareness, 76
Career-vocational skills
    and early childhood special
        education curriculum, 81
Carl Perkins Vocational Act, 48
Carnegie Corporation, 29
Carolina Abecedarian Project, 28
CBA. *See* Curriculum-based
    assessment
CBI. *See* Community-based
    instruction
CDC. *See* Centers for Disease
    Control
CDF. *See* Children's Defense Fund
CEC. *See* Council for Exceptional
    Children
Center for the Study of Autism, 120
Centers for Disease Control (CDC)
    National AIDS Hotline, 119
*Central York District vs.
    Commonwealth of
    Pennsylvania Department of
    Education,* 47
CFR. *See* Code of Federal
    Regulations

CHADD: Children and Adults with Attention-Deficit/ Hyperactivity Disorder, 120
Charles, Ray, 6
Charter schools
    and special education children, 91–92
    and teachers unions, 107
Cher, 101
Chicago Board of Education, 105–106
Chicago Federation of Labor, 105
Chicago Teacher's Federation (CTF), 105–106
Child Behavior Checklist (Achenbach), 15
Child Care Bureau, 136
Child Find, 11, 89, 94
Child prodigies, 71
Child Welfare League of America (CWLA), 120
Childcare subsidies, 103
Children
    and health insurance, 103
Children Experiencing Developmental Delays, 57
Children of a Lesser God, 100, 102
Children's Brain Tumor Foundation, 120
Children's Defense Fund (CDF), 133
Children's Hope Foundation: Childcare Necessities Program, 138
Children's Hopes and Dreams Foundation, 141
Children's Institute International, 133
Children's Personality Questionnaire (CPQ), 15
Children's Wish Foundation International, 141
Chugani, Harry, 31
Churchill, Winston, 5–6
Circle of Friends, 24
Circle of Support, 24
Citizen advocacy, 99

Civil Rights Act of 1965, 137
Civil rights movement, 98
Clark's Integrative Education Model, 75
Class projects, 83
Class Size Reduction Act, 57–58
Class Size Reduction Program, 110–111
Clearinghouse on Disability Information, 121
Cleburne vs. Cleburne Living Center, Texas, 49
Coach, 25
Code of Federal Regulations (CFR), 7–8
Cognitive psychology
    and multiple intelligence, 71
Collaborative consultation
    and special and regular education teachers, 35–36
Common school movement, 105
Community volunteers, 83
Community-based curriculum, 73
Community-based instruction (CBI), 81, 84
    and curriculum, 74–76
Community-based projects, 84
Community-referenced curriculum guides, 81
Community-referenced projects, 84
Compassionate Friends, 121
Competence
    and integrated curriculum, 65
Competency-based curriculum, 72
Comprehensive Test of Adaptive Behavior (CTAB), 16
Compulsory school attendance, 1, 4, 43. *See also* School attendance
Computer-assisted instruction (CAI) programs, 22
Computers
    and special education technology, 22–23
Concrete experiential learning activities, 83

Conflict resolution curriculum, 67
Congress
    and education, funding for, 91
    and Education for All
      Handicapped Children Act,
      funding for, 87, 108
    and IDEA, funding for, 93–94
    and interagency coordinating
      council, 94–95
    and school, bringing weapons to,
      110
Consortium for Citizens with
    Disabilities, 133–134
Consortium on Inclusive Schooling
    Practices, 111–112
Consumer Information Bureau, 134
Controlled substances
    and curriculum, discipline as
      part of, 78
Cooperative learning structures, 83
Cooperative Research Act, 44
Core curriculum, 72
Corporate Angel Network, 143
Council for Exceptional Children
    (CEC), 33, 35, 95, 121, 122, 134
County of San Diego vs. California
    Special Education Hearing
    Office, 54
CPQ. *See* Children's Personality
    Questionnaire
Creative Publications Base Ten
    Block Program, 80
Creative Publications Hands-On,
    80
Creative Publications Mathematics
    Their Way, 80
Creative Publications WorkMat
    Math Story Problems Series,
    80
Crime prevention/law-related
    curriculum, 67
Criterion-referenced assessment, 9
Critical learning periods
    and brain research, 30–31
Cruise, Tom, 101

CTAB. *See* Comprehensive Test of
    Adaptive Behavior
CTF. *See* Chicago Teacher's
    Federation
Curriculum, 59–60
    approaches, 72–73
    and community-based
      instruction, 74–76
    direct instruction, 109–110
    and discipline, 76–78
    Distar, 110
    and dual exceptionalities, 81–82
    and early childhood special
      education, 78–81
    enriched, 109
    and inclusion, 82–84
    instructional approaches, 83–84
    and multiple intelligence, 69–72
    and peaceful environment, 66–68
    and regular and special
      education teachers, 72–74.
      See also Curriculum
      construction; Curriculum
      development; Curriculum-
      based assessment; Integrated
      curriculum
Curriculum construction
    and politics, 112
Curriculum development
    and multidisciplinary team,
      60–63
    process of, 60
    and students and learning,
      beliefs about, 84
    See also Curriculum; Curriculum-
      based assessment; Integrated
      curriculum
Curriculum-based assessment
    (CBA), 63–65. *See also*
      Assessment; Curriculum;
      Curriculum construction;
      Curriculum development;
      Integrated curriculum
CWLA. *See* Child Welfare League of
    America

David and Lisa, 101, 102–103
Deaf, school for the, 3
Deborah Heart and Lung
     Association, 138
Debra P. vs. Turlington, 47
DEC. *See* Division of Early
     Childhood
Democratic Party
     and education, funding for, 91
Department of Health and
     Rehabilitative Services
     and State Board of Education,
     16–17
DeSilva, Howard, 102
Detroit Tests of Learning Aptitude
     (DTLA-2 and DTLA-P), 16
Development Test of Visual-Motor
     Integration–Revised, 16
Developmental Delay, 57
Developmental psychology
     and multiple intelligence, 71
Devereaux Adolescent Behavior
     Rating Scale, 15
Devereaux Child Behavior Rating
     Scale, 15
Devereaux Elementary School
     Behavior Rating Scale, 15
*Diana vs. State Board of Education
     of California,* 45
Direct instruction curriculum,
     109–110
Disabilities Issues Task Force
     (DITF), 123
Disabilities, persons with. *See*
     Persons with disabilities
Disabilities Rights Office, 123, 134
Disability
     definition of, 89, 90
Disability Government, 134–135
Disabled Children's Relief Fund,
     138
Discipline
     and curriculum, 76–78
Distar curriculum, 110
Distar Language, 79

Distar Math, 80
DITF. *See* Disabilities Issues Task
     Force
Division of Early Childhood (DEC),
     33, 95
Division of Mental Retardation and
     Developmental Disabilities,
     122
Dix, Dorothea, 4
DLM Cove Reading Program, 79
DLM Dolch Reading and
     Vocabulary, 79
DLM Math Problem-Solving Kits, 80
DLM Mathematics Big Box Kits, 80
DLM Moneywise, 80
DLM Survival Words Program, 79
DOT. *See* U.S. Department of
     Transportation
Dream Factory, 141
Drugs
     and at-risk children, 27
     and curriculum, discipline as
        part of, 78
DTLA. *See* Detroit Tests of Learning
     Aptitude
Dual exceptionalities
     and curriculum, 81–82
     for the gifted, 13
Duke, Patty, 102
Dullea, Keir, 102

Early childhood education (ECE)
     and at-risk children, 29
     and brain research, 25
     and parental involvement, 36
Early childhood intervention, 94–95
Early childhood special education
     (ECSE), 31–32, 33, 88
     and brain research, 25
     and curriculum, 78–81
Early Head Start programs, 31
Early intervention, 33
     and parental involvement, 38–39
Early intervention services
     and at-risk children, 29–30

ECE. *See* Early childhood education

Ecological environment
  sensitivity to, 71

ECSE. *See* Early childhood special
  education

Edison, Thomas, 5

Education
  funding for, 7–8, 87–88, 90–91,
    93–94, 109–111
  parent, 36–39
  regulation of, 7–8, 87–88
  and technology programs, 92–93
  See also Regular education;
    Special education

Education Commission of the
  States, 122

Education for All Handicapped
  Children Act, 46–47, 87, 100,
  108

Education of the Handicapped Act
  (EHA), 45, 49, 51

Education of the Mentally Retarded
  Children Act, 44

Education planning
  and parental involvement, 38
  and student involvement, 39

Educational Excellence for All
  Children's Act, 57, 75

Educational Research and
  Dissemination (ERD)
  Program, 109

Educational Resources Information
  Center (ERIC), 122

EEOC. *See* Equal Employment
  Opportunity Commission

EHA. *See* Education of the
  Handicapped Act

"El Nono de Vallecas" (Velazquez), 3

"El Primo" (Velazquez), 3

Elementary and Secondary
  Education Act (ESEA), 2,
  44–45, 52, 57–58

Eligibility, 11–13

Elks, 140

Engelmann, Sigfried, 109–110

Enriched curriculum, 109

Environment, peaceful
  and curriculum, 66–68

Epilepsy Foundation of America,
  122–123

Equal Employment Opportunity
  Commission (EEOC), 123, 137

ERD Program. *See* Educational
  Research and Dissemination
  Program

ERIC. *See* Educational Resources
  Information Center

ERIC Clearinghouse on Disabilities
  and Gifted Education (ERIC
  EC), 122

ERIC Clearinghouse on Elementary
  and Early Childhood
  Education, 129

ERIC EC. *See* ERIC Clearinghouse on
  Disabilities and Gifted
  Education

Erickson Institute Program, 109

Erskine, Roger, 107

ESEA. *See* Elementary and
  Secondary Education Act

Ethical concerns, sensitivity to,
  71

Evaluation, 8–11

*Evans vs. Board of Education of
  Rhinebeck Center School
  District*, 55

Exorcisms
  and disabilities, persons with, 2

Family Education Rights and
  Privacy Act, 46

"The Family of Philip IV"
  (Velazquez), 3

Family systems theory, 38

Family-focused intervention
  services, 78

FAPE. *See* Free, appropriate public
  education

FCC. *See* Federal Communications
  Commission

Federal Communications
    Commission (FCC), 134
    and Disabilities Issues Task
    Force, 123
Federal funding. *See* Education,
    funding for
Federal government
    and education, regulation of, 7–8,
    87–88
Federal minimum standards, 8
Federal Resource Center (FRC) for
    Special Education, 123
Federation for Children with Special
    Needs, 123–124
Films
    and advocacy, 100–102
Finger spelling, 2
Fitzgerald, F. Scott, 6
Florida
    and full-service schools, 16–17
Formal assessment, 9
Fourteenth Amendment, 7, 8
FPB. *See* Functional behavioral
    assessment
FRC. *See* Federal Resource Center
    for Special Education
Free, appropriate public education
    (FAPE), 8, 47, 49, 87, 89
French vs. Omaha Public Schools,
    51–52
Friends of Karen, 141
Fuerstein, Reuven, 10
Full-service schools, 16–17
Functional behavioral assessment
    (FBA), 9–10
Functional curriculum, 73–74
Functional secondary school
    curriculum, 76
Funding, federal. *See* Education,
    funding for
Funds, distribution of
    and teachers unions, 106

Gallaudet, Thomas Hopkins, 3
Gang prevention/reduction

    curriculum, 67
General education teachers. *See*
    Regular education teachers
GFSA. *See* Gun-Free Schools Act
Gift of Life, 138
Gifted and Talented Students
    Education Act, 57
Gifted children, 4
    and curriculum development,
    75
    dual exceptionalities for, 13
    teaching models for, 75
Give a Limb Program, 138
Give Kids the World, 141
Goals 2000: Educate America Act,
    50, 53–54, 57, 95
Goggin, Catherine, 105
Goodenough-Haris Drawing Test,
    15
Gooding, Bill, 94
Grade-level curriculum, 72
Greer vs. Rome City School District,
    20, 52
Guidance counselor
    and curriculum development, 61
Gun-Free Schools Act (GFSA), 53
Guns
    and curriculum, discipline as
    part of, 78

Haley, Margaret, 105
"Half" intelligence, 71
Hall, James, 48
*Hall vs. Vance County Board of
    Education*, 48
Handgun violence prevention
    curriculum, 67–68
Handicapped Children's Early
    Education Program (HCEEP),
    88
Handicapped Children's Protection
    Act, 49
Harassment, 67
HCEEP. *See* Handicapped Children's
    Early Education Program

Head Start, 2, 8, 26–27, 32–33, 44, 87, 103
  goals of, 33
Health insurance
  for children, 103
Health professionals
  and curriculum development, 62
Hear Now, 139
Hearing Aid Foundation, 139
High School Personality
    Questionnaire (HSPQ), 15
High-order thinking, 75
HIV/AIDS, 119–120
Hobson vs. Hansen, 45
Hoffman, Dustin, 101
Home environment
  and at-risk children, 27
Honig vs. Doe, 49
House Education and Welfare
    Committee, 110
Howe, Samuel Gridley, 3
HSPQ. *See* High School Personality
    Questionnaire
Humane treatment, 3–5
  and persons with disabilities, 2–3
Humphrey, Hubert, 5
Hurt, William, 102

IASA. *See* Improving America's
    Schools Act
ICC. *See* Interagency coordinating
    council
IDEA. *See* IDEA 1990; IDEA 1997;
    Individuals with Disabilities
    Education Act
IDEA 1990, 75, 87, 90–91, 94
  and discipline, school, 76
IDEA 1997, 38, 75, 76–78, 82, 88, 90, 91
  and discipline, school, 76–78
Idiocy, 2
IEP. *See* Individual education plan
IFSP. *See* Individualized family
    service plan
Improving America's Schools Act
    (IASA), 52

Inclusion, 18, 19–21
  and curriculum, 72, 82–84
  definition of, 82–83
  and teachers, 24–25
  and teachers unions, 108
  and technology, 22–25
India
  inclusion in, 21
Individual education plan (IEP), 48,
    49, 50–51, 55, 56, 87
  and assessment, 13–14
  and curriculum, 74, 75
  and curriculum, discipline as
    part of, 77
  and curriculum-based
    assessment, 63
  and family-focused intervention
    services, 78
  and parental involvement, 38–39
  and regular education teachers,
    33
  and school to work transfer
    process, 76
  and special education
    technology, 23
Individual student assessment, 87
Individualized family service plan
    (IFSP), 35, 56, 78
  and parental involvement, 38
Individualized intervention, 2
Individuals with Disabilities
    Education Act (IDEA), 8,
    13–14, 31, 33, 47, 48, 49, 51,
    55–56, 57, 74, 75, 88–89, 94,
    107–108, 110, 111, 127
  and charter schools, 92
  funding for, 90–91, 93–94
  and inclusion, 20
  and individualized education
    plan, 78
  and special education
    technology, 23
  and technology related
    assistance, 93
  See also IDEA 1990; IDEA 1997

Infants and Toddlers Intervention
   Program, 88
Information assessment, 9
Innovative Learning Concepts, Inc.,
   Touch Math, 80
Insanity, 2
Institute on Community Integration,
   124
Integrated curriculum, 59–60
   and affective domain, 65–66
   See also Curriculum; Curriculum
      development; Curriculum-
      based assessment
Intellectual functioning, individual
   tests of, 15
Intelligence
   types of, 69
   See also Intelligence quotient;
      Intelligence tests; Multiple
      intelligence
Intelligence quotient (IQ), 1, 43. *See
   also* Intelligence; Intelligence
   tests; Multiple intelligence
Intelligence tests, 4, 43. *See also*
   Intelligence; Intelligence
   quotient; Multiple intelligence
Interagency coordinating council
   (ICC), 94–95
Interpersonal intelligence, 69, 71
Intrapersonal intelligence, 69, 70,
   71
IQ. *See* Intelligence quotient
IQ test scores, 47
Itard, Jean Marc, 2

Janklow, Bill, 103
Judgment
   and integrated curriculum, 65

K-ABC. *See* Kaufman Assessment
   Battery for Children
Kaufman Assessment Battery for
   Children (K-ABC), 15
Kaufman Infant and Preschool
   Scale, 15

Kaufman Test of Educational
   Achievement (K-TEA), 15
Keller, Captain, 4
Keller, Helen, 4, 102
Kennedy, John, 5
Key Math, 15
Kindergarten, establishment of, 43
Kiwanis International, 140
K-TEA. *See* Kaufman Test of
   Educational Achievement

Labeling, in schools, 19
*Lachman vs. State Board of
   Education,* 49–50
Language
   and at-risk children, 28
Language arts/reading
   and early childhood special
      education curriculum, 78–79
Lanham Act, 109
Larry P. vs. Riles, 47
"Las Meninas" (Velazquez), 3
*Lascari vs. Board of Education of the
   Ramapo Indian Hills Regional
   High School District,* 50
Laws, 92–93. *See also* Education,
   regulation of; *under specific
   laws*
Laws, public. *See* Public laws;
   Education, regulation of;
   under specific laws
LCCE. *See* Life Center Career
   Education
LEA. *See* Local education agency
Learning, beliefs about
   and curriculum development,
      84
Learning disabilities
   concept of, 7
Learning Disabilities Association of
   America, 124
Learning potential assessment,
   10–11
Learning styles, 71
Learning-disabilities research, 4

Least restrictive environment (LRE), 18
and inclusion, 19–20
Legal advocacy, 99
Legislation
and advocacy, 99
Lennon, John, 6
Leonardo da Vinci, 6
Lezcano, Francisci, 3
Life Center Career Education (LCCE), 81
Life management curriculum, 73
Life skills training curriculum, 68
Lifeline Pilots, 143
LinguiSystems No Glamour Grammar, 79
Lions Club, 141
Local education agency (LEA), 111
Local government
and education, regulation of, 8, 87
Locke, John, 2
Logical-mathematical intelligence, 69, 71
Logue vs. Shawnee Mission Public School Unified School District, 55
LRE. *See* Least restrictive environment

Magnetic resonance imaging (MRI), 25
Mainstreaming, 18–19
Make a Wish Foundation, 142
Maker's Integrated Curriculum Model, 75
Making Action Plans (Maps), 25
Manifestation determinations, 77
Maps (Making Action Plans), 25
Margolin, Janet, 102
Martinez, Matthew G., 94
Martinez vs. School Board of Hillsboro County, Florida, 50
The Marty Lyons Foundation, Inc., 142

Mask, 100–101
Massachusetts Bay Colony, 105
Math proficiency, 2
Mathematics
and early childhood special education curriculum, 80
Mathematics and Science, 54
Mathematics for Daily Use, 80
Matlen, Marlee, 102
McCarthy Scales of Children's Abilities, 15
Medicaid, 140
Mental illness, 2
Mental institutions
reforms for, 4
Mental retardation, 2
Merrill Linguistic Readers, 79
Mild disabilities, 65
Mills vs. Board of Education, 46
Minimum competency test, 48
Minnesota Multiphasic Personality Inventory (MMPI), 15
Miracle Ear Children's Foundation, 139
The Miracle Worker, 100–101, 102
MMPI. *See* Minnesota Multiphasic Personality Inventory
Montessori, Maria, 4
Moving Up in Grammar, 79
MRI. *See* Magnetic resonance imaging
Multidimensional student grouping, 83
Multidisciplinary team
and curriculum development, 60–63
Multilevel instruction, 83
Multimedia presentations, 83
Multiple intelligence
and curriculum, 69–72
See also Intelligence; Intelligence quotient; Intelligence tests
Muscular Dystrophy Association—USA, 124
Musical/rhythmic intelligence, 69, 71

NADDC. *See* National Association of
   Developmental Disabilities
   Council
NAEYC. *See* National Association for
   the Education of Young
   Children
NAF. *See* National Amputation
   Foundation
NAGC. *See* National Association for
   Gifted Children
NAPAS. *See* National Association of
   Protection and Advocacy
   Systems
NARC. *See* National Association for
   Retarded Children
NASBE. *See* National Association of
   State Boards of Education
National AIDS Hotline, Centers for
   Disease Control, 119
National Amputation Foundation
   (NAF), 125
National Association for Retarded
   Children (NARC), 99
National Association for Retarded
   Citizens, 99
National Association for the
   Education of Young Children
   (NAEYC), 125
National Association for Visually
   Handicapped, 125–126
National Association of Child
   Advocates, 103
National Association of
   Developmental Disabilities
   Council (NADDC), 126, 135
National Association of Protection
   and Advocacy Systems
   (NAPAS), 135
National Association of School
   Superintendents, 105
National Association of State Boards
   of Education (NASBE), 19, 111
National Brain Tumor Foundation, 126
National Campaign to Fully Fund
   IDEA, 93

National Center for Learning
   Disabilities (NCLD), 126–127
National Council on Disabilities, 45,
   135
National Defense Education Act, 44
National Disability Policy, 91
National Down Syndrome Congress,
   127
National Early Childhood Technical
   Assistance System (NECTAS),
   127
National Education Association
   (NEA), 1, 4, 43, 105–106
National Education Goals Panel,
   107
National Educational Service, 127
National Head Start Association,
   127–128
National Hearing Aid Society, 139
National Hydrocephalus
   Foundation (NHF), 128
National Information Center for
   Children and Youth with
   Disabilities, 136
National Information Clearinghouse
   on Children Who Are Deaf-
   Blind, 128
National Maternal and Child Health
   Clearinghouse (NMCHC), 136
National Organization for Rare
   Disorders (NORD), 128
National Organization of Parents of
   Blind Children, 129
National Organization on Fetal
   Alcohol Syndrome, 129
National Parent Information
   Network (NPIN), 129
National Parent Network on
   Disabilities (NPND), 129–130
National Patient Air Transport
   Hotline, 143
National Pediatric and Family HIV
   Resource Center, 130
National School Age Care Alliance
   (NSACA), 130

National School Boards Association, 94

National School Lunch Act, 44

National Society for Crippled Children, 99

National Teachers' Association, 105

"The naturalist," 71

NCLD. *See* National Center for Learning Disabilities

NEA. *See* National Education Association

NECTAS. *See* National Early Childhood Technical Assistance System

Neurological psychology and multiple intelligence, 71

Neuroscience, 30

Newton, Sir Isaac, 6

NHF. *See* National Hydrocephalus Foundation

NMCHC. *See* National Maternal and Child Health Clearinghouse

NORD. *See* National Organization for Rare Disorders

Norm-referenced assessment, 9

NPIN. *See* National Parent Information Network

NPND. *See* National Parent Network on Disabilities

NSACA. *See* National School Age Care Alliance

Nursing practices and brain development, 26

Nutrition, 1–2

Oberti vs. Board of Education of the Borough of Clementon School District, 20, 52

Occupational therapist and curriculum development, 62

Office of Civil Rights, 89 and harassment, 67

Office of Special Education, 22, 111, 128, 130 and harassment, 67

Old Deluder Satan Laws, 105

Operation Smile, 139

Orton-Gillingham instructional procedure, 55

Osteogenesis Imperfecta Foundation, 131

Outcomes-based instruction, 83

Parallel curriculum, 73

Parent counseling and training, 56

Parent education, 36–39

Parent Resource Network, 133

Parental involvement, 36–39, 54 and education planning, 38 and Head Start, 31

Parents and advocacy, 99–100

Path (Planning Alternative Tomorrows with Hope), 25

Patton, George S., 6

Peace education curriculum, 68

Peaceful environment and curriculum, 66–68

Peer mediation programs, 68

Peer supports, 83

Pennsylvania Association for Retarded Citizens (PARC) vs. Commonwealth of Pennsylvania, 45–46

Perkins Institute, 3

Perry Preschool Project, 28

Personnel Development Program, 88

Persons with disabilities and humane treatment, 2–3

PET scans. *See* Positron emission tomography scans

Pharmaceutical Manufacturers Association, 139

Phoenix Society for Burn Survivors, 131

Physical therapist and curriculum development, 62–63

Piers-Harris Children's Self-Concept Scale, 15

P.L. 85-926, 44
P.L. 87-276, 44
P.L. 89-10, 44
P.L. 89-750, 44–45
P.L. 90-247, 45
P.L. 91-230, 45
P.L. 93-112, 46
P.L. 93-516, 46
P.L. 94-142, 31, 46, 47, 50, 87
P.L. 94-457, 49
P.L. 94-942, 100
P.L. 98-524, 48
P.L. 99-372, 49
P.L. 99-457, 31, 78
P.L. 101-17, 55
P.L. 101-336, 51
P.L. 101-476, 51, 55
P.L. 103-227, 53
P.L. 105-17, 37–38, 55
P.L. 106-113, 57
Placement, 11–13
    and curriculum, 72
    and curriculum, discipline as
        part of, 77
Planning Alternative Tomorrows
    with Hope (PATH), 25
Politics
    and advocacy, 103
    and curriculum construction, 112
    and special education, 109–112
Ponce de Leon, 2
Popular culture
    and advocacy, 100–103
Portfolio or "authentic"
    assessments, 84
Positron emission tomography
    (PET) scans, 25
Prejudice reduction/cultural
    awareness curriculum, 68
Prereferral consultation, 35–36
Preschools
    funding for, 109
Presidential Task Force on
    Employment of Adults with
    Disabilities, 135

Preterm infants
    and brain development, 26
Project Math, 80
Project Read, 79
Promoting cooperation approach,
    68
Psychological processes, assessment
    of, 16
Psychologists
    and curriculum development,
        61
Psychology, 30
Public laws, 7–8. *See also under
    specific laws*

Rain Man, 100–101
Rainbows Hope, Inc./Wish Is
    Granted Foundation, 142
REA Program. *See* Reading
    Excellence Acts Program
Reading Excellence Acts (REA)
    Program, 111
Ready To Learn, 53
Reauthorization Act, 82
Reciprocal teaching, 84
Referrals, 11–13
Regional Intervention Program
    (RIP), 31–32
Regular education, 7
    development of, 1–2
    See also Education; Special
        education
Regular education initiative (REI),
    20, 24
Regular education teachers
    and American Federation of
        Teachers, 108–109
    and curriculum, 72–74
    and curriculum development, 60
    and inclusion, 24–25
    and individual education plan, 33
    and mainstreaming, 18–19
    and special education teachers,
        collaborative consultation
        with, 35–36

See also Special education
teachers; Teachers
Rehabilitation Act, 14, 46, 51
REI. *See* Regular education initiative
Renzulli's Enrichment Triad Model,
75
Republican Party
and education, funding for, 91
Research and development
funding for, 88
Rhode Island
and compulsory school
attendance, 1, 43
Riley, Richard W., 110, 111
RIP. *See* Regional Intervention
Program
Roads to Recovery, 144
Rockefeller, Nelson A., 6
Rodriguez Pereire, Jacob, 2
Role model curriculum, 68
Role playing, skits, and plays, 83
Roosevelt, Franklin D., 7
Rotary Club, 141
Rowley vs. Hendrick Hudson School,
47, 49, 55

*Sacramento City Unified School
District vs. Holland,* 20, 53
Safe and Drug-Free Schools and
Communities Act (SDFSCA),
52–53
Safe, Disciplined, and Alcohol- and
Drug-Free Schools, 54
Salary benefits
and teachers unions, 108
Scales of Independent Behavior
(SIB), 16
School achievement
and Binet test of intelligence, 43
School attendance, 1. *See also*
Compulsory school
attendance
School Completion, 53
School districts
and teachers unions, 106

School nurse
and curriculum development, 62
School reform, 108
School to work transfer process, 76
Schools
and advocacy, 97–98
segregation and labeling in, 19
weapons in, 110
See also Special schools
Science proficiency, 2
Science/social studies
and early childhood special
education curriculum, 81
Screening, 11, 35
and Head Start, 31
SDFSCA. *See* Safe and Drug-Free
Schools and Communities Act
"Sebastian de Morra" (Velazquez), 3
Segregation, in schools, 19
Self-advocacy, 99
Self-concept, 65
Self-esteem, 65, 71
Self-esteem development
curriculum, 68
Sensory motor method, 4
Sensory stimulation, 2
Sequin, Eduoard, 3–4
Short-term skill-based grouping,
84
Shriners Hospitals for Crippled
Children, 139
SIB. *See* Scales of Independent
Behavior
Sign language, 2
SIM. *See* Strategies Intervention
Model
Skinner, B. F., 109
Social Security Office, 140
Social skills
and integrated curriculum, 65
Social worker
and curriculum development,
60–61
Social/emotional behavioral
assessment, 15

Software, computer
  and special education
    technology, 22–23
Special education, 7
  definition of, 56
  development of, 2–7
  and politics, 109–112
  and teachers unions, 105–109
  See also Education; Regular
    education
Special Education Act, 44
Special education teachers, 10
  and American Federation of
    Teachers, 108–109
  challenges facing, 35
  and curriculum, 72–74
  and curriculum development, 60
  and inclusion, 24–25
  and regular education teachers,
    collaborative consultation
    with, 35–36
  role of, 33–36
  See also Regular education
    teachers; Teachers
Special education technology,
  22–23. *See also* Assistive
  technology; Technology
Special institutions, 3–5. *See also*
  Schools
Special needs, 5–7
Special schools, 3–5. *See also* Schools
A Special Wish Foundation, 142
Specialized curriculum, 73
Speech-language pathologist
  and curriculum development, 61
Spina Bifida Association of America,
  131–132
SRA Corrective Reading Program, 79
SRA Cursive Writing, 79
SRA Expressive Writing, 79
SRA Reading Mastery Series, 79
SRA Reading, Writing and Math for
  Independence, 81
SRA Reading, Writing and Thinking
  Skills, 79

SRA Spelling Mastery, 79
SRA Your World of Facts, 79
SRA/Distar, 79
SSI. *See* Supplemental Security
  Income
St. Jude Children's Research
  Hospital, 140
Stand For Children, 136
Standardized achievement tests
  and curriculum-based
    assessment, 64
Stanford Binet Intelligence Scale,
  4
Stanford-Binet Intelligence
  Scale–Fourth Edition, 15
Stanford-Binet Scale of Intelligence
  Tests, 1, 43
Starlight Foundation, 142
Starting Points Initiative, 29
State Board of Education
  and Department of Health and
    Rehabilitative Services, 16–17
State departments of education
  and teachers unions, 106
State government
  and education, regulation of, 8,
    87–88
State Special Education Law, 8
Steck-Vaughn Health and You, 81
Steck-Vaughn Mastering Math, 80
Steck-Vaughn Phonics, 78
Steck-Vaughn Reading
  Comprehension Skills Series,
  78
Steck-Vaughn Sight Word
  Comprehensive, 79
Steck-Vaughn Spelling, 79
Steck-Vaughn Succeeding in
  Mathematics, 80
Steck-Vaughn The Wonders of
  Science Series, 81
Stepping Out, 81
Stoltz, Eric, 101
Strategies Intervention Model (SIM),
  79

Strauss, Alfred, 4

Strauss Syndrome, 4

Structure

and curriculum, 59

Student Achievement and
Citizenship, 53–54

Student involvement
in education planning, 39

Student presentation and projects,
83

Students, beliefs about
and curriculum development, 84

Subject-area curriculum, 72

Substance abuse
and at-risk children, 27

Sullivan, Anne, 4, 102

Sunshine Foundation, 142

Superstition
and persons with disabilities,
treatment of, 2

Supplemental Security Income
(SSI), 140

Systematic instruction, 2

Systems advocacy, 99

Teacher Education and Professional
Development, 54

Teachers
and inclusion, 24–25
requirements for, and teachers
unions, 108
See also Regular education
teachers; Special education
teachers

Teachers Union Reform Network
(TURN), 107–108

Teachers unions
and charter schools, 107
development of, 105–109
and funds, distribution of, 106
and inclusion, 108
and salary benefits, 108
and school districts, 106
and state departments of
education, 106

and teachers, requirements for,
108

and universities, collaboration
with, 107

Technology
and inclusion, 22–25
See also Assistive technology;
Special education technology

Technology programs
and education, regulation of,
92–93

Technology Related Assistance, 93

Teen-dating violence/family
violence/sexual assault
curriculum, 68

TEMA–2. *See* Test of Early
Mathematical Abilities–2

Tenth Amendment, 1, 8, 43

TERA–2. *See* Test of Early Reading
Ability–2

Terman, Lewis, 4, 43

Test of Adolescent Language
(TOAL–2), 16

Test of Early Mathematical Abilities
(TEMA)–2, 15

Test of Early Reading Ability
(TERA)–2, 15

Test of Early Written Language
(TEWL), 15

Test of Language Development–2
(Primary or Intermediate), 16

Test of Written Language 2 (TOWL-
2), 15

Test of Written Spelling (TWS), 15

Tests, 15–16. *See also* Assessment;
under specific tests

TEWL. *See* Test of Early Written
Language

Thematic Apperception Test, 15

Thematic, integrated approaches,
83

*Timothy W. vs. Rochester School
District*, 50

TOAL–2. *See* Test of Adolescent
Language

TOWL–2. *See* Test of Written Language 2
Tracking system, 45
Transfer
    and curriculum, 72
Transition models
    and curriculum, 75–76
Travel training, 56–57
TS Alliance. *See* Tuberous Sclerosis Alliance
Tuberous Sclerosis Alliance (TS Alliance), 131–132
TURN. *See* Teachers Union Reform Network
TWS. *See* Test of Written Spelling

UCP Association. *See* United Cerebral Palsy Association
Union Institute, 107
Union Ministry of Welfare (India), 21
United Cerebral Palsy Association (UCP), 99, 132
United Teachers of Dade (UTD), 107
Universities
    and teachers unions, collaboration with, 107
University of South Florida
    and special and regular education teachers, 36
Urbanski, Adam, 107
U.S. Architectural and Transportation Barriers Compliance Board, 111
U.S. Department of Education, 8, 22, 57–58, 89, 107, 111, 122, 128, 131, 132
    and early childhood special education, curriculums for, 78
    and technology programs, 92–93
U.S. Department of Health and Human Services, 136
U.S. Department of Justice, 134–135, 137
U.S. Department of Labor, Wage and Hour Division, 75

U.S. Department of Transportation (DOT), 132
U.S. Office of Education, 43
U.S. Secretary of Education, 52
UTD. *See* United Teachers of Dade

VABS. *See* Vineland Adaptive Behavior Scales
Velazquez, Diego, 3
Verbal/linguistic intelligence, 69, 71
Vineland Adaptive Behavior Scales (VABS), 16
Violence prevention curriculum, 67–68
Vision
    and curriculum, 59
Visiting teacher
    and curriculum development, 60–61
Visual/spatial intelligence, 69, 70, 71
Vocational Rehabilitation Act, 47, 87
    Section 504, 88–90, 92, 111
Vocational rehabilitation counselor
    and curriculum development, 61–62
Volunteer Pilots Association, 144
Vygotsky, Lev, 10

WAIS–R. *See* Wechsler Adult Intelligence Scale–R
Walker Problem Behavior Identification Checklist, 15
Wall vs. Mattituck-Cutchogue School District, 54–55
War on Poverty, 109
Weapons
    and curriculum, discipline as part of, 78
    in school, 110
Wechsler Adult Intelligence Scale–III (WAIS-R), 15
Wechsler Intelligence Scale for Children–Revised (WISC-R), 15

Wechsler Preschool and Primary
Scale of Intelligence–Revised
(WPPSI-R), 15
White House Conference on Child
Youth and Protection, 43–44
Wiley, Richard W., 92
Wilson, Woodrow, 5
Window of opportunity
and brain research, 30–31
Wings for Children, 144
Wings of Mercy, 144
WISC-III. *See* Wechsler Intelligence
Scale for Children–III
Wisconsin
kindergarten in, establishment
of, 43
Wish Is Granted, 142
A Wish With Wings, 142
Witch hunts
and disabilities, persons with,
2
Wonder, Stevie, 7
Woodcock Language Proficiency
Battery, 16

Woodcock Reading Mastery Test-
Revised, 15
Woodcock-Johnson Psycho-
Educational Battery–Revised
(achievement), 15
Woodcock-Johnson Psycho-
Educational Battery–Revised
(cognitive), 16
Work experience, 76
Works Progress Administration
Program, 109
World Council for Gifted and
Talented Children, 132
WPPSI-R. *See* Wechsler Preschool
and Primary Scale of
Intelligence–Revised
*Wyatt vs. Stickney/Wyatt vs. Aderholt,
Alabama,* 45

Yale Child Welfare Research
Program, 28

"Zero reject" policy, 87, 88
Zero to Three, 137

⚫⟩ About the Author

Arlene Sacks is the Academic Coordinator of the Ph.D. Program at The Union Institute. Previous to this she directed graduate programs at Barry University and St. Thomas University, both located in Miami, Florida. She received her doctorate at West Virginia University in 1974. Previous publications include "Social and Educational Family Empowerment Program Cooperates to Ensure Academic Success," in *The Developmental Process of Positive Attitudes and Mutual Respect: A Multicultural Approach to Advocating School Safety,* R. Duhon-Sells, S. Cooley, and G. Duhon (eds.), 1999; "The Full-Service School: A Holistic Approach to Effectively Serve Children in Poverty," in *Reaching and Teaching Children Who Are Victims of Poverty,* A. Duhon-Ross (ed.), 1999; "Brain Research: Implications for Early Intervention—Theory, Research, and Application," in the *Journal of the International Association of Special Education,* 1998; "Children in Protective Services: The Missing Educational Link for Children in Kinship Networks," in *Multisystem Skills and Interventions in School Social Work Practice,* E. M. Freeman, C. G. Franklin, R. Fong, G. L. Shaffer, and E. M. Timberlake (eds.), 1998; and "Positive Peace Education: From Philosophy to Curriculum," in *Exploring Self Science through Peace Education and Conflict Resolution,* R. Duhon-Sells (ed.), 1997.